Jesse Chisholm

This only known photograph of Jesse Chisholm was taken in 1867 at Leavenworth, Kansas, after an illness and a long wagon trip. *Courtesy of the Oklahoma Historical Society.*

Stan Hoig

Jesse Chisholm

Ambassador of the Plains

University Press of Colorado

Copyright © 1991 by the University Press of Colorado
P.O. Box 849
Niwot, Colorado 80544

The University Press of Colorado is a cooperative publishing enterprise supported,
in part, by Adams State College, Colorado State University, Fort Lewis College,
Mesa State College, Metropolitan State College of Denver, University of Colorado,
University of Northern Colorado, University of Southern Colorado, and Western
State College.

Library of Congress Cataloging-in-Publication Data

Hoig, Stan.
    Jesse Chisholm, ambassador of the Plains / Stan Hoig.
    p.   cm.
    Includes bibliographical references and index.
    ISBN 0-87081-198-3
    1. Chisholm, Jesse. 2. Frontier and pioneer life—Great Plains. 3. Great
Plains—Biography. I. Title.
F593.C523H65 1991
979'.02'092—dc20
[B]   90-27722
                                                     CIP

10 9 8 7 6 5 4 3 2 1

To My Brother
MELVIN E. HOIG, JR.

Contents

Preface

Jesse Chisholm lived most of his life on the far frontier and, often, beyond. Though he left behind no diary, letters, or other personal record, it is possible to follow the trail of Jesse Chisholm in his long and interesting journey through the early West and to document the role he played in its history. Indian and military documents, memoirs and recollections of those who knew him, early-day newspapers, and other research instruments that bear his imprint allow us to learn much about Chisholm through his participation in the events of his day and through what his contemporaries said about him. However, in the interest of honest history, I restrain myself from speculative interpretation of his character.

A special problem embedded in a study of Chisholm's life is that a good deal of faulty information and romantic speculation has surrounded him during the century and more since his death. Much of this has been repeated so often, and by legitimate historians, that it has become accepted as fact. My search for the truth about Chisholm has been extensive and deep; it has uncovered a great deal of long-buried and forgotten information regarding this important frontiersman. Where I challenge accepted information, I stand upon my sources, which have been traced to their most primary point whenever possible.

A researcher can only be dismayed at losses of irreplaceable material. Historian Grant Foreman relates: "I located a daughter of Jesse Chisholm, named Mrs. Thomas, living a mile or two south of Prague, Oklahoma. I asked her if Jesse Chisholm left any old papers when he died. She said, 'Yes there was a trunk full that we kept in the house for many years until the house burned and they were destroyed.' "

As always, successful research depends greatly upon the professional and generous assistance of those who store and maintain historical records. Particularly I wish to thank the persons who have been helpful at the following institutions: the Oklahoma Collection,

Oklahoma Department of Libraries; the Western History Collections, University of Oklahoma; the Knox County, Tennessee, Archives; the Washington County, Tennessee, Clerk's Office; the University of Central Oklahoma Library; the Special Collections of the University of Arkansas; the Pike Collection of the Scottish Rite Temple, Washington, D.C.; the Fort Worth Branch of the National Archives; the Archives Division, Texas State Library; the Barker Texas History Center; the Oklahoma Historical Society Library and Division of Archives-Manuscripts; the Gilcrease Institute; the Library of Congress; and the National Archives.

I also wish to express my appreciation to my wife, Pat Corbell Hoig, for her contribution in the preparation of this book.

Prologue

The Chisholm Cattle Trail, the route by which hundreds of thousands of Texas longhorn cattle traveled northward across the Indian Territory (now Oklahoma) to Kansas railheads, was named for Cherokee half blood Jesse Chisholm. By this alone, he has become an essential part of the lore of the American Southwest. Today his name graces rivers, landmarks, museums, public schools, and other sites and institutions. Though much of his fame rests upon the naming of the cattle trail, Jesse was a principal participant in the history of the early Southwest. For over thirty years Jesse Chisholm rode the southern prairies as a trader, hunter, emissary, scout, guide, peacemaker, and trailblazer. His life's occupation was that of an Indian trader, a merchant of the mesquite; but the scope of his activities was far broader than that. His involvement in the Indian affairs of his day was extensive. No man with white blood in his veins better knew and associated more harmoniously with the Comanches and other tribes of the region than did Jesse Chisholm; and no one better held their confidence.

He lived much of his life on the Canadian River in Oklahoma, but he ranged from the Arkansas River of Kansas to the Guadalupe River of Texas long before there was a Wichita, an Oklahoma City, a Dallas, or a Fort Worth. His trading grounds were along the North and South Canadian rivers, the Arkansas, the Washita, the Red, the Brazos, the Colorado, the San Saba, and countless other streams where the nomadic tribesmen of the Plains located their villages. Jesse Chisholm played a significant role in the events of early Arkansas, Oklahoma, Texas, and Kansas.

Chisholm was also an explorer, and during his lifetime he not only broke new trails across the Plains but saw both the Pacific and Atlantic oceans, trod the soil of Mexico, visited New Orleans, and traveled up the great Mississippi River on his way to Washington, D.C., where he interpreted for the president of the United States as he had so often for other government officials.

Chisholm traversed the prairie by horse, pack mule, and wagon,

sometimes alone, sometimes with his Cherokee and Delaware comrades, and sometimes with his large entourage of family, rescued
Mexican children, and hired hands. He hauled trade goods of the
white man's world to spread upon a buffalo hide before an Indian
tepee, where he would sit cross-legged and patiently barter "Indian
style." He was adept with sign talk as well as in the many tribal
tongues he knew as one of the most expert linguists in the West. He
gathered robes, peltries, Indian ponies, and Mexican mules to take
back to forward trade centers such as Torrey's Trading House in
Texas; Fort Smith, Arkansas; and Leavenworth City, Kansas.

Jesse Chisholm was an unobtrusive, modest man who was
known for his intelligence, generosity, and kindness, a man of
untainted honesty and integrity. Missionary J. S. Murrow, who
knew Chisholm well, said of him: "He was a man of commanding
presence and character. He was a born leader . . . always neatly
dressed, intelligent, well informed, spoke good English and was
evidently a man above the ordinary."[1] But at the same time he was
an intrepid adventurer, willing to plunge far beyond the bounds of
societal protection, risk the dangers of frontier life, and endure the
privations of a harsh life miles from comfort of town or lodging.
Chisholm, in fact, spent far more time in the field and with the
prairie Indians than he did at home. His wife Eliza once said that
he would visit her about once a year and remain a week or two, and
then he would be off again.

As a man of mixed blood — half white, half Cherokee — Jesse
was more accepted as an Indian and thought of himself as one. He
knew the tricks and turns of life in a wilderness world ruled by
natural laws and was as adept in the art of survival as any man of
his day. A large part of that survival depended upon his ability to
accommodate the temperament of militant, scalp-hunting warriors
and to avoid an ambush by any of the warring bands that regularly
scoured the Plains for the chance of a coup.

A great portion of the western North America that Chisholm
knew was populated by a multitude of small nations of native
tribesmen who fought isolated battles to hold on to their land and
way of life. In truth he was at the advance of the march of American
empire as it swept harshly across the cultures of those tribes, and

upon him was thrust much of the difficult task of cooling the passions aroused by white transgressions.

Those who knew Chisholm well have left behind testimonials to his intelligence as well as his courage. James R. Mead stated that he had been present during councils with Indian leaders when Jesse would converse in five or six different tribal languages.[2] He was considered to be one of the most knowledgeable men on the Plains and one who could be relied on for sound decisions. His opinion was valued highly by leaders among both the whites and Indians, and they listened to him in important matters. Chisholm was respected and trusted by all. Mead lauded him as "an honest and good man."[3] To men such as Comanche Chief Ten Bears, he was a beloved brother. As a Cherokee he shared a historic, and perhaps a personal, relationship with the leader of Texas independence, Sam Houston.

In his service to the white man, Jesse Chisholm often rode hundreds of hard miles out onto the wild prairie to find and persuade Indian leaders to come in to meet in council. It was an unpleasant and dangerous assignment even for Chisholm, to enter the camp of angry Comanches after the whites had abused them. Yet, for the sake of peace on the Plains, he did so. It was he who in numerous peace councils translated the words of white and red men as they attempted to settle their disputes.

It would be wrong to paint Jesse Chisholm as a hero. He fought no great battles, was no Prometheus, and the Chisholm Cattle Trail, for which he is remembered in history, was merely a by-product of his many treks. Yet, he has long been one of the unsung shapers of the American West, a man who played a significant role in an exciting, colorful period of the frontier, a faithful friend to both the white man and the Indian. He would have asked for no more.

Jesse Chisholm

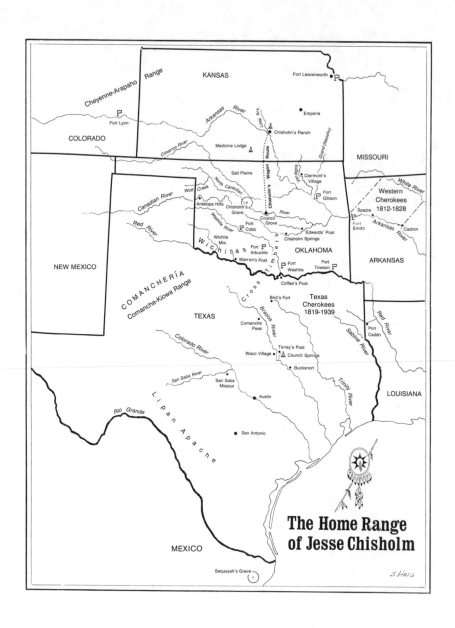

The Home Range
of Jesse Chisholm

The Chisholms and the Cherokees

The land seemed to be especially still on this spring morning of 1868. The bumping of the wagon and the occasional cawing of sentinel crows along the cottonwood-lined river were the only sounds that broke the quiet of the green countryside. The burial retinue that escorted the wagon holding the blanket-wrapped body of Jesse Chisholm was silent except for the soft, mournful death song of Comanche Chief Parasawamano, or Ten Bears, who rode behind on his cream-colored pony.

At a chosen place across the North Canadian River from the dominant red butte known to the Indians as Little Mountain, where the river bent eastward, the procession halted. Some of the Chisholm men carried Jesse's body to the hole that had been dug for it. The body was unwrapped and laid out beside the grave for all to take a final look at the man they had known and depended upon for so long.

Ten Bears seated himself at the head of the grave and continued his song. When he had finished, the Comanche patriarch rose and took from his neck the gold peace medal that had been given to him by President Abraham Lincoln.[1] It was his most prized possession. Tears trickled down from behind the old Indian's steel-rimmed spectacles and ran along the creases of his weatherworn face as he slipped the leather thong over Jesse's head and laid the medal gently on Chisholm's chest.

Without further ceremony, the body was wrapped again with the blanket, then with a buffalo skin, and lowered into the ground. Dirt was shoveled into the hole, mounded, and covered with rocks. A small enclosure of freshly cut poles was built, and a headboard was

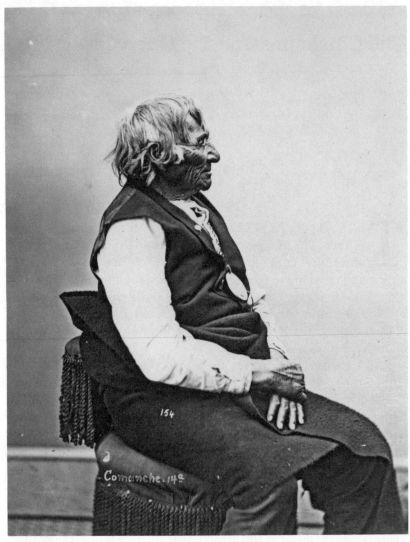

Comanche Chief Parasawamano, or Ten Bears. The peace medal Ten Bears is wearing here he later placed around the neck of the body of his beloved friend Jesse Chisholm. *Courtesy of the Smithsonian Institution National Anthropological Archives, Bureau of American Ethnology Collection.*

erected bearing an inscription of Jesse's name and date of death. Ten
Bears mounted his pony and rode off to the west where his band was
camped on some distant stream.

The others, Jesse's family and his Indian trader friends, continued on southeastward down the North Canadian to Jesse's cabin at
Council Grove. There Dutch Bill Greiffenstein dug a jug of
Kentucky's best from a flour barrel. The traders held a wake in the
memory of their departed comrade, toasting Jesse and firing to him
with their buffalo guns. They were men of the frontier, and death
was no stranger to them. Yet somehow they sensed that even as
Jesse departed the scene, an era of western history was ending. They
were pleased that their friend would be well remembered in the new
order of things. Already Texas cattlemen were crossing the Indian
Territory by way of the soon-to-be famous Chisholm Trail.

Not even his friends knew the full story of Jesse Chisholm's role
in the early American involvement on the vast prairie land that
stretched from the Arkansas River to the Rio Grande in the period
preceding settlement and the rise of the great range-cattle industry.
Nor likely did they know of the part that he and his family had
played in the saga of American advance as it swept westward from
Tennessee through Arkansas, the Indian Territory, Texas, and Kansas. Two of Jesse's forebears, one a Cherokee chief and the other an
ambitious Scottish immigrant, took major roles in the struggle of
the Cherokee Nation of the South to resist the onslaught of white
intrusion and the taking of its lands. Jesse's roots are firmly planted
in the events of that clash and the eventual Cherokee migration
westward. As the arena of conflict between native Indians and
advancing whites moved beyond the Mississippi to the central
Plains, Jesse became deeply involved in its resolution. Much of his
life was spent in efforts to work out peace arrangements with the
Indian tribes of the western prairie.

Jesse's maternal grandfather may well have been Corn Tassel,
the famous Cherokee principal chief and "Beloved Man."[2] The great
chief, reputed as the Benjamin Franklin of the Cherokee Nation,
was noted for his sagacity, his honesty, and his efforts to bring about
peace and understanding between his people and the whites.
"Throughout a long and useful life in his own country," observed
William Tatham, who came to know Corn Tassel during the forging

of the Treaty of Long Island, "he was never known to stoop to falsehood."³

Again and again, the Americans had come to the Cherokees with demands for new treaties, each time slicing off more and more of the Cherokee lands in Virginia, Kentucky, Tennessee, North Carolina, Georgia, and Alabama. The treaties were made, but nothing satisfied the Americans. They always wanted more. Old Tassel had observed this fact in dismay: "In every treaty that we have had that a boundary is fixt, we always find your people settle much faster than before. It is well known you have taken almost all of our country from us without our consent . . . truth is, if we had no land we should have fewer enemies."⁴

During negotiations for the Treaty of Long Island in July 1777, Tassel had sagely observed:

> The great God of Nature has placed us in different situations. It is true he has endowed you with many superior advantages; but he had not created us to be your slaves. *We are a separate people!* He has given each their lands, under distinct considerations and circumstances: he has stocked yours with cows, ours with buffaloe; yours with hog, ours with bear; yours with sheep, ours with deer. He has, indeed, given you an advantage in this, your cattle are tame and domestic while ours are wild and demand not only a larger space for range, but art [skill] to hunt and kill them.⁵

In 1788 renegade southern Cherokees from the Chickamauga Creek area murdered a family named Kirk on Little River below what is now Knoxville. The American militia under John "Noli-chucky Jack" Sevier came to Old Tassel's home at Chote, Tennessee, looking for revenge. The chief explained to them it was not his people of the Cherokee northern towns who had committed the murders.

Chucky Jack went back to his camp, but while he was away for a time Major James Hubbard came back to see Old Tassel. Hubbard promised him safe conduct if he would attend a council with other Cherokee chiefs. The chief agreed, fearing if he refused his village would be attacked by the militia, which was not noted for its discipline. He and his son rode with Hubbard under a white flag of truce to the home of Chief Abram. When all of the chiefs were gathered inside Abram's small house, Hubbard treacherously sprang his trap. He ordered his men to close off the windows and doors so no one could escape. Then John Kirk, a surviving member of the massacred Kirk family, came forward with a war ax. Corn Tassel knew the end had come and bowed his head to the death blow. The old chief, his son, and the rest of the Cherokee leaders were killed in the same manner.[6]

During this period of conflict between the Indians of the South and the pressing forces of American civilization, Jesse Chisholm's paternal grandfather was also playing an active and significant role. In personality and character, John D. Chisholm was virtually the opposite of Old Tassel; and the image that historical records leave of the Scot is largely of a determined, opportunistic rogue. Nonetheless, he was deeply involved in both the early history of the South and in the destiny of the first major group of Cherokees to migrate westward.

By his account, John Chisholm had arrived in North America in 1777, going first to Charleston, South Carolina, where his father, an earlier emigrant to the American colonies, resided.[7] The pressures of the American Revolution soon forced him to migrate on to Florida, then into the Creek country of Georgia and back northward with Indian traders into the Holston River country of east Tennessee.

A redheaded, contentious, "blasty" man, Chisholm quickly won himself a place among the over-the-mountain frontiersmen. He received an appointment as justice of the peace in the Washington District of North Carolina. Chisholm took part in the State of Franklin headed by the cavalier Nolichucky Jack and was a delegate to the Jonesboro Convention of 1784. Later he served as a Franklin legislator.[8]

In 1790 Chisholm was reappointed justice of the peace, this time of Washington County in the newly created Territory South of the Ohio River by its governor and superintendent of Indian affairs, William Blount. The following year Blount employed him to haul goods for the Treaty of Holston, which was conducted with the Cherokees at the site of present-day Knoxville. Chisholm's name appears on the treaty document as a witness.[9]

When Blount moved his headquarters to this location a short time later, Chisholm followed, thus becoming one of the earliest settlers of Knoxville. He was awarded a contract to build the first

Chisholm Tavern, Knoxville, Tennessee. This tavern, no longer standing, was one of the many enterprises of John D. Chisholm, Jesse's feisty Scottish grandfather. *Courtesy of the Barker Texas History Center, The University of Texas at Austin.*

courthouse there.[10] At the same time he was busy with other enterprises, erecting the first tavern in Knoxville next to the capitol, establishing a private postal route in east Tennessee, operating a beef market, and selling slaves.[11] Chisholm continued to act for Blount as an emissary to the Indian tribes of the region, helping to quiet disturbances and, on occasion, rescuing captured whites. He served with the local militia and was with Sevier's militia on a number of campaigns against the Indians.

During his first year in the region Chisholm had helped to probate the estate of William Fauling, whose widow Betsy he soon married. Of her at least three children — Ignatius, Elizabeth, and Deborah — were born.[12] One son, Thomas, was born to Chisholm's second wife, a part-Cherokee woman named Martha Holmes. It is not known what ended either of these marriages, but by 1797 Chisholm had taken as his third wife another part Cherokee named Patsy Brown, sister to Cherokee leader Richard Brown.[13]

At this time John Chisholm became enmeshed in a grandiose plan that, had it succeeded, would have drastically affected the history of the United States. From extensive travels he had made throughout the South and by virtue of the military intelligence received through his father-in-law by his second marriage, a British colonel, Chisholm conceived a plot to wrest Florida from the hands of the Spanish, who then held it.[14]

Blount, now elected as one of the first two senators from the State of Tennessee, was deeply involved in land speculation and expressed great interest in Chisholm's scheme. Chisholm, however, became fearful Blount was eventually going to cut him out. Brazenly, he set sail alone for London to secure the assistance of the British government. On the eve of his departure he penned a letter to a friend expressing his resolve: "I now tell you in Ernest at nine o'clock to-morrow I go aboard the ship favorite & saile for forein Climes. . . . I will conquer or be Damd."[15] Even as he was in England, however, a message from Blount to Cherokee interpreter William Carey at Hiwassee Garrison in Tennessee found its way into the hands of U.S. government officials and revealed the Florida scheme. Congress began impeachment proceedings against Blount.

When word reached England that Chisholm's plot had been made public, the British rejected his overtures out of hand. The ambitious Scot eventually ended up in debtor's prison in London. His release was secured and passage home was provided by U.S. officials only after he had made a written confession of the whole affair.[16]

Because he had named names in his confession, Chisholm felt great trepidation about his return. He obtained a passport containing a false description of himself and added the middle initial, D, to his name.[17] When Chisholm returned to Tennessee he had few friends and many enemies. Patsy Brown, whom he had deserted, divorced him.

But Chisholm's historical involvement was far from done. He now secured permission to enter the Indian country. Heading south down the Tennessee he relocated himself among the southern Cherokees at the Muscle Shoals in northern Alabama. There he became an advisor to the notorious Chickamaugan chief Doublehead, a nephew of Old Tassel. The vengeful Cherokee had once axed a group of helpless whites to death without mercy. Unable to defeat Doublehead in the field, the United States had decided to try bribery in lieu of force. Doublehead was invited to visit the president at the capital at Philadelphia. There a treaty was signed whereby the Cherokees made certain land cessions. Both Doublehead and John Chisholm, who accompanied the chief on the trip, were personally rewarded.[18]

The Cherokees of the Upper Towns were greatly incensed over this, and they were further enraged by reports that Doublehead and Chisholm were involved in selling Cherokee land to whites. The Ridge, an upper-village chief, headed a plot to assassinate the two men when they came upriver to attend the Cherokee ball games at Hiwassee, Tennessee. Doublehead was brutally murdered. For some reason, either by good fortune or forewarning, Chisholm did not accompany the chief to Hiwassee and escaped a similar fate.[19] However, his situation was as precarious as that of the lower Cherokees. There was no hope of his returning to reside among the whites of Knoxville and east Tennessee, and he had been banished by the Creeks from their country in Georgia.

Chisholm now became an advisor to Chief Tahlonteskee, brother to Doublehead and another half-blooded nephew of Old Tassel. Chisholm worked with Cherokee agent Return J. Meigs to promote Thomas Jefferson's policy of removing the Cherokees west of the

Mississippi to the Arkansas River country of the recently acquired Louisiana Territory.[20]Accordingly, Meigs and Chisholm persuaded Tahlonteskee to take his villages of Cherokees westward in the spring of 1810. The emigrants crossed the Mississippi, stopping for a time with another group of Cherokees who had settled on the St. Francis River of southeastern Missouri a number of years earlier.[21]

Following the great midcontinental earthquake in 1811, the combined group of Cherokees moved south to the Arkansas River. There they established several settlements, namely Dardanelles (named for the large mounds of rocks on either side of the river), Point Remove, Illinois Bayou, and Spadra Bluffs. No rolls were kept of these first Cherokee migrations, but Cherokee Agency correspondence definitely establishes the presence of John D. Chisholm with Tahlonteskee's group. On June 28, 1812, he wrote from Arkansas: "I have been constant with Tollantisky and party since he left the Old Nation and doing their business and instructing in the best manner I know how."[22]

Jesse's father, Ignatius Chisholm, had been involved with his father John's business enterprises in Knoxville during the 1790s. As a mere boy of less than sixteen years in 1793, he had taken part in a militia campaign against the Creeks in Georgia. At one time he was employed as a "patroller" in Knoxville and vicinity. A dealer in slaves like his father, Ignatius was one of three men who prior to 1800 were charged with invading a man's property on horseback, entering the slave quarters, and there abusing a Negro man.[23] As a result, Ignatius fled Knoxville and took up residence with the Cherokees in the Hiwassee area, there marrying Jesse's mother.

By her he sired three sons — Jesse, who was born in 1805 or 1806, and his two younger brothers, John and William. Prior to the Cherokee migration west, he separated from Jesse's mother and remarried. It is generally believed that his new wife was the half blood Martha Rogers, a member of the large family of trader John Rogers. The marriage is thought to have produced a half sister to Jesse, named Martha, who was born in Tennessee in 1812.[24]

The presence of Ignatius Chisholm in Arkansas is first indicated in an 1813 letter by a man who complained of a "notorious villain who ran away from Tennessee, and who has resided as a trader &c with the Cherokees since they have been on the Arkansas by the name of Lig Chisholm."[25] Evidently, Jesse had already been brought west by his mother with Tahlonteskee's group of 1810,[26] and he lived from the age of five or six until he was beyond the age of twenty along the Arkansas River of present-day Arkansas State. Possibly he assisted and learned from his father, who operated as a trader among the Arkansas immigrants. In this way he could have gained the knowledge and vocational skills he employed the entirety of his life as a trader. Ignatius Chisholm's name is listed in the records of Arkansas Post on the Mississippi, and it may well have been that Jesse accompanied him on canoe or flatboat voyages down the Arkansas River to swap furs for trade goods.

Jesse shared much the same boyhood experiences and training as other Cherokee youths: hunting and trapping in the game-rich forests to the south; joining Cherokee groups on adventurous forays westward; and participating in tribal dances and clan rituals. Importantly, he learned the art of survival in the wilderness, developing skills that would later mark him as a leader among men.

In Arkansas the immigrant Cherokees at once commenced erecting homes, clearing farmland, and building up herds of livestock. As the settlers became more established and as more people arrived from the Old Nation, their farms spread westward up the Arkansas to Frog Bayou and Mulberry Creek. This Western Cherokee culture was a unique mixture of American and tribal ways. On the one hand, the Western Cherokees followed the lives of independent planters and livestock owners. They cultivated crops of cotton, corn, and other foodstuffs, many keeping a few chickens, cows, and hogs. Some men earned their livelihood by hunting deer, bear, and small game for food; others trapped for pelts to sell to white traders. The women tended gardens, wove baskets, carded and spun cotton, and did other domestic chores about their log cabin homesteads.

However, the Arkansas immigrants soon discovered they had entered into a new world that was even more violent than that they had left behind. The most dangerous adversaries by far were the Osages, who ruled southwestern Missouri. Long before the first Cherokee move westward, Cherokee hunting parties had crossed the Mississippi and run afoul of the Osages, and a tradition of enmity already existed. The setting was ripe for the ferocious warfare that almost immediately developed between the two nations.

The mores of clan and warriorship were still strong among the Western Cherokees. Revenge expeditions against enemy tribes often involved horse stealing, slave taking, killing, and scalping, followed by tribal dances of celebration.

Despite efforts by U.S. officials to end the bloody intertribal warfare, it would continue throughout the Cherokee stay in Arkansas. One band of Osages under Chief Clermont had been encouraged by trader Auguste Pierre Chouteau to settle on the Verdigris River west of the Cherokees. Clermont's band became a barrier to Cherokee hunting excursions to the prairie buffalo range beyond, a situation that greatly incensed the Cherokees and would eventually lead to brutal resolve.

Young Jesse enjoyed special stature among the Cherokees by virtue of the prominence of his Scottish grandfather in Western Cherokee affairs. John D. Chisholm continued to act as an advisor to Tahlonteskee and others. There is some indication he may have operated virtually in the capacity of a chief himself, though being no part Cherokee he was never elected to that post. He and Ignatius also influenced Cherokee subagent William Lovely, who located at the mouth of Illinois Bayou in 1813.[27]

When Lovely arrived in Arkansas, he acted to keep peace between the Indians and the white settlers by issuing a decree establishing a separate territory for the Cherokees. It ran north from the Arkansas River to the White River and west from Point Remove to what is now the eastern border of Oklahoma. White settlers complained bitterly, claiming that Lovely had given the Cherokees the richest and best farming land.[28]

In 1814 John D. Chisholm was selected by the Cherokee council to go to Washington, D.C., for the purpose of making legal claim to the Arkansas lands and the right of the Western Cherokees to establish a government separate from that of the Old Nation Cherokees.[29] He also accompanied a Cherokee delegation to St. Louis in 1815 to express concern to Governor William Clark over their Arkansas lands being assigned as a county of Missouri Territory. In the spring of 1816 Chisholm headed still another delegation to St. Louis to protest Osage depredations.[30]

On July 9, 1816, agent Lovely and a delegation of Cherokees met with the Osages at Clermont's village and signed an agreement by which the Osages gave up their claim to all the land between the Cherokee country and the Verdigris River. Though the pact was never ratified by the United States, it and the area involved became known as Lovely's Purchase.[31]

In July 1817, despite the displeasure of the Old Nation leaders — especially of his former brother-in-law and then principal chief Richard Brown — John Chisholm represented the Arkansas Cherokees at a treaty-making council held at the Cherokee Agency at Calhoun, Tennessee. The Western Cherokees wished to maintain themselves as a separate government from the Old Nation; however, the United States was principally interested in encouraging Old Nation removal to the west. Chisholm exercised great influence upon the Western chiefs; too much for General Andrew Jackson, U.S. commissioner at the treaty, who later complained, "We were compelled to promise to John D. Chisholm the sum of one thousand dollars to stop his mouth & obtain his consent."[32]

Despite the Lovely agreement, the war with the Osages continued unabated, coming to a head in the fall of 1817. Following the murder and decapitation of a Cherokee who had been lured to the camp of some Osages, the Arkansas Cherokees were determined to mount a formidable, well-planned strike upon Clermont's village (near present-day Claremore, Oklahoma). In July they wrote to forewarn Governor Clark of their intentions of revenge, and fighting men from the Old Nation were recruited during the treaty council at Calhoun. Led by Tahlonteskee and silver-headed, eagle-faced war chief Takatoka, the Arkansas Cherokees gathered together a large contingent of white men and half bloods as well as Indians of other tribes who held grievances against the Osages.[33]

Jesse Chisholm was barely in his teens, and it is very doubtful he was among the Cherokee attackers, even though other "Chissoms" were.[34] Clermont and most of his fighting men were away on their fall buffalo hunt at the time, and their village lay defenseless as the Cherokees swept up the Arkansas River and launched their attack. Over eighty Osages were killed, and nearly one hundred women and children were taken prisoner, with the loss of only one of the Cherokee force killed and a few wounded. Some Osages were said to have drowned in the Verdigris River while trying to escape. The thatched-hut town was burned, crops destroyed, and a large amount of livestock and other plunder carried away.

John D. Chisholm died the following year,[35] and his half-blooded son Thomas came west the same year. Thomas would eventually rise to prominence and serve briefly as a third chief among the Western Cherokees. Tahlonteskee followed Chisholm to the grave in 1819, and a new set of leaders took over.

The first decade for the Western Cherokees in Arkansas had often been violent as the immigrants contended for their territorial rights. But the roots of more peaceful ways were spreading among the Cherokees along the Arkansas River. When the English botanist Thomas Nuttall came up the river in 1819 he noted the prosperity of fenced farmlands, good stocks of cattle, and well-furnished homes along the Arkansas.[36]

However, the shadow of Clermont's Osage warriors still loomed across the Cherokees' path leading west to the prairie. The Arkansas Indians aggressively demanded an outlet to the west by which their hunters could reach the buffalo herds as they felt the U.S. government had promised them. Chief Takatoka set about to form an alliance of Indian nations that had been removed from east of the Mississippi by the government. He and other Cherokees hoped also to secure title to the area of Lovely's Purchase, which would give them the "clear opening to the setting sun" promised them by President James Monroe.[37]

Corn Tassel, the brother of Jesse's mother and probably a son of the former principal chief, was among those who in October 1824 accompanied the aging Takatoka to a grand council at Kaskaskia, Illinois, in his quest for an Indian confederacy. Takatoka died at Kaskaskia; but, as he had requested from his deathbed, the other Cherokees continued on to Washington, D.C., in an effort to secure title to Lovely's Purchase.[38] But, in response to demands made by Arkansas whites, the government attempted to persuade the Cherokees to trade their present holdings for new land, to give up their lands in Arkansas and move to the country of Lovely's Purchase. The delegation rejected the idea out of hand and returned home. The Cherokees watched with increasing alarm as whites began to settle west of them following the establishment of cantonments (soon to become forts) Gibson and Towson in 1824.

In late 1827 another delegation was dispatched to Washington. One of its members was George Guess, or Sequoyah, the famed inventor of the Cherokee alphabet who had come west prior to 1820. Though never achieving the status of chief, Sequoyah often took part in important Western Cherokee decisions. It was during his visit to Washington that Sequoyah's portrait was painted by artist Charles Bird King.[39]

The Cherokee council had no intention that this delegation would become involved in a treaty to exchange their Arkansas lands for those of Lovely's Purchase. But once they were in Washington, U.S. officials held them as virtual prisoners in their hotel for several weeks until they were cajoled and bribed into signing an agreement for the exchange. The Treaty of 1828 caused much animosity among the Western Cherokees in Arkansas. Poles were erected at the delegates' homes as a threat that their heads might well be placed there when they returned.[40]

With great suffering and loss of property and stock, the Cherokees began making their move westward along the Arkansas River in present-day Oklahoma from Fort Smith to Fort Gibson. There they formed small new communities at sites such as Skin Bayou, the Illinois River, Sallisaw River, Webbers Falls, and Bayou Menard. Behind them the whites of Arkansas quickly moved into the Cherokees' homes; but other whites residing in Lovely's Purchase were unwilling to vacate their holdings, placing even more hardship upon the Cherokees.

Young Jesse Chisholm had already made his way to Gibson, and by the time he had crested twenty years he had become part of the frontier legion populating the fort and nearby trading posts.

In September 1826, twenty well-armed men on horseback rode out of the rectangular log fort that had been established two years earlier near the mouth of the Grand River as Cantonment Gibson. They towed seven pack mules heavily loaded with food and supplies, plus shovels, picks, and pans for gold mining. Each man carried a long-barreled hunting rifle across his saddle, with ball pouch and powder horn dangling at the side. At their head was the much-respected Nathaniel Pryor, former member of the Lewis and Clark Expedition and now the Osage subagent and operator of a trading post near Gibson. A few of the men wore military uniforms, but most were civilians garbed in the buckskins of the frontier. One of these, the only man among them with Indian blood, was Jesse Chisholm, still with a youthful look in his early twenties.

The group moved up the Verdigris River to Clermont's Osage village. Pryor was married to an Osage woman and spoke her language well. After informing Clermont that he and his men were headed out to search for gold that was believed to be there, Pryor led the way northwestward until they struck the Arkansas River. The men traveled cautiously now, for this little-known country was regularly trespassed by war parties of Pawnee, Kaw, and other tribes from the north. They rode steadily up the Arkansas, making about twenty-five miles a day, stopping now and then to hunt and to pan the river sands. After traveling for fifteen days, the gold seekers went into camp on the river near the mouth of Walnut Creek. Now they began their search in earnest.

There was a special mystique about the early American West that drew men irresistibly to explore its secrets, to find a place to settle and build homes, and, ever hopefully, to reap the rewards of its great cornucopia of wild game and mineral wealth. This was true not only of white men but also of the eastern Indians who roamed much farther and wider on exploring, hunting, and marauding expeditions than is generally believed. Jesse Chisholm was among those who, discontent to remain within the relative safety and comfort of the more civilized areas, was constantly drawn to the distant horizon.

Early on, Jesse had become acquainted with the area of Lovely's Purchase, which included an important site, near the juncture of the Verdigris and Grand (or Neosho) with the Arkansas, known to Indians as the Ten Bulls and to the whites as the Three Forks. By 1819 three trading posts were maintained there. The cabin of Joseph Bougie was located a mile and a half above the mouth of the Verdigris; Pryor, Samuel Richards, and Hugh Glenn had a post a mile up the same river; and Captain Henry Barbour and George W. Brand were situated on the east side of the Verdigris above its falls. Some thirty miles up the Grand was the original trading house of Auguste Chouteau, and not far from there was a salt-mining operation, which would be owned temporarily a few years later by Samuel Houston. In 1824 two important frontier forts were created beyond Fort Smith: Cantonment Towson on the Red River and Cantonment Gibson near the mouth of the Grand. These trading and military posts did much to extend the operating area of the Arkansas Cherokees and frontier whites and led to adventures such as Pryor's 1826 gold-seeking expedition.

This hunt for gold on the Arkansas River had been prompted by intriguing rumors and reports of military explorers, traders, and others who had visited the area. During the preceding year, while on a visit to New Orleans, Pryor had met a wealthy merchant who said he had been with the Pike expedition in 1807. He had been taken prisoner by the Mexicans, the merchant claimed. He and another man had escaped and made their way to the Arkansas River, which they followed eastward. At the mouth of Walnut Creek they had discovered signs of a mining operation. They had halted their march to examine the area, discovering a large quantity of gold.

With a makeshift forge they had melted it and formed it into bars, which they carted on downriver to Natchez, where the two men had separated. It was this gold, the merchant asserted, that had enabled him to embark on his commercial success in New Orleans.

The idea of precious metal on the Arkansas River was augmented by another story recounted by a Spanish surgeon in Havana. He told of being with a group of Spanish explorers who in 1783 had found large quantities of silver ore at the mouth of Walnut Creek. The Spaniards had been attacked by a party of Indians, the surgeon being one of eight who escaped. Later the men had returned, built furnaces to melt their ore into bars, then floated it downriver in canoes made of buffalo hides.[1] This account, though varying in details and date, is similar to the story that a group of Spaniards transporting a cargo of gold and silver was attacked by Indians at the mouth of the Little Arkansas; all were killed except one man who buried the bullion before making his escape. The incident, which is reflected on the Antoine S. Le Page du Pratz map of 1757, is believed to have taken place long before that date.[2]

Also adding fuel to the gold legend was Pratz's claim that "I found, upon the river of the Arkansas, a rivulet that rolled down with its waters, gold dust."[3] Such stories stirred the blood of men, and some were fully convinced that precious metals were to be found up the Arkansas.

In addition to Jesse, Pryor's party consisted of men from Arkansas and the Gibson area. Colonel Matthew Arbuckle, who authorized the exploration, sent a few of his officers and soldiers along.4 Other members of the party were Dr. John W. Baylor, post surgeon at Cantonment Gibson; W. M. Black of Crawford County, Arkansas; G. C. Pickett; Joseph Tomlinson; Frederick Fletcher; Reuben Sanders and his son Richard; a Fort Gibson sergeant named Griggs; a private named Mixen; and two other men named Hodges and Butler. Another officer from Gibson, a "scientific man," was along but soon became ill and turned back.

A letter, written by W. M. Black during the California gold rush excitement and published in the May 19, 1849, *Arkansas Intelligencer* of Van Buren, Arkansas, gives an account of this interesting expedition. Responding to a request by an Evansville, Arkansas, group that had asked him to lead them to Walnut Creek, Black recalled the 1826 gold-seeking venture, telling how he and the others had gone up the Arkansas. He recounted how two of Pryor's party had discovered large quantities of shining particles in the riverbed near the mouth of the Walnut. They thought they had found the "golden sands" of the Arkansas, and there was great excitement in the camp. However, the soldier named Mixen, who was from the gold-mining region of North Carolina, had doused their hopes, saying that he had never seen gold in that form. Jesse and his comrades had continued their exploration along the river without luck. After seven weeks in the field, many of the men had become tired and discouraged. It had been decided to give up the venture, though some still fervently believed there was gold to be found. The weary gold seekers had killed sixteen elk, herds of which still roamed southern Kansas at the time, cured the meat, and then had returned home to the joshing of friends.

However, the lure of a possible gold mine on the Arkansas caused one member of the party to return soon after, without success. He was followed later by a company under Richard Bean, who with his brother operated a saline on the Illinois River, and on still another occasion by a group of Cherokees. Whether Jesse accompanied any of these explorations is not known, though his trading associate, James Mead, later claimed that Jesse led a gold-seeking detail to the mouth of the Little Arkansas in 1836.[5]

Jesse Chisholm is listed on the Western Cherokee Old Settler rolls as one of those who migrated from Arkansas in 1828, probably to the Fort Gibson area. He is shown to have been single at the time. Ignatius Chisholm is listed as having two members in his family — probably himself and his second wife.[6] Ignatius resettled at Webbers Falls, residing with George Chisholm. George, a son by Ignatius's second wife and thus a half brother to Jesse, had been born in Arkansas around 1814. Jesse's mother lived nearby just up the Arkansas until she died in 1837.[7] Besides George and half sister Martha, it is possible that Jesse had another half brother named Nelson.[8]

Also on the Arkansas emigrant rolls was the widow Diana Rogers Gentry, daughter of trader John Rogers who had come west in 1817. Diana would either marry or take up conjugal relations with

Sam Houston, who had recently resigned as governor of Tennessee.[9] Houston arrived among the Western Cherokees in 1829 and first located with Chief John Jolly, with whom he had resided for a period as a young boy in Tennessee and who had informally adopted him as a son. Jolly, the rotund brother of Tahlonteskee and nephew of old Corn Tassel, now owned a large, slave-operated plantation at Webbers Falls and ran a sizable mercantile business there.[10]

Houston later moved to the Fort Gibson area and established a trading post known as the Wigwam Neosho. Jesse Chisholm, too, was conducting trading operations in the Fort Gibson area, buying corn from the Cherokee and Creek farmers and reselling it to the military post. At Gibson he would come to know the man, eight years his senior, whom he would later serve in Texas.[11]

The warring activities of the Cherokees and Osages against one another had largely subsided by now, though both had become involved in conflict with the tribes that resided on the vast prairies extending south of the Arkansas River well into central Texas. During 1828 a party of thirty-five Cherokees set out on a hunting expedition to the west. They were met by a party of Pawnee Picts who surrounded and rushed them. The Cherokees lost three men before escaping. When seven Cherokees made a revenge attack on the Pawnee Pict village, three more warriors were killed.[12]

Jesse was undoubtedly involved in many adventures with the Cherokees of which there is no historical record. His known history as a peacemaker makes it doubtful that even as a young man he indulged in the incessant intertribal warfare. He was, however, either involved in, or close to, a bloody battle between Cherokees and Tawakonis on the Brazos River of Texas in 1830.

Eleven years earlier a sizable group of Cherokees under half bloods Richard Fields and John Bowles had cut away from the main body on the Arkansas and moved southwestward to southern Arkansas. In 1820, at the invitation of the Mexican government, they moved to the headwaters of the Trinity River at the site of present-day Dallas, Texas. Conflicts with the prairie tribes, however, caused them to move back east to the sweet gum and pine woodland along the upper Neches and Sabine rivers of northeast Texas. There new conflicts, both external and internal, soon developed. The Cherokees were resisted by both the native tribes and by Texas whites. Accusing Fields of treachery in dealing with the Mexican government, Chiefs Bowles and Big Mush had him assassinated.[13]

In 1824 the noted Cherokee war chief Dutch had been angered by a decree ordering the Cherokees living in the forested area south of the Arkansas River to remove to the relatively gameless land north of the river. In response he had taken his band of followers and moved to the Caddo country south of the Red River. Dutch, with whom Jesse may well have held a clan relationship, was a commanding figure.[14] Possessed of an erect and powerful six-foot build and a wild, fierce countenance, the war chief was known to be brave and cunning. For his friends, it was said, he held great love; for his enemies, great hate. Against the Osages, he had proved an implacable foe, taking many of their scalps.

Parties of Arkansas Cherokees regularly made sojourns to Texas to hunt and visit with relatives, and Jesse spent enough time in the region to become adept in the Caddo tongue. His long association with Dutch also caused him to become caught up in the Texas Cherokee intertribal warfare against the Tawakoni Indians. This Wichitan tribe resided to the west on the Brazos River, having earlier been driven from north of the Red River by the Osages. During 1826 Stephen F. Austin, on behalf of the Mexican government, contacted the Texas Cherokees, asking them to supply a hundred warriors for a joint attack against the Tawakoni villages on the headwaters of the Navasota River. The Cherokees were willing; but the plans were canceled by the Mexican government, and the proposed campaign did not take place.[15]

However, trouble between the Tawakonis and the Cherokees developed in 1827 when a party of six Cherokees and Creeks attempted to steal some horses from the Tawakoni village. The group was discovered and ambushed. Three of the horse thieves were killed, scalped, and their corpses tied to a pole for a victorious scalp dance celebration. The Tawakoni victory was reported to the Bowles colony by warriors from another tribe who had been witness to it. The Texas Cherokees wrote a letter to the northern Cherokees, who by the time they received it had moved to the area of Lovely's Purchase in what would soon become the Indian Territory.

Cherokee leader Tahchee, or Dutch. A close friend of Jesse Chisholm, Dutch was well known in Arkansas, the Indian Territory, and Texas as a determined and resourceful warrior. *Courtesy of the Smithsonian Institution National Anthropological Archives, Bureau of American Ethnology Collection.*

In the spring of 1830 John Smith, another athletic-looking
Cherokee who was noted as a warrior captain,[16] called together a
war dance and council at Bayou Menard east of Fort Gibson to
organize a reprisal expedition against the Tawakonis. Chief Jolly,
who strongly opposed the action, was too ill to attend the affair, but
he sent Sam Houston in his stead. Despite his efforts to dissuade
the war faction, Houston could not prevent "the raising of the
Tomahawk of War" by some of the Cherokees.[17]

Smith gave a detailed account of the affair to John Ridge at
Washington in 1836. Before he and his father were assassinated by
followers of Chief John Ross in 1839, John Ridge put the story on
paper. He tells how Smith and a Creek warrior headed south for
Dutch's village. On the way they met with a group of Cherokee
hunters, who led them on southward across the Sabine River to "the
field and Cabins of my friend, the Great Cherokee Warrior, whose
name is Dutch."[18] It is not clear, but accounts seem to indicate that
perhaps Jesse Chisholm was already in Dutch's village.

Dutch welcomed his guests heartily, providing a dinner of boiled
pork, bread, beans, and sweet potatoes, and a drink made from
ground Indian corn. After two days had passed, eleven warriors from
the Fort Gibson area arrived. When Dutch learned of Smith's plan
to strike against the Tawakonis, he volunteered himself and nine-
teen of his men to go along.

In support of Smith and Dutch, a council was held by Chief Big
Mush, whose settlement was only fifteen miles distant. There it was
promised that in eleven days warriors of this village would join
Smith and Dutch at Marshall's saline, two days' journey toward the
setting sun. Dutch led the way to Marshall's place. The Cherokee
force was now sixty-three strong. After a brief rest, they moved on
westward, some mounted and some on foot, crossing the Trinity
River (probably in the vicinity of present-day Corsicana) and proceeding on with six spies in front and six to each side until the
Tawakoni village was reached.

While their scouts reconnoitered the village and beyond, the
Cherokee warriors stripped themselves of all but their shirts, which
they kept to distinguish themselves from the enemy during battle,
painted their bodies and heads, and adjusted their headdresses.
During the early hours of morning, the predators crept up on the

sleeping village, so silently that the rattle of their powder horns was the only sound. Men were posted outside the doors of lodges to begin the attack by slaughtering anyone who came out.

The massacre that followed, as described by Smith, was ruthless. The Cherokees gave the Tawakonis no quarter. They shot and tomahawked men and women alike. A large portion of the village, however, made it to the protection of their great lodge. Twelve by forty-five feet, half buried and supported mainly by a long ridgepole, the structure's cornstalk and dirt roof extended to the ground. An attempt was made to burn the occupants out, but it was successfully repelled by the arrows and gunfire that poured forth from the redoubt.

Another battle erupted when a large force of Waco warriors appeared on the scene, mounted and well armed. Three Cherokees on horseback and several on foot were lured off in pursuit and ran into a deadly trap. Their scalped corpses were later found pierced by lances and spiked with barbed arrows. Still unable to burn out the refugees in their earth-protected lodge, the Cherokees made their retreat with some fifty-five to sixty Tawakoni scalps, leaving behind five dead of their own. Upon their return to Dutch's village, the victorious war party was welcomed with great feasting and shaking of hands. The Cherokee celebration was visited by a Texas settler who was told in detail of the Tawakoni fight by "a very intelligent man, a half-breed, named Chisholm."[19] It is not clear if Jesse had been with the Cherokee war party as an eyewitness or had simply heard accounts of the fight.

In September 1831 Dutch and ten other Cherokees guided an American named Aaron B. Lewis on an expedition up the Red River as far as the Washita River.[20] Dutch, who wished to hunt and trap along that river, parted from Lewis there. Jesse may well have been a member of this expedition. His presence in this same region with Dutch's party as a guide for the Leavenworth-Dodge expedition three years later indicates that he was familiar with the country.

During that same year, following word that the reward for him had been revoked, Dutch agreed to move back north of the Red River. The strong tie between Dutch and the Chisholms was apparent when the U.S. government hired John Smith, Ignatius and Nelson Chisholm, Thomas Ogden (a discharged Fort Gibson soldier who

worked for George Chisholm), and forty other men to move Dutch
and his people to the Canadian River.[21] There Dutch settled down
to live in peace, building a home around which a sizable Cherokee
community developed.

Jesse also became involved in more pacific pursuits. Both the
whites and Indians at Fort Towson had been after the government
to construct a road to their locale from Fort Smith. It would cross
the Kiamichi Mountains through country that was still infested with
renegade Indians. During February 1832 Jesse assisted Arkansawyer Robert Bean in laying out a trace from Fort Smith to Fort
Towson via the sites of present-day Spiro and Poteau, Oklahoma.
The road, constructed by U.S. troops, was the first in the Choctaw
Nation.[22]

Jesse would soon be riding with Dutch again, this time as a scout
for a U.S. military expedition that would introduce him to the prairie
tribes — the Comanches, Kiowas, Wichitas, and others. He would
spend much of his life among these Indians as a trader, often serving
as a valuable link between them and the white man.

For several years prior to 1836, Jesse Chisholm frequented Fort Gibson, which then was a jumping-off place for the unknown prairie frontier. He, like other hunters, traders, and voyagers, drifted in and out of the post, buying his supplies and trade goods there, learning the latest news from eastern arrivals, and hearing stories of western adventure told by frontiersmen who came and went at the fort. By now Gibson had become a mecca for an assortment of whites, Indians, and half bloods, a last outpost of civilization sitting on the far western edge of what until 1830 had been Crawford County, Arkansas Territory.

A new boundary line had been established, giving the Cherokees, Creeks, and Osages possession of the country surrounding Gibson. The fort had thus become a military and trade outpost connected to the East by steamboats that, water level permitting, worked their way up and down the Arkansas River from and to Fort Smith, Little Rock, and Arkansas Post on the Mississippi.

In 1827 a military road had been opened between Smith and Gibson, and the following year saw the mass emigration of the Arkansas Cherokees to the Lovely's Purchase area and the establishment of Webbers Falls as a small trading center between the two forts.

To the north the military trace leading to Fort Leavenworth would soon lead to the development of the Texas Road, which would extend on southward as a route for settlers and others headed for Texas. Otherwise there were only Indian trails, such as the path followed by the Osages along the Arkansas and Cimarron leading

Fort Smith, Arkansas. The town and military base of Fort Smith, founded by Captain John
Rogers, served as a vital link in the chain of outposts in the newly acquired Indian Territory.
Jesse Chisholm often visited Fort Smith, seen here from the north bank of the Arkansas River.
Courtesy of the Archives and Manuscripts Division of the Oklahoma Historical Society.

westward to the buffalo country and the Salt Plains. Clermont's
village on the Verdigris and Union Mission on the Grand were the
only neighboring settlements until Tahlequah was established with
the arrival of the Cherokees.

Fort Gibson sat on the east bank of the Grand River just above
its conflux with the Arkansas. On the opposite bank of the Grand
was Nathaniel Pryor's old trading post. Built originally in 1819, it
now served as an agency for both the Creeks and Osages, who came
there to trade and while away the days between hunting excursions.
Another gathering point was at the sutler's store, operated by half
blood John Rogers (son of the Tennessee trader of the same name)
whom Chisholm had known in Arkansas, and General John Nicks.
Not far away, between the Grand and the Verdigris, which joined
the Arkansas close by, Sam Houston operated his Wigwam Neosho
trading house until he departed for Texas in the fall of 1832.

It was an interesting and colorful conglomeration of humankind
among which Jesse Chisholm mingled at the fort. Tall Osage warriors, with their shaved heads and crested scalp locks that set them
apart from all others, were joined by the brightly turbaned and
sashed Creeks whom the government had only recently moved into
the area from Georgia. The Cherokees, having finally made peace
with the Osages, were present, too, beginning their new existence
among the rocky, forested hills of present-day eastern Oklahoma.

Their mixed garb revealed a closer attachment to white culture than was common among the other tribes.

Among the crowds of Indians strolled white and half-blooded frontiersmen, some in green frock coats made from blankets, others in soiled buckskins and moccasins. Almost all had a rifle in hand and a bowie knife at the waist. Sweating slaves worked at the forge pounding horseshoes into shape, as garrison soldiers, some recent immigrants to the United States, lolled about the fort in boredom, chatting, whittling, and chewing tobacco. From these many strains came an assorted babble of tongues — Americanized English, French, Spanish, Osage, Creek, Cherokee, and others — to produce a "frontierese" of language.

Jesse Chisholm listened with interest to the stories that frontiersmen told of their experiences on the boundless Plains. There a man could find the adventure of exploring, the excitement of hunting among buffalo herds so huge that they often blackened the landscape, and the opportunity of trade with the Indian tribes that roved the country of the Canadian, the Red, the Brazos, and the Colorado rivers. Herds of wild horses flitted across the grassy prairies, joined by an abundance of deer, elk, black bear, wolves, and a bountiful supply of small game.

Those who were accepted among the Indians could reap rewards of Indians goods — handsomely worked moccasins, buckskins, and robes. The tribal herds were filled with valuable ponies as well as mules taken from the corrals of Mexican rancheros. Nor did the older frontiersmen fail to describe the fetching beauty of the young raven-haired Indian girls. Like other traders, Jesse was interested in the profits that could be made in bartering among these people with the many goods of the white man that the Indians craved — coffee, sugar, pots and pans, beads, vermilion, cloth, knives, guns and ammunition, plus hundreds of other items. A horse or mule procured in an Indian camp could be sold for thrice or more at a trading post.

While the products of the prairie offered much reward, there was also considerable risk in going after them. Always there was the danger of falling victim to the deadly game of war and scalp taking practiced by young tribal males out to win their laurels among the war societies. During the summer of 1826 a small party of white men from Miller County, Arkansas (now southeastern Oklahoma), had traveled up the Red River to the Washita to capture mustangs. Indians caught five of the men who were away from the main party and killed them. The culprits wore Spanish uniforms and carried muskets. They were believed to have been Pawnees from the north who had been visited and courted by a Spanish military command in earlier days.[1]

In 1830 Forts Gibson and Towson were the two most forward outposts facing the southwestern portion of the country that the United States had secured as part of the Louisiana Purchase. Beyond the Red River to the south and the 100th parallel to the west lay the Mexican provinces of Texas and New Mexico; but north of the Red River was a large body of land over which U.S. officials wished to exercise influence for the peace and security of the white frontier and immigration across the Plains. This was still a largely unexplored region dominated by a little-known population of nomadic, warring Indian tribes. Thus far there had been but slight U.S. penetration of the area, and it held the aura of mystery and danger. During the early 1830s, this country would be invaded by several U.S. military expeditions operating out of Fort Gibson as well as by Cherokee hunters. In light of his ensuing history, it is difficult to believe that Jesse Chisholm did not take part in some of these adventures.

Lieutenant James L. Dawson, who led one such exploration as far as the Washita River, reported crossing a trail blazed by Captain John Rogers, a trader and founder of the town of Fort Smith. Rogers (no kin to the Cherokee trader of that name) had been purchasing peltries from a group of Cherokees who were camping and hunting on the Washita.[2]

A group of U.S. Rangers — actually a ragtag group of young Arkansas frontiersmen — under Captain Jesse Bean made a journey through what is now central Oklahoma in 1832. Accompanying them were Indian Commissioner Henry Ellsworth and writer Washington Irving, who had just returned from Europe. Irving would later make the excursion famous with his book *A Tour of the Prairies*. Further, his description of Fort Gibson provides an excellent view of the frontier in which Chisholm lived.[3] The explorers advanced westward up the Cimarron to the famed Cross Timbers, the thick mass of low trees and brush extending southward well into

Texas and serving as a landmark separating the forested land to the east and the buffalo prairie to the west. From the Cimarron the Rangers turned southward to the Canadian River, hunting, chasing wild horses, and enduring adventures of the trail but returning to Gibson without encountering any danger from hostile Indians who hunted this region.

Danger there was, however. From 1832 to 1834 several serious incidents had involved Americans, causing the government much concern. It had not yet made treaties of friendship with either the Comanches or the Wichitas, whose warring branch, then known as the Pawnee Picts, dominated the region. Now began a series of events that would directly affect the course of Jesse Chisholm's life.

In December 1832 a party of twelve men returning from New Mexico, led by Judge W. C. Carr of St. Louis, was attacked in the Texas Panhandle by Indians. Two of the Americans were killed during a thirty-six-hour siege, and the others escaped only by leaving behind all of their goods and Mexican silver. Five of the survivors later stumbled into Fort Gibson after a torturous journey over the prairie.[4] Troubles continued to escalate during the summer of 1833 when a force of mounted Rangers under Colonel James B. Many of Fort Gibson was scouring the country along the Washita River in an attempt to overawe the tribes there. The opposite result occurred when Ranger George B. Abbay was captured and carried off by a band of unidentified Indians.[5]

Then, in the spring of 1834, Judge Gabriel Martin, a planter who resided along the Red River in what was then Miller County, Arkansas (now southeastern Oklahoma), went on a hunting excursion to the west with his young son Matthew and some of his slaves. They were attacked by Indians, the judge and one of the black men were killed, and the boy was carried off into captivity.[6]

Secretary of War Lewis Cass was concerned that these assaults on U.S. citizens threatened the development of American trade into the Southwest. He issued orders to General Henry Leavenworth, commanding the newly formed 1st Regiment of U.S. Dragoons at Fort Gibson, to display a "respectable force" in the region north of the Red River controlled by the Comanches and Pawnee Picts.[7] The Cherokee warrior Dutch, who had already visited the country of the Washita River, was selected to lead a party of eight Cherokee guides for the expedition. Jesse Chisholm rode with Dutch, thus becoming a member of this first official meeting between the Americans and the Comanches. At this point in history, the populous tribe, whom the Spanish recognized as Lords of the Plains, ruled the prairies from the Arkansas River to the Rio Grande, an area known generally as the Comanchería.

It was an impressive display of horse-mounted military that Jesse Chisholm witnessed at Fort Gibson as he prepared to join the expedition. Each company of the Dragoon regiment was mounted on horses of one color: one of all bays; others of all blacks, whites, sorrels, grays, creams, and so on. The Dragoons themselves sparkled with color as they marched in review wearing their smart new uniforms of dark blue jackets and lighter blue-gray pants, both trimmed with yellow; white horsehair pom-poms dancing above their dress hats; sabers dangling to the left; the new Hall single-shot, breech-loading carbines to the right; and the muzzle-loading flintlock pistols strapped to their waists. On another occasion, dressed in their battle fatigues, the whooping Dragoons performed a series of charge-and-repulse maneuvers before a large audience of garrison soldiers, Indians, and others.

The Dragoon regiment consisted of nine companies and some five hundred men when it departed Fort Gibson on June 15, 1834. The expedition followed along the Arkansas River for a short way, accompanied by its long train of supply and equipage wagons and a herd of seventy beef cattle. Also with the expedition were over thirty Indians and half bloods from the Cherokee, Osage, Delaware, and Seneca nations to serve as guides, hunters, and interpreters. Jesse Chisholm rode in the advance with Dutch's group of scouts. Notable among the Osages was the Frenchman Pierre Beatte, a celebrated hunter and frontiersman of whom Washington Irving had made special mention during the excursion two years before.[8]

A Wichita girl of eighteen years and a Kiowa girl of fourteen and her brother, all captives of the Osages, had been purchased to serve as tokens of friendship when their parent bands were met. Tragically, the young boy, whom George Catlin had painted while at Gibson, was killed by a belligerent ram at a trading post near the fort. Portraits of the two Indian girls were also painted by Catlin, who accompanied the expedition in order to add to the canvas record of American Indian life he had already begun while on the upper Missouri River.[9]

The officer ranks of the Dragoon regiment listed a number of men whose names would become well known in the years ahead. Second in command to Leavenworth was Colonel Henry Dodge, later to be noted for his explorations of the West. Others included Lieutenant Colonel Stephen Watts Kearny, Captain Edwin V. Sumner, First Lieutenant Philip St. George Cooke, Captain Nathan Boone (son of Daniel Boone), and a young lieutenant from Kentucky named Jefferson Davis. Leavenworth, for whom Fort Leavenworth, Kansas, is named, was an affable, gentlemanly person who was well liked by his officers and men.[10]

The regiment was in high spirits as it broke bivouac at Camp Rendezvous on June 21 and took up its march for the Washita River. Dutch, Jesse, and the other Cherokee scouts led the way. Though no one yet recognized it for the omen it was, already twenty-three men had been pronounced too ill to continue by the regimental surgeon and sent back to Gibson. Wagons constantly broke down; they also required the help of thirty to forty men to ascend the banks of every stream, rivulet, and draw along the way. Still, the expedition crossed the North Fork of the Canadian near its mouth and proceeded down its north bank to Little River.

Here they found Lieutenant Theophilus H. Holmes with a company of 7th Infantry troops constructing a log fort and quarters for two companies of soldiers on the east bank of Little River near its conflux with the Canadian. Jesse would later make his home at this site and reside there for many years to come. Leaving twenty-seven sick men behind at Camp Canadian, the regiment crossed the nearly dry Canadian River on June 25 and proceeded on southwestward. Ten miles from their crossing, they encountered a buffalo-hunting excursion of five to six hundred Osages under Chief Black Dog. Two of the Osages joined the march as scouts.[11] When the first herd of thirty to forty buffalo was seen on Bois de Arc Creek just beyond the Blue River, Jesse and the other guides rode out and killed six of the animals.

The advance of the Dragoon regiment reached the Washita near its juncture with the Red River on June 29, there joining the camp of a 3rd Infantry unit from Fort Towson that was in the early stages

of building a new military post — Fort Washita. The main body of
the regiment arrived two days later, already suffering badly from
exposure to the scorching heat and from the bilious fever that
plagued horses and men alike. Forty-five of the men and three of the
officers were reported ill at this camp, while seventy-five of the
horses and mules were disabled.

Jesse was one of those who thus far had escaped the scourge.
The symptoms of high fever, severe stomach cramps, and excessive
vomiting, accompanied by complete debility, plus a cholera epidemic
among the Missouri Osages at the time, point strongly to this
disease as being the cause of the extensive sickness and death
among the 1st Dragoons. The regimental surgeon, however, seemed
unaware of the possibility of cholera and blamed the long marches
through intense heat for the illness. The delirious victims began to
think that they were cursed with some mysterious malady of this
strange and unknown land.

On July 3 the crossing of the narrow but deep Washita began.
Unlike the Canadian, a lively stream of muddy red water flowed in
the Washita. A platform was mounted on two canoes to ferry across
the baggage wagons, while a gum resin–covered canvas boat, owned
by Lieutenant Colonel Kearny, was employed for some of the expedition members. The horses and mules were made to swim across.
A few of the army animals drowned in the swift, murky stream; but
by dark that evening the regiment was safely across, as were Jesse
and his friends.

The Dragoons lay in camp through the Fourth of July, and
Sergeant Hugh Evans of Company G mused in his diary: "[H]ow
many Thousand are enjoying themselves in all the magnificence and
grandeur feasting on all the luxurious production of the Earth
without the least feeling of compassion for those travelers in the
forest. . . . I made my 4th of July dinner upon some venison soup
without Bread."[12]

By this time many more men had fallen seriously ill. However,
by dividing Companies C and K among the other units, it was
possible to organize a 250-man force. Colonel Dodge took command
of the unit in place of the stricken Leavenworth, who was too weak
to ride. Dutch, Jesse, and the other scouts rode in advance of the

troops as the Dragoons headed on west with ten days' provisions, eighty rounds of cartridges per man, and baggage reduced to its minimum allowance.[13]

With the command divided into three columns — the right under Major Richard B. Mason (later to be a military governor of California), the center under Captain David Hunter, and the left under Captain Sumner — the Dragoons moved forward across rolling prairie broken by brushy ravines and scrub-oak ridges. Jesse and other hunters furnished buffalo to eat as they went.

The decimating sickness had not been left behind, and daily the march became more and more encumbered with incapacitated men and floundering stock. Catlin, who stayed with the march all of the way, described the deterioration of the expedition: "[W]e traveled happily, until our coffee was gone, and our bread; and even then we were happy upon meat alone, until at last each one in his turn, like every other moving thing about us, both man and beast, were vomiting and fainting, under the poisonous influence of some latent enemy, that was floating in the air, and threatening our destruction."[14]

On July 13 the Dragoons entered a beautiful, well-watered "grand prairie." Now were seen immense accumulations of buffalo, large droves of wild horses, and an occasional glimpse of distant riders who were believed to be Pawnee Picts. When a party of riders was seen approaching on the fourteenth, Dodge ordered a halt to his columns and moved forward with his staff officers under a white flag. The Indians proved to be Comanches, led by a man of Mexican blood who had been captured as a boy and had risen to prominence in the tribe as a warrior. Dodge conversed with him in Spanish through a Cherokee member of Dodge's command. There was a general shaking of hands among the Comanches and the Indian scouts.

The meeting was conducted amicably, and afterward the Dragoons were escorted onward to where a Comanche village lay back-dropped serenely to the northwest by a range of foothills of the Wichita Mountains. Several hundred bleached skin lodges with smoke curling from their tops stood surrounded by not less than 3,000 horses and mules that speckled the slopes of the surrounding

valley. The Comanches welcomed their visitors with open hospital-
ity, showing no great concern over the presence of U.S. troops among
them.[15]

The Dragoons went into camp on the banks of a clear stream
half a mile from the Comanche village, resting from the march and
enjoying the sights of the peaceful encampment of Indians on the
far prairie. They watched with admiration the displays of superb
horsemanship by the bronze Comanche warriors; noted the pleas-
ing, dark-haired beauty of the buckskin-clad women; and indulged
in trading blankets, tobacco, and butcher knives for the Comanche
horses. It was not lost upon Jesse Chisholm that an item worth less
than $4 could be bartered for a horse worth from $80 to $100 at Fort
Smith.

A principal interest of the expedition was to locate Ranger Abbay
and the Martin boy. Such a boy and a black man, the Comanches
said, had been seen among the "Toyash" (or Taovaya, a militant
branch of the Wichitas) beyond the mountains, but they claimed to
know nothing of Abbay. A guide was offered to lead the Dragoons to
their village, and Dodge put his command in the saddle again,
advancing around the southern flank of the Wichita Mountains. The
detachment's number of effectives was now reduced to 183 men.
After a day's march, Dodge halted and ordered the erection of a
breastwork of logs for a sick camp. Leaving behind thirty-nine sick
troopers and about that many more to care for and protect them, the
remainder of Dodge's diminishing force continued on.

Dutch and Jesse were still with this group that worked its way
through the rugged foothills of the mountains, over ravine-slashed
terrain, and through difficult passes strewn with sharp-edged granite. On the twentieth they struck the North Fork of the Red River.
Here a lone Wichita man was captured by two of the officers and
brought to camp. The badly frightened Indian was kindly treated
and released to tell his village that the Dragoons were coming in
peace. But when the Wichitas failed to come out to greet them as
they advanced upstream, Dodge ordered his troops to fix bayonets
and prepare for a fight.

Within a mile or two of the village, a well-armed party of Wichita
men appeared. Though they displayed much consternation, the
Wichitas led their visitors through a long, narrow defile along the

Wichita Village by George Catlin. Artist Catlin and Jesse Chisholm were with Colonel Henry Dodge and his Dragoons when they entered this village to parley with the Wichitas in 1834. *Courtesy of the Archives and Manuscripts Division of the Oklahoma Historical Society.*

river to where their community of more than two hundred thatched huts nestled beneath a towering mountain of granite. Artist Catlin made a sketch of the matted-grass Wichita houses surrounded by neatly cultivated fields of corn, beans, melons, and squash.

The Dragoons bivouacked a short way from the Wichita settlement. There the visitors were generously treated to dishes of corn and beans dressed with buffalo fat, dried buffalo meat, watermelons, and wild plums that the tattooed, bare-breasted Wichita women brought them in liberal quantities. The soldiers also found a ready market for trading knives, tobacco, tin cups, shirts, buttons, and even the yellow stripes from their trousers in exchange for roasting ears, muskmelons, and other foodstuffs. When money was offered as a bartering item, the Wichitas merely pushed it away in scorn.[16] It was Jesse's first encounter with the Wichitas. In the years ahead he would become well known and highly respected by the Wichitas and be as much at home in their camps as in those of the Comanches.

Dodge and his staff met in council with the Wichita chief, Wetarasharo, his subchiefs, and the Comanches, who had since arrived. The officer stated the desire of the Americans and the eastern Indians to live in peace with the prairie tribes. When he demanded to know what had happened to Ranger Abbay, the Wichitas answered that he had been captured by Indians from south of the Red River and killed. However, they were able to produce the Martin boy and a Negro man who had been taken on the Red River some time earlier. In return, Dodge presented the Wichita girl to her people.

Dodge was visited the following morning by Wetarasharo and two of his principal men. The officer urged them to send a delegation back with the Dragoons to visit "the great American captain" in Washington and make peace with the Indians to the east. Dodge rewarded a Wichita man with a rifle and a pistol for his having prevented his war party from killing young Martin. He also permitted speeches to be made to the prairie Indians by Dutch for the Cherokees, Beatte for the Osages, and George Bullet for the Delawares. The talks were interrupted by the sudden arrival of a war party of twenty to thirty bold, bellicose warriors whose bows were strung and whose quivers were filled with arrows.[17] They were Kiowas, and this was likely Chisholm's first acquaintance with this tribe.

When the Kiowas learned of the presence of Osages, the band became extremely agitated. They had good reason for being disturbed. Only the year before, in 1833, a large group of Osages had backtracked a Kiowa war party and located its village, totally unprotected, near the Wichita Mountains. Falling upon the encampment without mercy, the Osages had slaughtered the women, children, and elders of the village, then compounded their deed by cutting off the heads of the victims and placing them in buckets around the sacked camp. The Osages had committed an even more serious crime — they had stolen the Kiowas' medicine bag, a vital religious symbol to the tribe.[18]

Dodge managed to pacify the war party by presenting the captured Kiowa girl whom he had brought from Fort Gibson. An uncle of the girl threw his arms around Dodge and wept on his shoulder in gratitude.[19] Though they greatly feared to travel through the forests that edged the prairie, the Wichitas, Comanches, and Kiowas pledged themselves to send representatives back to Fort Gibson with Dodge.

Jesse Chisholm served as a translator during this council. Though he as yet spoke neither the Comanche nor Wichita tongue, he used his knowledge of the Caddo language to assist in talks with the Indians. In his journal of the expedition Lieutenant Thomas B. Wheelock reported: "[A] Toyash Indian who speaks the Caddo tongue communicated with Chisholm, one of our Cherokee friends who speaks English and Caddo."[20] This was the beginning of Chisholm's long and valuable service as a contact for both the United States and the eastern Indians with the Plains tribes.

On July 25 the Dragoons, accompanied by some members of the prairie tribes, began their return. Dodge had at first intended to strike northeasterly for Fort Leavenworth but, because of the extreme difficulty of the march, chose instead to return to Fort Gibson. It was, indeed, a torturous march — probably the worst that Jesse Chisholm would ever make — across a treeless, waterless country through the torrid heat of late July and early August. The men were still plagued by deadly illness and mouth-parching thirst that left many too weak even to ride their horses.[21]

While in camp on the Canadian near present-day Oklahoma City, the despairing Dragoons received news that distressed them even more. A courier from the bivouac at the mouth of the Washita arrived to report the deaths of General Leavenworth, Lieutenant George W. McClure, and ten to fifteen other Dragoons. The feverish and feeble Leavenworth, intensely desirous of being with his command in meeting with the Indians, had ridden some fifty or more miles on the trail of Dodge before he had finally succumbed.[22]

Death continued to stalk the detachment as it straggled down the Canadian past the mouth of Little River, where Lieutenant Holmes and his company of 7th Infantry were also suffering sickness and fatalities. Incapacitated soldiers were left along the way, and even after the regiment reached Fort Gibson the malady continued to reap a heavy toll. Catlin, himself near death in the Fort Gibson hospital, heard the mournful sound of the Scottish dirge "Roslin Castle" and muffled drums as they passed "six or eight times a-day under my window on their way to the burying ground."[23] Among the dead was a German botanist and his aide who had accompanied the expedition the entire distance before dying at Gibson.

The cost of this peacemaking and exploring venture had been high, indeed, with nearly a third of the original command lost, including several officers. Fort Gibson earned an unenviable reputation as the Charnel House of the Army.[24] Some of the troops at Gibson were moved to a temporary post up the Arkansas to escape the scourge; and Catlin, as soon as he was barely able to sit his horse, headed off alone for St. Louis, preferring to risk death afield rather than at the disease-ridden post.

Though he had suffered badly during the expedition, Chisholm fared well enough that on September 2 he attended a huge meeting of eastern and prairie Indians in a makeshift council house at the fort. Couriers had been sent to the various tribes in the vicinity — the Cherokees, Osages, Creeks, Choctaws, and Senecas — to invite them to meet with the visiting Comanche (only the Mexican-captive warrior came all the way), Kiowas, Wichitas, and Wacos who had accompanied Dodge to Gibson.[25] Several days of speechmaking, smoking the calumet, dancing, and assertions of friendship followed. Jesse Chisholm served as interpreter for the Western Cherokees, who were represented in part by his half uncle, Third Chief Thomas Chisholm. Thomas had only that spring been elected to replace the deceased Walter Webber. He, too, died not long after the council, succumbing to typhoid at his home near Beatte's Prairie in November 1834.[26]

When the council was done, the prairie visitors were given Dragoon escort back beyond the Cross Timbers. Fort Smith trader Holland Coffee had built a post on the Texas bank of the Red River opposite the mouth of the Washita, initiating trading operations with the prairie tribes.[27]

Now, having been introduced to the world of the Plains Indians, Jesse Chisholm, too, would commence a lifelong career as a trader on the grand prairie.

During the 1830s Jesse Chisholm helped lead the advance of American civilization westward up the Canadian River, spearheading exploration of the country beyond the Cross Timbers. He also began to play a significant role in the affairs of both the United States and the Cherokee Nation in their developing relationships with the tribes of the area. He would soon win a reputation as one of the most knowledgeable and capable contacts on the Canadian River frontier.

Jesse was not the first to conduct trade with the Comanches. As early as 1821 trader Thomas James had led a party from Arkansas across the Comanche lands to New Mexico. He had returned in 1822 to hold a winter's trade at a log fort near the junction of Wolf and Beaver creeks, in present-day northwestern Oklahoma, where the North Canadian River is formed. James's partner Robert McKnight, whose brother was killed by the Comanches during James's second visit, entered the area the following year to trade for horses and robes with the Comanches.[1] Chisholm was, however, one of the very first to win the privilege of coming among Comanches' camps regularly and to earn the permanent friendship of their leaders. For over thirty years he would prove an invaluable instrument of contact between the prairie tribes and those who pressed aggressively against the borders of the Comanchería — the Americans, the Texans, and the immigrant Indians from the East.

The United States, anxious to extend its commerce to the rich trading area of New Mexico, had followed up its initial contact with the Comanches, Wichitas, and Kiowas, made by the Leavenworth-

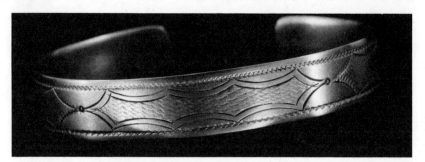

Silver bracelet presented to Jesse Chisholm by the Comanches. Thirty years of service as interpreter and counselor to the Comanches earned Jesse the deep and lasting friendship of their leaders. *Courtesy of the Barker Texas History Center, The University of Texas at Austin.*

Dodge expedition, by laying plans for treaty talks with them during the forthcoming spring. U.S. officials had promised then that a treaty would be concluded "when the grass next grows after the snows have melted away."[2] In March 1835 Holland Coffee arrived at Fort Gibson from his post on the Red River to report that the Indians were anxious to know just when the council would be held.

During that same month the secretary of war appointed a three-man council and appropriated $11,000 for conducting peace talks with the Comanches, Kiowas, Wichitas, and other tribes of the southwestern frontier. This commission — consisting of General Matthew Arbuckle; former governor of North Carolina Montford Stokes; and Choctaw agent Major F. W. Armstrong (who died on his way to join the commission) — held preliminary talks with the Osages and other tribes, including two Comanches who had been brought in, at Fort Gibson. It was hoped that a general peace between the eastern and prairie tribes could be worked out.

The Osages were indifferent to the pending council, saying that the plunder of Comanche horses on the Plains was more profitable to them than anything the government would do. Later, when Major Richard Mason, commanding the 1st Dragoons, sent for a Comanche horse stolen by Clermont's warriors, the Osage headman replied contemptuously that Mason and his officers were not chiefs and were "as the dead grass of the prairie — good for nothing."[3] They reluctantly agreed to attend the Fort Gibson council only when lured there with a keg of gunpowder.

Mason, accompanied by Colonel Auguste P. Chouteau and four Osage hunter-guides, led a detachment of seventy troops to the head of Little River in advance of the commission.[4] He selected a site for the council at a location just north of the Canadian River between present-day Norman and Purcell, Oklahoma. The prairie tribes — Comanches, Kiowas, Wichitas, and Plains Apaches — began arriving in large numbers, establishing their camps for miles along the banks of the Canadian and Chouteau Creek in wait for the commission party.

Though no record of it has yet been found, there can be little doubt that Jesse Chisholm attended the council. Quite likely he either accompanied Dutch, who was appointed by Western Chief John Rogers to represent the Cherokees at the proposed treaty, or came as a member of the large caravan of traders who accompanied the commission party with more than a hundred wagons of merchandise.[5]

Later, after Chouteau had established a trading post near the site of what would be known as Camp Holmes (taking up the name of the defunct post at the mouth of Little River), Jesse would use this location at the far edge of the Cross Timbers as a base for his own trading operations. Intermittently, troops would be stationed at Camp Holmes before it was abandoned. Four years after the treaty council the deserted site would be visited by Josiah Gregg, who described it as a "wild, romantic spot" with a beautiful spring.[6]

The long wait was eased by games and by the presence of the daughter of the Comanche head chief Ichacoly (The Wolf). He was a tall, handsome man himself, and the girl was a young beauty with raven-dark braids, flashing eyes, and a sparkling smile. She wore deerskins fringed with elks' teeth, and she was further bedecked with silver bracelets. Her ebony hair was parted with a vermilion-painted seam that matched her eyelids and lips. She immediately caught the attention of the male-populated camp and enhanced the Indian-white relationship considerably.

Wrestling contests and footraces were held between the soldiers and the Osages. When a buffalo herd appeared in the area, Major Mason, an avid sportsman, joined the Indians in the hunt. In a letter to a friend, Mason told how one Osage hunter had driven an arrow

completely through a buffalo and how another had shot a buffalo on
a dead run, the arrow penetrating within two inches of the feather
shaft. When the buffalo did not fall, the Indian jerked out the arrow
while riding at a breakneck gallop and reshot the animal, this time
killing it in its tracks.[7]

If Jesse was indeed present, he undoubtedly witnessed these
games and heard the din of wailing that awakened the camp one
night. The keening came from the Wichitas, who had just learned
that one of their war parties had suffered the loss of a number of
warriors in a fight with whites at a Texas settlement. Likely, too, he
observed the Comanche who was in mourning over the loss of a
daughter. The bereft father, painted black with charcoal, wore
draped about his neck trinkets that had belonged to his child. Among
them was a little buckskin doll whose head was covered with a lock
of the dead girl's hair.

As the hot days of July 1835 burned away, the Indians became
more and more impatient and angry. They had been promised that
the white chiefs would be waiting for them there at the western edge
of the Cross Timbers with presents and food. But the days passed
one into another, and the commissioners did not appear. For a time
there were buffalo to hunt and eat, but not enough to feed for long
the 7,000 or so tribespeople. The chiefs complained to Mason that
the white man had agreed to come when the grass was in the blade,
not in the leaf.[8] Soon after, the Osage scouts reported that there was
much unrest among the prairie tribes. They said that a Comanche
chief, the dark-skinned, battle-scarred Tabaqueena (or The Big
Eagle), was trying to get other bands to join him in wiping out the
small force of U.S. Dragoons at the newly established Camp Holmes
and stealing their horses.

Major Mason dispatched couriers back to Fort Gibson in an
urgent call for reinforcements, but Gibson was a week away at the
very least. The situation seemed desperate for the greatly out-
numbered soldiers. However, the day was saved by Ichacoly, who
opposed Tabaqueena and persuaded the tribes to be patient for a
while longer.

Still, with their people facing starvation, the Kiowas and many
of the Comanche and Wichita bands struck their lodges, packed the

buffalo-hide shelters onto their lodge-pole travois, and headed back to the prairie to hunt for food.[9]

The late-arriving commission party was chagrined to discover that the Kiowas had already departed. Troops were sent to locate them but without success, for the Kiowas were said to be like the wolves on the prairie — hard to find.[10] Nonetheless, an effort was begun by the remaining Indians to meet with the whites on friendly terms.

The Treaty of Camp Holmes accomplished little. Unrealistic commitments were made by the various tribes to forgive and forget when others did injury to them. The government also made a futile promise that it would pay for stock stolen from the prairie tribes by whites. The principal agreement concerned permitting the eastern tribes and whites free access onto and across the buffalo grounds. Further consideration of this critical issue would later cause the Comanches to tear up the pact in anger.[11]

In 1836 Jesse, now some thirty years of age, married fifteen-year-old Eliza Edwards, the half-Creek daughter of trader James Edwards.[12] They took up residence at Edwards's newly established trading post at the mouth of Little River, from which Jesse would launch his extended trading excursions far into the Comanche-held ranges of Texas. Edwards's post was on the west bank just across from where Lieutenant Holmes had built his short-lived fort, and here for a time was the advance edge of white settlement on the Canadian River and in what is now Oklahoma — a scattering of log houses surrounded by gardens of corn and sweet potatoes and populated by an assortment of whites, mixed bloods, Creek Indians, and Negro slaves.[13] The post stood almost as a port on the coast of an unexplored prairie-ocean that challenged the courage of those who dared to venture onto it. There were few havens of safety from the pirate parties of warriors who plied the region at will, ready to take all, including scalp trophies.

Jesse Chisholm undertook that risk in his service as a trader afield for the firm of Edwards and Shelton. He would load his wagons with trade goods and set forth to locate the villages of the Indians where he could barter for horses, mules, robes, and peltries. Upon his return to Edwards's, the fruits of his trade — furs, robes, horses, and mules — would be taken on to Fort Smith. Traders there would then boat the wares down the Arkansas and Mississippi rivers to the port of New Orleans.

Jesse soon built a house on the north bank of the Canadian River at its crossing a mile from Edwards's place, and his son William Edwards Chisholm was born there on September 15, 1837.[14] Jesse's claim regarding the theft of some of his horses by the Osages this same year places him at Tallassee Town, a Creek settlement later known as Tallahassee Mission; but likely this was only a temporary camp.[15]

Jesse and the Chouteaus continued to be the major contacts for the government with the prairie tribes through 1837 and 1838. Colonel Chouteau accepted the task of trying to gather a delegation of Comanches and Kiowas to take to Washington, D.C. He arrived at Camp Holmes in the fall of 1837 but reported back that it was impossible for him to contact the tribes until spring and that he would remain at Holmes through the winter.[16] He also indicated that the Wichitas and Wacos were being constantly harassed by the Pawnee Mahas from the Loup River of Nebraska.[17]

In the spring of 1838, Chouteau sent his nephew, Edward L. Chouteau, with an escort of Dragoons northwestward up the North Canadian to interview the Comanches. The party arrived just two days after a big fight had taken place between Wolf and Beaver creeks. A large force of Cheyenne and Arapaho warriors from north of the Arkansas River had attacked a Comanche village in retaliation for the killing and scalping of some Cheyenne Bow-String soldiers the year before.[18] The attackers had wreaked havoc on the Comanche camp. The Comanche women had attempted to escape by digging holes in which to hide themselves and their children. When it was reported that the Dragoons were on the way with Osage scouts, the Cheyennes and Arapahos had retired, leaving some fifty-eight Comanches dead in addition to hundreds of slain horses.[19]

The Battle of Wolf Creek was significant in that it set the stage for a great peace council at Bent's Fort on the Arkansas. At this council, gifts were exchanged and a peace agreement made by which the Kiowas and Comanches consented to let the northern tribes range unmolested south of the Arkansas.

John Conner *(center, seated with arms folded)* and Black Beaver *(standing, second from left)*. The Delawares traveled widely over Chisholm's home range, and these two men particularly were his comrades. *Courtesy of the Western History Collections, University of Oklahoma.*

In December 1838 Colonel Chouteau died following a lengthy illness, and the vacuum in friendship left by this man so highly respected by the Comanches and others would ultimately be filled to a large degree by Jesse Chisholm. General Ethan Allen Hitchcock, who toured eastern Indian Territory, proclaimed that Jesse Chisholm was the one person who could induce the Comanches to send a delegation to Washington in an attempt to end their war with the Texans.[20]

An effort in this direction was made in the spring of 1839 when Jesse gave aid to a delegation on its way to a prearranged meeting with Chouteau. The Indians, seventeen Comanche and Kiowa chiefs along with seven of their women, had expected to meet with Colonel Chouteau at Camp Mason around the first of May. Before they reached the post, however, they fell in with Jesse's friend, Delaware half blood John Conner, who told them of Chouteau's death. Conner took the Indians on to Little River where Jesse provided them with beef, corn, and bacon.[21] The two frontiersmen then escorted them on up the Canadian River to Webbers Falls where the party was halted by the flooded Arkansas River. Jesse's half brother George Chisholm supplied the Indians with three beef cows to eat.

The Comanches and Kiowas were taken to Fort Gibson and from there to the Choctaw Agency at Skullyville (near present-day Spiro, Oklahoma). Major William Armstrong, Indian superintendent, decided not to send them on, feeling that it would be impractical at that time. The prairie Indians attended a Choctaw-Chickasaw celebration and were spectators at an intertribal ball game, which they enjoyed immensely. After being presented with blankets, knives, tobacco, scarlet cloth, and other gifts, they were sent back to their homes under the guidance of Conner and Chisholm.[22]

In September of that same year Jesse Chisholm undertook one of his most extensive adventures. Securing a passport from General Arbuckle at Fort Gibson, he led an exploring party to the Mexican province of California. Traveling with him were Delaware Principal Chief George Bullet; George Conner, another Delaware who was a highly regarded frontiersman; Robert Beckham, a resident of Edwards's settlement; John Caunot of Missouri; and Nicholas Miller and Robert May, both Cherokees.[23]

This roster reflects the long association that Jesse Chisholm maintained with the Delawares, including the famous chief Black Beaver, who had resided close to the Western Cherokees in Arkansas during the 1820s. The Delawares' love for adventure and curiosity took them off on excursions to the Rocky Mountains, the Pacific Coast, and virtually every area of the American West. Black Beaver claimed that he had seen the Pacific Ocean at various points on seven different occasions.[24]

Josiah Gregg had made his famous journey to Santa Fe, one that produced his classic book, *Commerce of the Prairie,* along the Canadian River during the spring of 1839. It is believed, however, that Jesse and his companions took the southern route, breaking a new trail southwestward across the townless, roadless plains of northern and western Texas.

Little is known about the excursion except that on their return Jesse and his party met with an encampment of Comanche Indians at the old stone fort on the San Saba River, near present-day Menard, Texas.[25] This was the former Spanish mission of San Saba that the Comanches and Taovayas had ravaged in 1758, killing two priests. From there the following year, Spanish Governor Diego Ortiz Parilla had marched with an army to attack the Wichita villages on the Red River (at the site known today as Spanish Fort, Texas). The Spaniards were severely defeated. The San Saba mission was reconstructed of stone in 1761; but the Spanish had abandoned it about 1766, and the place had since fallen into ruin.[26]

In the Comanche camp Chisholm discovered a captive Negro boy, ten or so years of age, whom he purchased with some guns and other goods that he procured from his comrades, an equivalent value of $150. This boy, Aaron, and a brother had been taken from the plantation home of Dr. Joseph W. Robertson of Bastrop County, Texas. The brother, Manuel, was found and purchased by a Creek Indian while on a hunting tour with some Cherokees along the Colorado River.[27] Both boys were taken to Edwards's place at Little River, and both ultimately became the property of Lucinda Edwards, the younger sister of Eliza. Jesse sold Aaron to his sister-in-law for $400.[28]

Somehow Robertson learned that his two slave boys were at Edwards's, and in December 1840 he went there in the hope of retrieving them. At that particular time, however, there happened to be a large party of Cherokees encamped near Chisholm's house. These were remnants of Bowles's band that had been attacked by Texas forces on the Neches River, badly mauled, and driven out of Texas. Chief Bowles himself had been killed and his body mutilated by the Texans. Some of the survivors had fled to Mexico, some to southern Arkansas, and others to the Canadian River, first settling near Dutch, then moving on downriver to where Chisholm provided them as much subsistence as he could.[29]

Robertson made no effort to contact either Edwards or Chisholm, at first hoping to slip the boys away. However, he realized that if he, a Texan, were discovered by the refugee Cherokees he would very likely be killed. He hurried back to Texas, looking over his shoulder all the way, fearing that he was being followed. Once safely back he applied through the channels of government of the Republic of Texas to regain his property.[30] Eventually, in 1844, the boys were returned to him.

During the government's investigation into the matter, General

Hitchcock noted, "This man Chisholm is very intelligent, and is, I believe, a man of sterling integrity."[31] Jesse also received plaudits from the officer who visited the Little River settlement in February 1842. He spoke of Chisholm as one "who trades among the Comanches and has great influence among them."[32]

This was not Jesse's only brush with fugitive slaves on the Indian Nation frontier. The wealthier Cherokees, who owned slaves, held to the rigid concept of the South that the blacks were property. In fact, most owners considered their slaves to be their most valuable possessions, and their loss or defection was a matter of most serious consequence.

The harsh treatment of slaves by Cherokees such as Rich Joe Vann and the influence of newly arrived Seminole blacks from Florida, where General Thomas S. Jesup had promised them their freedom for their help during the Seminole War, contributed to a small mutiny in November 1842. Some twenty-one Negroes banded together near Webbers Falls. Taking horses and mules belonging to the Cherokees, the party of blacks struck out for Mexico, where slavery had been banned.[33] It was a dangerous undertaking for runaway slaves to venture forth onto the prairie. If they did not starve first, they were often killed or taken captive and made slaves anew by the prairie Indians.

The Webbers Falls defection was soon discovered, and a courier was sent flying to the Cherokee National Council, then in session at Tahlequah. The council hastily enacted a measure authorizing the organization of a company of men to go after the escapees. On November 21 ninety men under the command of Cherokee merchant John Drew left Webbers Falls in feverish pursuit.[34] Purchasing provisions at Edwards's place, they hurried on. Ten miles beyond the crossing of the Canadian the posse reached a place where a few days earlier a small party of Creeks had encountered the runaway slaves. The fugitives had put up such strong resistance as to force the Creeks to abandon attempts to recapture them.

Some twelve or fifteen miles farther on the Cherokees came upon the bodies of two men, one a white man and the other an Indian. The dead men were identified as Billy Wilson, a Delaware, and a man named Edwards (whoever this man was, he was not Jesse's father-in-law).[35] The Cherokees pushed on at a hard pace for two days more and were within seven miles of the Red River in the vicinity of present-day Denton, Texas, when they caught up with the fleeing blacks. The slaves were near starvation and offered no resistance as the heavily armed Cherokees surrounded them and, with the exception of two men who were away hunting at the time, seized the entire party. From the captured group they learned the story behind the two dead men.

At a date prior to the mutiny, a white man who was married to a Choctaw woman had lost eight slaves — a man, two women, and five children. This family had escaped to the west and ended up as captives in a Comanche village. Jesse Chisholm, who arrived at the camp soon after, had taken charge of the black family and turned them over to Edwards, Wilson, and a Cherokee man for return to their owner. En route the Cherokee had become separated from the others. Edwards and Wilson had had the misfortune of encountering the fugitive Cherokee slave party, who had killed the two and freed the refugee family.[36]

After purchasing lead, powder, and percussion caps at the trading house of Abel Warren on the Red River, Drew and his men returned to Little River where a blacksmith was paid $20 to shoe their horses and place the unfortunate blacks in irons. The slaves were all returned to their respective owners, except for two who were turned over to the U.S. district attorney to face murder charges.[37]

Jesse Chisholm continued to reside at the mouth of Little River, but on numerous occasions his reputation as a man of esteem among the prairie tribes would cause him to be called away from his home base on the Canadian for service south of the Red River. There, during the following decade he would lend valuable assistance to Sam Houston in his effort to resolve the stubborn conflict between whites and Indians on the Texas frontier.

Just how close Jesse Chisholm and Sam Houston were is not revealed by the records. It is apparent that they knew one another when both were at Fort Gibson from 1829 to 1833. Further, it is possible, though not proved, that Houston's Cherokee wife Diana was a sister of Ignatius Chisholm's second wife, Martha Rogers. We do know that Houston and his Indian Affairs Bureau depended heavily upon Chisholm not only as an interpreter and as a liaison with the Indians but also to lend the weight of his immense influence in persuading the Comanches and others to hear and trust Houston's words.

The years 1839 and 1840 were eventful for the southwestern Plains. The government finally dislodged the Indian tribes of the South and conducted its tragic removal of them over what has come to be known in history as The Trail of Tears. For the Cherokees the tragedy of the death-ridden journey to the Indian Territory was compounded by an internal war of intense animosity between the ruling Ross faction on the one side and the Old Nation Treaty party and Western Cherokee leaders on the other. One bloody result was the assassination of the three Treaty party leaders — The Ridge (the assassin of Chief Doublehead in 1807), his son John, and Elias Boudinot — in the fall of 1839 by Ross loyalists.

It was during this year, also, that the Texas forces under General Thomas Rusk attacked and destroyed Bowles's Cherokee settlement on the Neches River. The conflict with the Comanches also had been excited to a considerable degree in 1840 when a visiting delegation of chiefs at San Antonio were trapped inside a courthouse and massacred by the Texans. The Texans, infuriated over the capture and maltreatment of white children, had attempted to arrest the Comanche leaders, whom they had invited to a peace council. The Comanches had resisted; and in the melee that followed, some thirty-five Comanches were killed, including three women and two children, and twenty-seven others captured. Seven whites were lost, with eight wounded.[1]

On the heels of these events, a group of Texas capitalists organized an ill-fated excursion to New Mexico on a route that would take them through the heart of the Comanchería and eventually into captivity in Mexican prisons and leper colonies. Also, groups of German immigrants, unsuspecting of the Indian resistance they would meet, were moving out of Austin and San Antonio to settle on grants of land in western Texas.

Jesse Chisholm played an important role in peacemaking attempts by Sam Houston. Now reelected president of Texas following the term of the Indian-hating Mirabeau B. Lamar, Houston sought to reinstitute friendly relations with the prairie tribes that were ravaging the defenseless frontier settlements of Texas. The destruction of Bowles and his Cherokee colony plus the massacre of the Comanche chiefs had caused the settlers on the Texas frontier to pay a high price in bloodshed, kidnapings, and thefts of stock.

The other tribes of the southwestern frontier were disturbed by warring between the aggressive Texans and the furious Comanches. A plea for peaceful relations was made to Houston by Creek agent James Logan on behalf of the Wichitas, Tawakonis (on occasion referred to as Tawacaros), and Kichais (or Keechies), who were among the sixteen or more tribes meeting at the Creek council grounds on May 15, 1841.[2]

When Houston resumed office in December 1841, he immediately turned his attention to the vast area of central, north, and west Texas, for which his debt-strangled Republic could provide little protection. He set about to make new treaties with the prairie tribes.[3] Jesse Chisholm, now recognized as one of the most qualified and highly respected men on the frontier, was among a select group of men to whom Houston turned in contacting and persuading the Comanches and other tribes on the Texas frontier to make peace.[4]

In the spring of 1843, Houston hired Jesse to lead a group of

Delaware scouts to scour the prairies of north Texas, search out the widely scattered bands, and arrange a grand council with both Texas and U.S. commissioners.[5] It was a physically demanding and dangerous assignment, particularly so because the Comanches still seethed with anger over the murder of their chiefs at San Antonio. Nonetheless, Jesse and the Delawares managed to arrange a council with the prairie tribes. It was to be held in March at the springs a few miles above where Tehuacana (a variation of Tawakoni, sometimes known as Tahuacarro) Creek empties into the Brazos eight miles below present-day Waco, Texas.

A deserted Waco village was located just up the Brazos on its west bank. During that spring of 1843 the Torrey brothers constructed a trading post on an oak-covered hill on the east bank of the Brazos near the mouth of Tehuacana Creek. It became widely known as Torrey's Trading House or as their Post Number Two.[6] The place consisted of a trading house, the inside of which was stocked with blankets, trinkets, paints, bright-colored calicos of which the Indians were fond, as well as bales of pelts and buffalo robes, many of which had been beautifully decorated by the Indian women with beads and design work. In addition to the trading house, there were dwellings for the manager and employees and several log huts for storing pelts. A few soldiers were stationed at the post, and a stockade served to hold the company's horses and mules at night against theft. The establishment, in which trader George Barnard and Sam Houston were shareholders, soon became the principal outpost north of Austin, a place where the Indians came to swap furs and robes for goods of the white man. Jesse's Delaware friend Jack Harry was hired as the post interpreter.[7]

Cherokee agent Pierce M. Butler, a former governor of South Carolina who was destined to be killed in battle during the war with Mexico, was sent from the Cherokee Agency at Tahlequah to attend the Tehuacana Creek council and lend the weight of the United States to the proceedings. Butler's party departed Fort Gibson and rode to Fort Towson, where it was joined by a fifteen-man Dragoon escort before proceeding on to the Waco village. He was met there by the Texas commissioner, General George W. Terrell, and escorted to the council grounds four miles up the creek from the post, a site that would become known as Council Springs.[8]

Among the whites present at the Tehuacana Creek council was a well-known painter of Indian life, John Mix Stanley. Stanley, who had been invited to the Cherokee country by agent Butler, produced numerous paintings of Indian subjects in the Fort Gibson–Tahlequah area.[9] Like Catlin nine years earlier, Stanley wished to go to the frontier in order to paint the Indians in their natural habitat, and he had seized on this opportunity to accompany the Butler group. During the trip to Tehuacana Creek, Chisholm served as a personal escort for the painter, helping Stanley arrange for the paintings he made during the trip.

On March 21, Chisholm, Luis Sánchez, and Jim Second-eye arrived at the proposed meeting site to report that Jim Shaw was coming behind them with chiefs of sundry tribes — Caddo, Delaware, Shawnee, Anadarko, Tawakoni, Waco, Ionie, Wichita, and Kichai. The Lipan Apaches and Tonkawas were also represented when the council finally got under way, but the Comanches had adamantly refused to come.[10]

The council began on March 28 with Commissioner Terrell addressing the Indians. "We will not deceive you," he told the chiefs, "or give you a crooked talk. . . . If they [the red men] make peace with us they may have their homes, and live with us as before."[11] He went on to warn that the game on the land would soon be gone. He said that if the Indians would settle down in peace and make farms, Texas would establish trading houses among them and buy their horses, mules, skins, and other things they wished to sell. He also promised they would be given powder and lead with which to hunt, in addition to other presents. Houston had already sent to Europe for three hundred fine lances to present as gifts to the chiefs.

The Waco Principal Chief Kakakatish (or The Shooting Star), an orator by reputation, was among those who answered Terrell:

> Amidst this assemblage I do not wish to utter falsehoods, and I believe that my Texan friend has spoken nothing but the truth. The soil I now stand upon was once mine; it is now the land of the Texans, and my home is far off in the west. I am now here on this soil, where in my young days I hunted the buffalo and red deer in peace, and was friendly with all, until the Texan came and drove me from my native land. I speak the truth — I wish for peace that shall last so long as the sun rises and sets, and the rivers flow. The

John Mix Stanley's rendering of the Council Creek meeting is one of the few of his western scenes that survive. Jesse Chisholm may well be among the people depicted here. *Courtesy of the Archives and Manuscripts Division of the Oklahoma Historical Society.*

wildfire of war has swept over the land, and enveloped my home and people in smoke; but when I return and tell them what I have heard, the smoke will be dissipated, and they can find their way to the council-ground of white brothers of Texas, and combine to quench this fire that heats our blood and impels us on to war.[12]

Butler also spoke, indicating the support of the United States for Texas. His words were translated by Chisholm[13] and the others into the various tongues represented at the meeting. On the following day the Indians responded in kind, expressing their desire for peace and willingness to do their part in keeping it. A letter from President John Tyler was read to the large circle of chiefs, and on the following morning an article of agreement was signed by the Texas commissioner and the chiefs.[14]

By this pact it was agreed by both sides that the warring in Texas would end, that the Indians would have the privilege of trading at Torrey's post, and that another council would be held in the fall with the United States as an active participant. Left unsaid was the imperative need to persuade the Comanches to participate; everyone knew full well that there would be no peace in Texas unless the Comanches were agreeable to it.

Houston assigned Texas Superintendent of Indian Affairs Joseph C. Eldridge the chore of bringing the Comanches in for a council. Accompanied by Thomas Torrey and guided by Jesse's close friend John Conner and other Delawares, Eldridge set out on a three-month pilgrimage in search of the Comanches. He took with him two Waco girls whom Sam Houston wished returned to their tribe as a token of his goodwill. On the Brazos Eldridge met with a Waco war party and returned to them the two girls, who had been held by the whites for a number of years. The girls, who had become adapted to white ways, wailed pitifully and pleaded not to be forced to go back to their tribe. Their pleas were ignored. They were put on the back of a Waco chief's horse and carried off to the prairie still screaming.[15]

Continuing on, the Texans crossed the Red River. After some wandering about, they finally located a Comanche village near the Wichita Mountains, returning a captive Comanche boy and girl to the band. Despite this gesture, the Texans were threatened by angry relatives of the chiefs who had been massacred three years earlier at San Antonio. The visitors were saved by the portly Comanche Chief Pahhauca, or The Amorous Man, who mounted his horse, rode about the encampment, and in a loud voice ordered that no one should harm the visitors or steal their horses.[16]

Eldridge won an agreement from Pahhauca to attend a council at Comanche Peak on the Brazos in four months and signed a temporary peace agreement with him on August 9. However, he failed to get the Comanches to attend a new council that met in September at Bird's Fort on West Elm Fork of the Trinity River seven miles north of present-day Arlington, Texas. The blockhouse fort had been erected by Jonathan Bird in 1841. There another treaty of friendship was signed by Texas with the various small tribes and bands of north Texas on September 29, 1843. Thomas Torrey died there during the council.[17]

Jesse Chisholm was not present at this treaty event. While Eldridge and Torrey had been searching about for the Comanches, Chisholm was involved in a huge gathering of Indians at Tahlequah. Though Jesse lent his assistance to the Cherokee Nation on

numerous occasions, he actually spent little time in the Cherokee
country and was seldom involved in the intense intertribal Cherokee
political conflicts. His name does appear on a September 14, 1843,
resolution by Western Cherokees asking for political and geograph-
ical separation from the Eastern Cherokees under Chief John
Ross.[18] Ross, who had now won control of the Cherokee government
in the West, arranged for an International Indian Council of tribes
living within the sphere of influence of the Cherokees. The purpose
of the council was to discuss how to get along with Texas and to
resolve the problems existing between themselves and the United
States. Some eighteen tribes were present, with some 3,000 to 4,000
people said to be in daily attendance at the meeting that lasted four
weeks. There was much dancing, singing, and drinking, though it
was estimated that the authorities destroyed some seventeen hundred gallons of whiskey, in the bottle and in the keg, during the
conference.[19]

Chisholm again aided Stanley in arranging for Indian leaders
at the council to sit for their portraits, according to an account by
Stanley's son:

> In attempting to paint the portraits of the Cherokee chiefs, Mr.
> Stanley found a difficulty in their caprice and superstition. They
> insisted that portraits should first be painted of Jim Shaw, a
> Delaware, and of Jess Chisholm, a Cherokee, under whose protec-
> tion Mr. Stanley had been conducted; if these men should consent
> to sit and should receive no harm from the operation, then the
> Cherokee chiefs would sit. It would be done this way. They came
> forward in the order of their rank and were delighted with the idea
> of being painted, considering it a great honor.[20]

While example setting may have been necessary for some of the less
sophisticated chiefs, it was hardly necessary for educated men such
as John Ross or Stand Watie, whom Stanley painted. Stanley's
painting of the Tahlequah conference features at its center the
image of Chief John Ross standing with General Zachary Taylor.

Iowa chief Wohumpa demanded that he be depicted shaking
hands with Stanley so that the Great Father in Washington would
know that he was a friend of the white man.[21] Of particular amuse-
ment to Stanley was the young Osage boy who followed behind the

artist and mimicked his every action as he painted. Stanley did the boy's portrait also.[22]

One well-known scene features a band of Osage warriors surrounding a captive white woman and her child. Quite possibly Jesse Chisholm is portrayed in some of the council scenes, but if his individual portrait was done by Stanley, it was not among those listed as being on display at the Smithsonian Institution in 1865, when many of Stanley's canvases were destroyed by fire.[23] Likely Chisholm was also Stanley's escort when the artist visited the Creek settlement at North Fork Town, located near the mouth of the North Canadian, where he did portraits of Chilly McIntosh, Opothle Yahola, and a scene titled *A Creek Buffalo Dance,* plus other paintings.[24]

Still hoping to induce the Comanches into signing a treaty, and with the promise that Sam Houston himself would attend the council, agent Butler departed Fort Gibson on November 20 for the mouth of Cache Creek on the Red River south of the Wichita Mountains. It was here that trader Abel Warren had located a trading post — a large, double-log fort with parapets at each corner and surrounded by a fifteen-foot-high palisade.[25]

This post, which Eldridge had visited during his tour of the area, operated as a trading center for the region. One government official held a dim view of Warren's post, reporting: "It is most admirably situated for carrying on all sorts of nefarious transactions, and I am informed by those who live near that those having it under management are not at all backward or slow to avail themselves of the results, and I know enough myself to satisfy me that the accusations against them are just."[26] Chisholm used the post for his own trading operations, as a base for his excursions out to the scattered prairie bands in northern Texas. An acquaintance later stated that Jesse had an interest in the post.[27] Butler selected a point with good grazing for his stock, just across from the mouth of Cache Creek in Texas for a council ground. He dispatched John Conner, Jim Shaw, and Cherokee Nick Miller to go afield and contact either the Indian tribes or the Texas commissioners who were supposed to meet them. Miller soon reported the presence of a band of Hoish Comanches nearby; and on the following day the commission camp was visited by Buffalo Hump, who explained why Comanche Principal Chief Pahhauca had not come in for talks. The chief's son had recently been killed in a fight with the Mexicans, and by custom the chief could conduct no business until the coming spring. In mourning he had burned five of his six magnificent lodges, killed nearly all of his horses and mules, thrown aside all of his ornaments and wearing apparel, and with new skins had gone to the Salt Plains to make a new home.[28] On December 11 Butler "sent a talk" to Pahhauca in a letter from himself along with a U.S. flag, some tobacco, and presents for the chief's wife and children.[29]

Chisholm is not mentioned in reports of the expedition. However, it may well be that instead of serving as a scout he acted solely in attendance to artist Stanley, who was along to paint the Comanches at home on the prairie, and Stanley had been busy while at Cache Creek. Buffalo Hump had been persuaded to sit for him. He also painted Pochonnahshonnocco (or the Eater of the Black Buffalo Heart); his wife, Ohahahahwahkee (or the Yellow Paint Hunter); and a Comanche mother and child. Other scenes included that of a Comanche warrior sleeping on the banks of the Red River and a Comanche gambling game in which the women competed for deerskins and dressed buffalo robes.[30]

Stanley also contributed to the council by making a badge that each Indian participant wore with a show of much distinction. When the Indians departed, Stanley was presented a riding crop by a very pretty Comanche girl of whom he had sketched a portrait.[31]

Butler failed to secure a pact with the Comanches on this trip, but efforts were continued in the spring of 1844. Acting in behalf of Texas, Daniel G. Watson and John Conner left the falls on the Brazos just below the mouth of Tehuacana Creek in early February and traveled to an Anadarko village in north Texas, then on to a Kichai village in their search for the Comanches. Watson carried the promise of Sam Houston that he would be present at Tehuacana Creek in May if the Comanches would attend. Meeting four Comanches, who had been on a war party and were themselves searching for their band, Watson and Conner followed along with them to the Colorado River. There they received word from the Comanche chief that he and his fellow chiefs could not attend a treaty council just then because his young men were out in all directions on war excursions.[32]

Returning to the Brazos, the emissaries were met at Red Bear's

Caddo village by Jesse Chisholm, who was at the head of a Cherokee party. While there, a Waco chief, known as Lame Arm because of a battle wound, was brought into camp by Anadarko Chief José María. José María told of how he and ten others had joined a Tonkawa war captain named David Warwick (who had been taken prisoner as a boy) in a horse-stealing raid on Texas settlements. The Texans had followed them and killed Warwick and one Waco. Because of this, the Tonkawas were afraid to come to the council. He said, however, that he would do so if Jesse Chisholm or John Conner would come to his camp.[33]

From Red Bear's village, the commission party proceeded to Tehuacana Creek. When Waco Chief Acaquash, who had come alone, was asked to bring in his people, Chisholm accompanied him in order to hasten the matter. Four days later Jesse returned with word that the Wacos and Tawakonis would be delayed a few days, they having found a large buffalo herd. Chisholm was sent out again to bring in those tribes. He returned two days later, and the two tribes soon followed.[34]

Finally, on May 13 a meeting was held with representatives of several prairie tribes. Chisholm and the Delawares interpreted the speeches avowing peace and friendship.[35] The chiefs all expressed disappointment that Houston was not there, as had often been promised to them. They said that if Houston would come out, all would be right.[36] Another effort would have to be made to persuade the angry, suspicious Comanches to come in for a council.

Once more Jesse Chisholm played a key role in Houston's peace efforts. In June Houston issued a commission for him to visit the Comanches in behalf of Texas and bring them in, authorizing the payment of $250 in specie for four months' service.[37] Colonel Leonard H. Williams was sent north to contact Jesse on the Canadian River and go with him into the Comanche country, treat with the chiefs, and bring them to Tehuacana Creek in September.[38]

En route from Austin, Williams witnessed a unique event — the hanging of two white men who had murdered some Delaware Indians hunting south of the Red River in Fannin County, Texas. Taking the horses and personal effects of the Delaware victims, Williams contacted Chisholm, who escorted him to the Delaware village where the property was given to relatives. Despite warnings that the Waco, Tawakoni, and Wichita bands were angry with whites, the two men and John Conner headed for the Wichita Mountains in search of the Comanches.

On the Walnut Creek branch of the Canadian, they met with some Waco Indians who told them that the Wichitas had recently deserted their villages north of the Red River and joined the Comanches in their camps on the Clear Fork of the Brazos. Chisholm and his companions also encountered some Caddos and Kichais who, having never made a treaty with the United States and being anxious to do so, escorted the three men to their village. There they found the Delaware Jim Shaw with a Comanche party in tow. Chisholm was able to persuade all of the tribes, including the reluctant Comanches, to attend the grand council at Tehuacana Creek, promising that Sam Houston himself would meet them. They all departed en masse for Council Springs on September 15.[39]

The long-hoped-for meeting between the Comanches and Sam Houston finally came about on October 7, 1844, with Jesse Chisholm playing a major role as an interpreter and a counselor.[40] The tribes had begun arriving, setting up their camps and waiting for the affair to begin, when the sound of horses galloping toward the council grounds caught the attention and concern of both the Indians and the whites there. In a moment a small group of horsemen dressed in the military attire of the Texas army appeared over a rise. Mounted on a fine horse at their head was a large, erect-postured man decked in the full uniform of a general. Even at a distance, Chisholm recognized the figure of the man he had once known as a hard-drinking Indian trader at Fort Gibson. It was Sam Houston.

It was a historic moment as Sam Houston, the former trader among the Cherokees who was now famous as the liberator of Texas, faced the assemblage of Plains Indian chiefs. Upon reaching the council grounds, Houston and his aides slowed to a canter and rode with grand display around the waiting crowd. At the far side, Houston dismounted and walked calmly through the crowd of Indians, commissioners, traders, and frontiersmen. There he greeted the chiefs individually with an Indian hug — one arm over and one arm under with an energetic squeeze. This done, the chiefs seated themselves cross-legged in a circle, and Houston had brought forth a calumet with a huge stone head and a cane stem so long that

Samuel Houston. Jesse Chisholm played a vital role in Houston's efforts to bring peace to the young Republic of Texas. *Courtesy of the Barker Texas History Center, The University of Texas at Austin.*

the pipe reached almost to the center of the circle.

After the pipe was filled with its kinnikinnick mixture of tobacco and sumac leaves and lighted, Houston took several long drags. Then, with his head tilted back, he sent the smoke puffs reverently skyward. When the pipe had made its way ponderously around the circle of chiefs, Houston called Chisholm and the other interpreters to his side and began his speech.[41]

Houston's capacity for diplomacy as well as showmanship was demonstrated when he honored the amenable Waco Chief Acaquash. Having Acaquash rise, he bound about the chief's head a silk handkerchief with a large gold-plated pin and pronounced him to be the head chief of the Wacos.[42] Then, with Chisholm at his side to interpret and lend his personal credence to the affair, Houston addressed the Comanches. "Six years ago I made peace with the Comanches," Houston said. "That peace was kept until a bad chief took my place. That chief made war on the Comanches and murdered them at San Antonio. He made war on the Cherokees, also, and drove them from the country. Now this has to be mended; war can do us no good."

Chisholm translated Houston's talk, and after a time Buffalo Hump, the ranking war chief of the Comanche Nation, arose. Those who had never seen him before were surprised to find a medium-sized, fine-looking man in his early fifties who spoke well and was at ease in council. Buffalo Hump pointed to the sky and then to the ground. "The Great Spirit above is looking down and sees and hears my talk; the ground is my mother, and sees and hears that I tell the truth. When I first heard the words of your emissary I felt glad. I was uneasy until I struck the white path and followed it here to see you. What I came for was to hear the words of peace. That is all I have to say."

The talks continued for two days. There was no doubt that both Houston and Buffalo Hump wanted peace, but settling the difficult disputes between them was impossible. Houston proposed a dividing line between the Comanches and the Texans, to run southward from the mouth of Cache Creek on the Red River past Comanche Peak on the Brazos and the old San Saba mission and from there southwesterly to the Rio Grande. He also wanted to build a series of forts and trading posts along the edge of the Comanche country.

But Buffalo Hump would not bend to these things, and finally Houston was forced to drop those matters and settle for a simple treaty of friendship. He had done the best he could do, so he said farewell to Jesse Chisholm and his other Cherokee friends of old and rode back down the river to his home at Washington on the Brazos. The Comanches and the other tribes packed their lodges onto their travois, gathered up their horse herds, and disappeared into the wilds of northern Texas.

The pact that was signed on October 9 declared an end to such things as horse stealing and captive taking by the Indians. In turn they would be furnished with gunpowder, lead, spears, and other arms with which to kill game. But the difficulties that lay between the white people of Texas and the prairie Indians were much too large to be overcome by this treaty effort.

Chisholm collected his pay from the Republic of Texas and with Watson and Conner purchased a large amount of trade goods, including powder and lead, from Torrey's. The three men then headed off to barter with the Mexicans who seasonally came into the Texas Indian country to conduct trade.[43]

When Texas agent Eleazer L.R. Wheelock prepared to make a trip into the Indian Territory in May 1845, Texas Commissioner of Indian Affairs Thomas G. Western warned that the Comanches were intensely angry with the Delawares over the killing of some Comanche warriors. He recommended the employment of Chisholm as one of "three excellent men, and competent" to serve as an escort, the others being Jesse's Delaware friends.[44]

There is no evidence that Chisholm was present at Council Springs that fall of 1845 when Texas agents met once more with the prairie Indians, among them the Comanches under Old Owl.

But still there was no solution found for the widening difficulties that existed between the whites and the Indians of Texas. As Houston once stated, he could build a great wall around the Indians and sooner or later whites would find a way to get over it. However, there would be other treaties, and Chisholm's service in Texas was far from done. He was now, however, involved in another mission, one that would take him beyond the Rio Grande into Mexico.[45]

I t was of great concern that Sequoyah, or George Guess, the half-blooded Cherokee who was so widely renowned for his invention of the Cherokee alphabet, had disappeared. Three years earlier, in 1842, he had simply vanished; no one seemed to know where he was. It was rumored that he had set out on a mysterious pilgrimage into the prairie wilderness. His friends were worried and fearful that harm may have come to the Cherokee intellect, who was now in his advanced years and in bad health. In the spring of 1845 Jesse Chisholm was called upon to make a search for Sequoyah, either to bring him back or verify his death. Just how close Jesse Chisholm was to the man who was some forty-five years his senior is not known. Undoubtedly the frontiersman not only felt the bond of blood and clan but was equally concerned.

Like Jesse Chisholm, Sequoyah was a descendant of the Corn Tassel family, his mother being Wurteh, sister to Old Tassel. His father, Colonel Nathaniel Gist, had been sent as an emissary to the Cherokees by George Washington; and Sequoyah was born near Fort Loudoun, Tennessee, about 1760. At the Treaty of Long Island on the Holston River in July 1777, Old Tassel had stipulated that Gist was the only white person who would be permitted to "sit down on Great Island when he pleased."[1]

Despite a crippled leg, Sequoyah had served under Captain John McLemore during the Creek war, his regiment being involved in the Battle of Horseshoe Bend in 1814. He was among the 331-member emigration party of Chief John Jolly that migrated to Arkansas in early 1818. It was during the ensuing years that he developed the

Sequoyah. The immortal inventor of the Cherokee alphabet was very likely kin to Jesse Chisholm. *Courtesy of the Smithsonian Institution National Anthropological Archives, Bureau of American Ethnology Collection.*

famous Cherokee alphabet that would win him immortality, taking his invention back to the Old Nation in 1821.[2] Upon seeing the alphabet successfully taught and used to translate the New Testament into the Cherokee language, Sequoyah had returned to Arkansas as a celebrity among the white people and a political leader of the Western Cherokees. In 1825 a medal was struck in Washington,

D.C., and presented to him by the Cherokee National Council as recognition for his great achievement.

Sequoyah had played a major role as a signator to the Treaty of 1828 whereby the Western Cherokees moved from Arkansas to the Lovely's Purchase area. He had also been a prominent figure in attempting to reconcile the Western Cherokees with the John Ross– led Old Nation group that arrived in 1838 and 1839. It was with Sequoyah's help that Ross had assumed control of the Cherokee government against the bitter opposition of Western leaders such as John Smith, Dutch, and John Rogers, Jr. For a time Sequoyah served as a schoolteacher for Cherokee children.

Sequoyah had grown much disturbed about the breaking away of Cherokees to settlements in distant places. Even as other Cherokees were searching westward for a new site to which they could move to escape white and Old Nation domination, he made his decision to go out and persuade the variant bands of Cherokees to return to the fold of their main body. He also had a curiosity about the land and peoples beyond the Cross Timbers and wished to learn more about them before he died. In the spring of 1842, Sequoyah had departed in secrecy from the Park Hill area near Tahlequah with eight other Cherokees, including his son Teesa and a prairieexperienced guide named Occheeah, or The Worm. Nothing was heard from them until September. Then Cherokee agent Pierce Butler learned from Seminole agent Marcellus Duval that a band of Kichai Indians west of the Cross Timbers had reported that George Guess and his son were on the Red River and were expecting Butler to come out.[3]

In November, Butler received further word that Sequoyah was on the headwaters of the Colorado River of Texas, some five hundred miles distant. The U.S. government, through the War Department and Indian Bureau, authorized $200 for the rescue of Sequoyah. Butler first considered sending Cherokee merchant John Drew after him.[4] In the end, however, it was Jesse Chisholm who undertook the task of making the search.

Sequoyah was now rumored to be in Mexico with the Cherokee settlement there. In March 1845 the *Cherokee Advocate* announced that a Cherokee party was preparing to leave for Matamoros to locate Sequoyah. Chisholm was at the head of the small group, which also included Cherokees John Spaniard and Daniel G. Watson. Even before the end of March, it was reported in the *Intelligencer* at Van Buren, Arkansas, that the searchers had been murdered by the Comanches, the account being based on a report by a visitor from the Little River settlements.[5]

The death of Chisholm and the others was confirmed by the paper in May when it announced that, indeed, Chisholm, Spaniard, Watson, Nick Miller, John and Bill Conner, John Kitchum, and several others were dead.[6] Both reports, however, proved to be false; and on June 26, 1845, the *Cherokee Advocate* published a letter that Butler had received from Warren's Trading Post on the Red River. Dated April 21, 1845, it read: "We the undersigned Cherokees, direct from the Spanish dominions, do hereby certify that George Guess, of the Cherokee Nation, Arkansas, departed this life in the town of Sanfernando in the month of August 1843, and his son is at this time on the Brazos River, Texas, about 30 miles above the falls, and intends returning this fall." The letter was signed by Standing Rock, a refugee Cherokee who had personally witnessed the death and burial of Sequoyah; Standing Bowles, another refugee from Texas who was probably a relation of Chief Bowles; and Watch Justice. The names of Jesse Chisholm and Daniel G. Watson appeared on the letter as witnesses. The *Intelligencer* corrected itself by announcing: "We are glad to hear that Jess. Chisholm and his companions have 'come to life'. . . . Jess. Chisholm has got home. Watson, Conner, and others are not dead as reported. Old Geo. Guess, inventor of the Cherokee Alphabet is certainly dead."[7]

That Chisholm and his party made the long journey to Mexico is further indicated in another report to Butler, written in the Cherokee language, stating: "After reaching Red River on my way, I met with the following Cherokees from Mexico — Jesse, the leader of the party, The Worm, Gah-na-nes-kee, The Standing Man and the Standing Rock. The last named, The Standing Rock, attended Sequoyah during his last sickness and also witnessed his death and burial. Isse-sa-de-tah, the son of Sequoyah, remains on Red River. He is very sorry that the remains of his father are buried so far from his own country, and remains where he is on this account."[8] It appears, also, that Jesse persuaded the refugees to Mexico under Standing Rock to comply with the wishes of Sequoyah and return to

Texas. These Cherokees relocated near the deserted Waco village at the falls of the Brazos above Tehuacana Creek, residing there in extremely destitute conditions.

In its June 26, 1845, issue, the *Cherokee Advocate* published an interesting and historically valuable account by Occheeah, who had served as a guide for Sequoyah on his odyssey among the prairie tribes and across the vast plains of Texas to Mexico, the country in which Jesse Chisholm roamed and conducted trading ventures during the 1840s. Sequoyah had directed the course of his small party southwestward along the well-worn trail leading to the Red River. When he became ill, the Cherokee was taken in and cared for by a kindly Kichai chief. After recuperating for a time, he sent all of his companions back except for Teesa and The Worm. The three then set out across Texas for Mexico.

When his horse was stolen by some Tawakoni Indians, Sequoyah was forced to take refuge in a cave near San Antonio while Teesa and The Worm went on to Mexico for help. They returned to find Sequoyah gone. Tied to a log was a note in the Cherokee language telling how a flood had washed away his provisions and driven him out. They eventually found him seated, lonely and in despair, beside a campfire. Sequoyah was taken on to Mexico where he was cared for at the Cherokee village near San Fernando until he died one day, quite suddenly. He had requested some food, and while it was being prepared he "breathed his last."[9] He was buried in a grave near the Mexican town.

Jesse returned home from Mexico just in time to become involved in another frontier problem. Earlier the Creeks had killed six Pawnee Mahas who had come south to steal horses. When the Creeks staged a scalp dance in celebration, the Pawnees murdered a Creek man in revenge and sent one of his amputated hands to the Creek Upper Towns. The worried Creeks called another "grand council" and asked Jesse's help in mediating between them and the Pawnee Mahas from the north.[10]

A short time later the Wichitas, also beset by the Pawnees who invaded their territory, killed six more of that tribe in a skirmish. The Wichitas contacted the Creeks in behalf of both themselves and the Comanches, who had only recently maltreated some Creek emissaries who had come to invite them to their council. Peace

This statue of the great Cherokee intellect Sequoyah stands in the U.S. Capitol's Hall of Statuary. *Courtesy of the Archives and Manuscripts Division of the Oklahoma Historical Society.*

emblems were sent by the Creeks to the Pawnees, who agreed to meet them and the other tribes of the area at the Great Salt Plains in the fall.[11]

These tribal feuds had the frontier alarmed, but even more disturbing was the killing of four Comanches by the Caddos on the

Red River. Already upset by the encroachment onto their hunting grounds of whites and other tribes, the Comanches demanded that Abel Warren abandon his post at Cache Creek.[12] Warren applied for troop protection; but, failing to get it, he departed the post, going east to his original home in Boston to marry his childhood sweetheart. He left in charge a man who reportedly sold all the goods and stock there and absconded with the profit.[13] The hostility of the Comanches and the closing of Warren's place caused Jesse Chisholm to take his trading operations even deeper into Texas to barter with Mexican traders.

His presence there was recorded by William Quesenbury (pronounced "*Cush*enbury," as in *cush*ion), a young Arkansawyer who kept a diary of a journey he made through central and western Texas with a party of Cherokees in the fall of 1845.[14] The group was made up of Old Settler Cherokees and members of the Treaty party. The two factions, both strongly opposed to the control of the Cherokee government by John Ross and his Old Nation party, wished to explore the vast, thinly inhabited regions of central and western Texas for a place to which they could migrate. Among the group were Teesa Guess, Ezekial and James Starr, and Albert Finney Chisholm, son of Thomas Chisholm.

Crossing the Red River at Coffee's post, the party entered the Cross Timbers country of north Texas and was guided through them by Jesse's son William (known to friends as Bill). It was probably along the Brazos that the group visited Jesse Chisholm's camp where one evening they "chatted and cracked pecans with Chisholm until near twelve."[15]

After touring the Texas country along the Colorado and San Saba most of the winter, the field-weary Quesenbury visited San Antonio. There he met with William Duval, an Arkansas slave trader and brother to the agent for the Seminoles in the Indian Territory. After a time, the two men headed north for Arkansas. On February 1 they again encountered "Jess" Chisholm and his party, who were waiting with their horses and pack mules to cross the flooded Guadalupe River. Chisholm was on his way back to the settlement of the former Mexican Cherokees on the Brazos, following a trading venture.

"Cush" Quesenbury joined with Chisholm's group as it moved north toward Austin. His diary of the journey provides interesting glimpses of the problems and events of travel that Chisholm normally faced in his trade excursions onto the prairie. The travelers forded streams by ferrying their saddles and packs across on rafts. On occasions they were delayed by having to search for mules that had strayed from camp, and their movement was slowed by the constant need to hunt for food as they went. Quesenbury noted that on one occasion he killed a rabbit, while Jesse bagged a wild turkey and another time brought in a large buck. When Quesenbury shot a raccoon, Chisholm tied it to his saddle and took it to camp for a meal. On February 6 Quesenbury and another man went into the infant settlement of Austin and purchased bread.

As they continued on north from Austin, the travelers spotted a herd of buffalo moving in toward them. Jesse and his companions took stands and waited on them, but the animals decided to lie down just out of gunshot range. Quesenbury reported the incident with some humor: "Jess Chisholm banged away and broke one's shoulder. We all then ran to our mules and took after it. William Duval brought it down after Jess had missed it when in about ten feet of its head."[16]

Upon reaching a place where the prairie had been burned off so badly that they could not follow the trail, Quesenbury rode to the site of a deserted Waco village, now the site of Waco, Texas, where he met an old Caddo Indian who put them on the right trail. Finally reaching the Brazos, they forded the stream and moved up its east bank to the mouth of Tehuacana Creek near Torrey's Trading House. Close by was the village of the Mexican Cherokees, and near it was a newly arrived encampment of a U.S. peace commission.[17] Among the commission's members were several old acquaintances of Chisholm, including a number of men from the Cherokee and Creek nations. They had come to help the commission carry out its task of making a new treaty with the prairie tribes. Thus far, efforts at getting the Comanches to attend another peace council had been unsuccessful. The commission sorely needed the assistance of someone for whom the Comanches held great trust and respect. The arrival of Jesse Chisholm at this moment was highly opportune for them.

When Texas entered the Union in 1845, the United States became responsible for the problem of conflict with the Plains Indians on the southern Plains. The Comanches were still the core of that problem, the tribe still dominating most of northern, central, and western Texas. Accordingly, the United States made arrangements for a large effort to make lasting treaties with the Comanches and other Indians of the region — treaties that would define territorial jurisdictions and secure peace for the embroiled frontier. Rescue of the numerous Mexican and American captives held by the prairie tribes was also a major consideration, as was the future safety of Americans who more and more were traversing the great central Plains to New Mexico and California.[1] In order to conduct these treaties, services of the most experienced frontiersmen were vital. But when officials looked about for Jesse Chisholm, he was nowhere to be found — off somewhere on a trading venture. Eventually, they would be fortunate to find that Chisholm was already in Texas.

In the fall of 1845 Cherokee agent Butler and Colonel M. G. Lewis had been named as U.S. commissioners to treat with the Indians at a Texas site known as Comanche Peak. The acting chief of the Cherokees, George Lowrey, also appointed two Cherokee delegates, William S. Coodey and Elijah Hicks, to attend the council and cooperate in negotiations.[2] As early as November, runners had been sent out from Gibson to invite the tribes to attend still another council. These envoys had been met with hostility by the Comanches and others who were still agitated with both Texas and the United

States. Some of the couriers had been made prisoner, and their lives threatened.[3] One set of runners encountered a large body of Comanches moving northward toward the Salt Plains to attend the Creek-arranged council. The Comanche chief refused to turn around, saying that he hoped to kill some Osages at the Salt Plains.[4]

The need for a good guide was paramount, for none of the group was quite certain just where Comanche Peak was located except that it was on the Brazos River in the wilds of central Texas. With Jesse Chisholm unavailable, the commission party employed Doublehead, son of the famous Chickamaugan chief, who claimed that he knew the country below the Red River. Agent Butler and his company of nearly thirty people, which included *Arkansas Intelligencer* editor Josiah W. Washbourne, left Frozen Rock (on the Arkansas River above Fort Smith) in late December and headed down the Texas Road. They were joined at Edwards's store by Seminole Chief Wild Cat and some of his men. At Preston, Texas, near Holland Coffee's trading post, they united with the party of Commissioner Lewis who, accompanied by his wife, had come overland by wagon from Shreveport.[5]

On January 11 the expedition of nearly fifty members, with seventy-five horses and pack mules carrying $1,200 worth of presents for the Indians, struck southwestward toward the Brazos. Coffee and some of his men accompanied the expedition as hunters to provide meat during the journey. A group of Chickasaw and Seminole Indians rode in escort against attack by the prairie tribes. The commissioners had hired them after being denied military escort by General Arbuckle.[6]

Drovers working for Coffee and Abel Warren headed for the treaty site on a separate route with a herd of beef cattle for which the commission had contracted. The beef would feed the Indians during the council.[7] Some of the Indian scouts rode out in advance carrying presents with which to lure the prairie tribes into attending the council. The peace commission party headed more directly southwestward across the Trinity River for the appointed rendezvous, breaking their own trail.[8]

The tribes were to have been invited to meet with the commissioners at the full moon in February. Unfortunately, Doublehead did not know the country as well as he thought and led the expedition across the Brazos almost to the Colorado River, nearly a hundred miles beyond Comanche Peak. This error, plus the delays caused by swollen streams, prevented the commissioners from reaching their destination by the time agreed upon. Their runners, however, had foreseen the possibility of this and had postponed the appointment until the full moon in March.[9] It was February 11 before the wandering commission party finally reached the Brazos and went into camp at Council Springs on Tehuacana Creek not far from the trading post, recently purchased from the Torreys by George Barnard.[10] Some twenty-five miles down the river, the frontier settlement of Bucksnort had sprouted into being. It was a rowdy, rough community that boasted a racetrack, hotel, and prostitutes.[11]

By chance, Chisholm and Quesenbury arrived at Council Springs only a few days later, and the commissioner quickly hired Chisholm to find Pahhauca and his people and bring them in to council. On February 22, Jesse and Nick Miller embarked on a search that would take them out onto the vast prairie beyond the Red River to the headwaters of the Washita.[12]

Shortly after their departure, Coffee arrived at the commission camp from Comanche Peak, where he had delivered the beef herd, and reported that Buffalo Hump and two hundred of his people were at the Peak. On March 1, the commissioners packed up their camp and made the seventy-five-mile, three-day ride to the Peak. They discovered with some disappointment that Comanche Peak was merely a "brushy hill" — a rectangular mound about a fourth of a mile in length.[13]

The commissioners made the contractor's camp some four miles from the Peak (near present-day Glen Rose, Texas) and were joined by arriving bands of Indians, who set up their lodges in the same vicinity. First to appear were the Lipans from the San Antonio region, their women decked in buckskin capes, petticoats, and bootees, all beautifully fringed. Then came a deputation of well-mounted Tonkawa chiefs and warriors, their stirrups dragging the ground. Long reputed on the Plains to be cannibals, the Tonkawas were each streaked with vermilion and armed with lance and bows. Their quivers were filled with arrows. These Indians were followed by the Wichitas from the Red River with their women and children, accompanied by their cousins, the Kichais from north of the Red.

The warriors and their war horses were daubed with paint. Wacos from their camps nearby and Caddos from their villages below on the Brazos also joined the encampment. A delegation of Creeks under Chiefs Chilly McIntosh and Tuckabatchee Mico from the Canadian River added their colorful costumes to this collage of Indian life. Wild Cat, the famed Seminole warrior-chief of the Florida Everglades, told stories of interesting battles with the white soldiers.

But the Indians drawing the most respect and attention were the Comanche party of nearly two hundred chiefs, warriors, women, and children led by the notorious Buffalo Hump. Some of the young Comanche dons who strutted haughtily about the encampment were heavily painted, trinketed, and fancily dressed. Their appearance was almost effeminate, but no one doubted their manhood or war-ring ability — every tribe on the Plains lived in constant fear of them.[14]

The mesquite prairie along the Brazos had become a sizable community of commission members, teamsters, scouts, Indians, tents, lodges, wagons, horses, and cattle. All waited upon the arrival of the remainder of the Comanche bands and chiefs, in particular for Chisholm to appear with Pahhauca. The Indians passed the time at their favorite games of bullet hiding and four-spike arrows, while groups of barefoot boys aged twelve to fourteen engaged in the combative sport of kicking an adversary's legs out from under him. The commission conducted preliminary conferences with the chiefs already there. Buffalo Hump pledged his cooperation but insisted that the main council be moved back down the Brazos to Council Springs where Sam Houston had met with the tribes in 1844.[15]

On March 15, Chisholm and Miller returned with Principal Chief Pahhauca in tow. The chief, cautious against another massa-cre such as that of the San Antonio courthouse, had not brought his other chiefs with him. On the day following, a council was held with the chief. Both Butler and Hicks made speeches calling for peace and brotherhood and recommending that a boundary line be estab-lished to separate the Indians and the whites. Pahhauca replied that he had come a long way and was pleased to hear the commissioners' talk. But, he said, he would need time to consider the matters that had been raised before making a reply.[16]

That night a feast was given the Comanches by the Kichais, who boiled, slightly, two kettlesful of beef and dumped it on a buffalo saddle skin. They also entertained Pahhauca with a concert of singing that was accompanied by the rattling of gourds. Pleased with his reception, the Comanche promised the commissioners that he would return to the prairie and bring in his people. On the eighteenth, the hefty "emperor of the desert" mounted his mule, gave a courtly hug or two, and rode off with Jesse and two other emissaries as his escorts. A week later Chisholm sent back word from the headwaters of the Washita that three bands of Comanches were on their way in and would arrive about the twelfth of May.[17]

On the same day that Chisholm and Pahhauca departed, the commission party decamped at Comanche Peak and began a return move to Council Springs. There they reestablished their camp, built stockades to hold supplies purchased for the forthcoming council, and erected a large arbor in which to meet with the Indian leaders. But the commission party had been long in the field, enduring many privations and suffering inclement weather. Sickness had begun to set in. Commissioner Butler was confined much of the time to his tent by illness, and Cherokee representative Coodey, also ill, departed for home.[18]

The stalemate continued into April, with Chisholm still afield. As the days passed the commission camp began to run out of food. By the twenty-fourth there was no bread, coffee, or sugar; and for breakfast the men were hammering the broiled but very hard buffalo meat with a stone to make it chewable.[19]

On April 27, couriers who had been sent to the Colorado River returned, bringing with them a four- or five-year-old German boy whom they had ransomed from the Comanches. The boy had been with a large colony of German emigrants on their way to settle a grant of land near the old stone fort of San Saba. The Comanches and Lipans had lost no time in attacking the group. The rescued child became very attached to Mrs. Lewis during the council.[20] The commissioners were much more concerned that the German intrusion into the Comanche buffalo range would upset their negotiations with the tribe. The Comanches on the Colorado were refusing to come in for another reason. They feared retaliation for the recent killing of some Texas citizens by one of their war parties. The commissioners sent back promises of a friendly reception for the Comanches if they would come to the treaty council.[21]

The Colorado River Comanches were finally persuaded. On May 9 some two hundred of them headed by Chief Old Owl and the famed war chief Santa Anna arrived at Council Springs. After canoeing their baggage and swimming their horses across the Brazos, the Comanches were escorted to the U.S. commission camp by a large welcoming party.[22] George W. Kendall, editor of the *New Orleans Picayune,* was on hand to describe the scene:

> They all came in, Mopechocopee [Old Owl] taking the lead, in regular order, followed by a raft of women and children, all mounted, and I would not have missed the spectacle on any account. The women sat their horses fearlessly, and astride after the manner of their lords and masters, while the children were clinging on anywhere and everywhere; and as well might one undertake to shake a squirrel from a limb as one of these small specimens of the genus Comanche from their horses. The women at once struck the camp, arranged all the buffalo skin wigwams, brought water from a delicious spring hard by, built fires, and in half an hour's time all were feasting themselves upon buffalo meat.[23]

That night a great celebration of Indian dancing took place. Cherokee Elijah Hicks wrote in his diary:

> A Cherokee dance was given at the Caddo lodges where there was a numerous party to witness the feat. There was considerable animation in the running around the fire encircled with a ring of three deep, of fine looking men and women. Within a rod was a Caddo party at the same pleasure, of the same form but tardy comparatively.
>
> Near our lodges was a Tonkawa dance, sung loud to a drum beat but with much vigor, and danced until sun rise this morning 10th — instant. This dance consisted of men & women, all singing three or four feet deep and from ten to twenty in length. Every moving creature appeared to be in animation, and may be looked [upon] as a jubilee of the tribes. The Comanches commenced a concert, by a Choir of singers, but of short duration.
>
> . . . the dance was continued by the Lipans & Tonks. Consisting

of a squadron of singers, men with drum, rattling gourd, and beating on a couple of raw Bison skins keeping time with the Song. The dance was by the women in front & some girls with a slow step, one foot down and the other, so as to make a rocking motion of the females, enlivenly [sic] every few minutes by a shrill yell of the females, and proceeded to & thro the Camanchee encampment. This feat I am told is given in honor of the Camanches congratulating themselves in their success of killing a Spaniard. This I term a military Ball or War dance.[24]

In addition to the German boy, several Mexican children were rescued from the Comanches. Chisholm purchased a Mexican slave boy, Emanuel Mariana Etuarte of El Torián, Chihuahua, who had been Pahhauca's personal servant, for a price of $150.[25] He also made efforts to rescue Cynthia Ann Parker, who had been taken captive in Texas in 1836 along with her younger brother. The girl, now about seventeen, and her ten-year-old brother had been seen by scouts. Cynthia Ann was now married to a Comanche man. Her husband scorned offers of up to $500 plus a large amount of goods for her return. Neither would the girl have it. Now over ten years into her captivity, she ran away and hid to avoid rescue.[26]

The whites, too, still held a number of Indian children, some of whom had been taken six years earlier during the San Antonio massacre of the Comanche chiefs. Hicks wrote a compassionate description of the exchange of captives and lamented upon the practice of slavery:

> Camanche girls & prisoners taken at a treaty of peace [at] San Antonio and elsewhere by the Texans have been brot to camp by the agents employed by Comrs. to be returned to their people. This is the Country of Captives, the weeping Camanche girls, held in duress by the Texans, the silvan face of anglo Saxon Sons & daughters and the Sons of the Montezumas & Guatimonzin cursed and driven, traded, as slaves by the roving & haughty Camanchee. O, what a country of freedom in name, a nations birthright to two miles [million] of African slaves.[27]

During the interim period the treaty party had a chance to observe the curiosities of Indian life. A young Lipan girl, clad in a buckskin-fringed wedding dress and belled boots, was married to a

Kichai man, the two marching through the camp wrapped in a blanket as friends accompanied them beating a drum.[28]

Hicks also told of humorous moments, such as the attempt by the corpulent Creek Tuckabatchee Mico and the equally weighty Pahhauca to greet one another by embracing Kichai style — one arm over the other's shoulder, the other arm under the armpit, then reversing the order of embrace. The two men could barely reach one another's shoulders because of their huge bellies that protruded between. The sight drew the laughter of both white and Indian onlookers.[29]

During this wait, also, the commissioners developed an appreciation for the huge amount of raw beef that a Comanche brave could consume in one day. Later, when it was necessary to justify expenditures for the council, the commissioners would call upon frontier experts to verify the amount. Estimates varied from five to ten pounds a day.[30]

George Kendall was on his second trip to the Texas plains. His first visit had been in 1841 when as a member of the Texas expedition to Santa Fe he and other members had been captured and imprisoned in Mexican leper colonies. Under the escort of Delaware Jim Shaw, who worked with the Texas Indian service, and Texas Indian agent Robert Neighbors, Kendall had traveled by horseback from Houston by way of Austin, Bucksnort, and Torrey's Trading House. Kendall sent back descriptive reports of the council and the Indians in attendance until news in camp arrived of the outbreak of hostilities between the United States and Mexico. The *Picayune* editor then dashed off for Matamoros, Mexico, to become an American war correspondent.[31] Another correspondent, using the pseudonym "Buffalo Hump," took over sending the *Picayune* accounts of the council. He reported that the Indians killed the time while waiting with their favorite pastimes of racing horses or gambling. "In one lodge you will find a party dealing monte with American or French cards; in another some other game of cards not familiar to Americans: under the trees a game of 'hiding the bullet,' of which they are all passionately fond and become extremely excited; men, women and children participate and often bet the last article they possess upon earth. Their children are early taught by the parents the art of throwing the arrow and gaming upon the result."[32]

On May 12, 1846, Chisholm arrived in escort of Pahhauca and his band. The Comanches pitched their lodges near the others, producing an encampment that gave the appearance of a small army. Now, after the peace commission had waited three long, tiresome months and endured much discomfort and illness, a treaty could finally be consummated with the prairie tribes. The chiefs were all gathered under the arbor erected for the occasion, and the calumet was smoked.[33] Through Chisholm and other interpreters, the commissioners told the assembly that they brought with them a talk from the president of the United States, which they would deliver at a meeting the next morning. That night a feast of large cakes of bread and chunks of boiled beef, all piled upon a tent cloth, plus coffee was served to a large crowd that ranged in dress from the finely attired Cherokees, Creeks, and Chickasaws to those who wore few clothes. Some were fantastically painted.[34]

In the council on May 13, the commissioners gave their talk from the president, Jesse and his companions again serving as linguists in translating the message into the various Indian tongues. Proposals for a treaty establishing a permanent peace and for boundary lines were submitted to the chiefs, who said that they would need a day or two to talk the ideas over among themselves.

When they returned to council on the fifteenth, Pahhauca spoke for all the Comanches. He said they were satisfied with the president's talk, and they had no objections to signing a peace treaty. However, as they had to Sam Houston in 1844, they objected to drawing boundary lines that would hamper their movement.[35] This matter remained unresolved when on May 16 the treaty papers were inked by the commissioners, chiefs, and witnesses. By the treaty the Comanches, Wacos, Tonkawas, Wichitas, and Tawakonis agreed to live in peace under the jurisdiction of the United States, to return all prisoners, and to give up tribal members guilty of murder or robbery of U.S. citizens. They accepted the establishment of trading posts on the borders of their land, and agreed to report anyone selling intoxicating spirits among the tribes. In turn the United States promised to send them blacksmiths, schoolteachers, and preachers.[36]

The issue of establishing borders would be taken up with Houston when a delegation of Indians from the council visited him. A number of the Indians were persuaded to make the long journey to Washington, Chiefs Buffalo Hump and Santa Anna among them. However, at the last moment Buffalo Hump changed his mind and refused to go.[37]

On the day following the treaty signing, there were, as Hicks described it, "Comanches in every direction Striking their tents, women packing, horses — recd. their goods & drawing off into the boundless desert."[38] It is easy to understand the feeling of Hicks, who after being afield for nearly five months, ended his diary of the Comanche Peak council on a plaintive note: "The end is now Come to go home. Is my wife and children alive? I pray to heaven to protect me home, away, away, away . . . 500 miles."[39]

Jesse Chisholm was not listed among the witnesses to the treaty. He was, however, contracted along with Jim Shaw to accompany the delegation as an interpreter. After riding many hundreds of miles on horseback across the prairie for the peace commission, he would now travel many hundreds more on a new and interesting sojourn to the nation's capital.

Throughout the history of white-Indian conflict, many Indian delegations were escorted to the seat of government in Washington, D.C., to meet their "Great Father," the president of the United States. American leaders believed that if the leading men of the tribes could see the advanced state of civilization of the United States, comprehend its overwhelming numbers, and know its great military power, they would return home and tell their own people, who would no longer resist American intrusion. Then the tribes would be persuaded more quickly to give in to white superiority, to take up civilized ways themselves eventually, and even to accept Christianity.

For these reasons it was decided that after the treaty agreement at Comanche Peak a delegation of Indian chiefs from the council would be taken to visit Washington, D.C. Jesse Chisholm, along with Delawares Jim Shaw and Matty Conrad, was chosen to accompany the delegation as an interpreter.[1] Jesse was probably just as awed by this sudden separation from the frontier and immersion into the world of white civilization as were his companions. It was an adventure to travel by horseback through the pined forests of east Texas to Fort Caddo, located just below the Great Raft that clogged the Red River above present-day Shreveport, Louisiana. It was even more exciting to take his first steamboat ride down that river to where it joined the broad, hurried waters of the Mississippi, and on south to New Orleans.

As they moved down the waterways of Louisiana, white and black faces alike on the banks, in boats, and at the river ports along their route gawked in astonishment at the sight of the travelers. The Indians, some blanketed, some with their bronze skins bare to the southern climate and decorated with silver trinkets, were as curious and as amazed at the sights offered by the delta land, plantation life, and Creole culture of the region as those who espied their first "wild Indians" from the prairie. Many of those along the shore stood and stared as the smoke-belching paddle wheeler churned past with its unique railside menagerie. Once beyond their initial surprise, they waved their hats or handkerchiefs in friendly salutes to the Indians and to the white men who were escorting them.

Upon reaching New Orleans, the Indians were quartered on Basin Street, their presence drawing many curiosity seekers who wished to view the "untutored sons of the Southwestern forests." The coastal port was overwhelming in itself.[2] Masses of smoke-stacked steamboats were lined row on row along its levees. The river port bustled with activity as passengers came and went and ebony-skinned slaves labored to load and unload the enormous cargoes of "King Cotton" between wharf and ship deck. Neither the Indians nor Chisholm had ever before witnessed, or even considered possible, the city's conglomeration of humankind, horses, carriages, and street vendors.

From New Orleans their route was by riverboat back up the Mississippi River past the place now called Memphis; it had been known as Chickasaw Bluffs when Jesse had crossed the river there as a mere child on his way to Arkansas. They left the Mississippi at Cairo, Illinois, and continued up the Ohio River, passing Louisville, Kentucky, on June 28.[3] Then it was on to Cincinnati, Ohio, and Wheeling, West Virginia, before finally disembarking to travel overland by stagecoach via Pittsburgh and Brownsville, Pennsylvania, to Cumberland, Maryland. The *Cumberland Civilian* reported their arrival in late June 1846, describing the Comanche chief Santa Anna as "a man of powerful limb and breadth. He has an honest face, and looks like a bold and daring leader."[4]

On June 26 the party of sun and wind-weathered visitors from the heart of the Texas plains, dressed in their blankets and buckskins, befeathered and trinketed, arrived at the capital city's Globe Hotel and took up residence there.[5] Colonel Lewis was in charge of the forty-one chiefs, plus several warriors and Indian women. Jesse

Chisholm and his Indian friends were, indeed, impressed with the many amazing and interesting sights. There was the nation's Capitol Building sitting high above the city with its copper-sheathed dome and magnificent pillars; the shining white executive mansion; and connecting them the tree-lined Pennsylvania Avenue busy with traffic. Officials always made certain that visiting delegations toured the Naval Yard, the Armory, and the Center Market — places, it was hoped, that would convince the tribesmen to change their wild mode of life. One scribe expressed the notion that when the Indians saw the wonders of civilization and understood the "various comforts of Christian life and duties; they will go home recounting them, and 'prepare the way of the Lord and make his path straight.' "[6]

The visit would not be a totally pleasant one for the red men, and it would do little to change their way of life. Mainly it was hoped the Indians would be impressed with the numbers and attainments of the white race. For Chisholm it meant not only the experience of witnessing eastern society but the honor of meeting and interpreting for the president of the United States, James K. Polk. In doing so he matched his grandfather, John D. Chisholm, who had once met Thomas Jefferson while in the Philadelphia quarters of Tennessee Senator William Blount in 1796,[7] and his half uncle, Thomas Chisholm, who, while on a visit to Washington in 1808, had been awarded a peace medal by President Jefferson.[8]

The White House was enclosed with an iron railing fence when the Indian delegation visited it in 1846. In front stood a contemplative statue of Thomas Jefferson neatly encircled by a brick walk. Men in silk hats and frock coats and women in long skirts and bonnets strolled the walkway along Lafayette Square, while horse-drawn omnibuses moved up and down the macadamized Pennsylvania Avenue along with commuters on horseback.

The Indians attracted "no little attention" as they were feted at a reception levee given by President and Mrs. Polk. They addressed the first lady as their "Great Mother."[9] Though they had been attired in American clothes for this visit to the president, the Indians and frontiersmen who had recently arrived from the wild prairies of far-off Texas still drew the curiosity of Washington citizens.

On July 1, Polk again received the delegation at the White

House, this time formally, inside the executive mansion. He noted the occasion in his diary:

> At 5 O'Clock P.M. Between 40 & 50 chiefs and braves of the Comanche and other bands and tribes of wild Indians from the prairies in the North of Texas, were presented to me by M. G. Lewis, Esq'r., who had been sent with Gov. Butler last fall to visit these tribes. I received them in the Ladies Parlour above stairs, in the presence of a few ladies and other persons. I held a friendly talk with them through an interpreter. . . . After the reception and talk were over Miss Pleasanton performed for them on the Piano. They were afterwards conducted to the East Room and through all the parlours below stairs.[10]

The entourage of Indian chiefs and their wives were awed in turn by the shining, columned home of the great father of the white people. The Indians were equally impressed with the inside of the building, particularly the large mirrors that delighted them when they saw their reflections.

President Polk addressed the visitors with a short speech, assuring them that they could rely on the friendship and protection of the United States as long as they themselves were friendly. Chisholm interpreted the president's words into the Comanche tongue for Chief Santa Anna. The Comanche war leader replied that once he had thought his nation could whip any nation in the world. But he had found that the white men were more numerous than the stars, so many he could not count them all.[11]

The delegation was escorted to the south grounds where a large crowd had assembled to hear the Marine Band perform its weekly airs. The Indians drew more attention than did the band, particularly when some of them discarded the uncomfortable shoes that had been laced on them.[12] On another occasion, an Indian warrior created a sensation when his breeches became too binding as he strolled up Pennsylvania Avenue. He simply removed them, put them on his arm, and continued on as Washingtonians gawked in amazement.[13]

When the delegation was taken on a tour of the Capitol, they were much impressed with the glistening dome and delighted with the statuary in the rotunda as well as the colorful specimens of stuffed birds on display. At the Congressional Library their attention was caught by the Indian paintings of George Catlin on exhibit there, some of the original sketches having been made twelve years earlier in their own camps. The prairie tourists gazed with varying emotions upon the scenes of buffalo hunts, chases after wild horses and wolves, and Catlin's extensive presentation of Indians in their native costumes. The women of the party conducted an animated conversation as they pointed to illustrated aspects of their prairie milieu. After touring the Capitol, the frontier guests were taken to visit the U.S. Patent Office.[14]

It was to be expected that sooner or later difficulties would arise in this mix of cultures. The most serious problem involved the matter of liquor, to which the citizens of the Plains were treated in Washington. A capital newspaper complained after one of the Indians had come to the door of a hotel and put his hand to his mouth to indicate that he would like a drink of whiskey.[15] A few days later the same paper reported: "The Indians in our city have been followed and hooted at by the boys. They have been gazed upon by citizens and strangers. They have been in our stores and dwellings, and we daily pass them on the streets. We have pitied their condition and we looked upon their blankets and paints and hideous ornaments. They have been made drunk in our shops and have been turned drunk into our streets."[16]

Usually, visiting Indians were taken to view the naval might of the United States and other evidences of the country's military power. Likely they were taken to the Plumbe National Daguerrian Gallery and Photography shop to have their photo taken "in exquisite style without regard to weather."[17] It is possible that a daguerreotype was made of Jesse Chisholm during this trip; it may be waiting, someday to be discovered.

The visiting tribesmen were also taken on a steamer excursion on the Potomac, which passed in full view of Fort Washington and Mount Vernon. Coincidentally, at the time of their visit, a meeting was being held in Washington between the Old Settler Cherokees and the Ross-led Old Nation Cherokees. The government was attempting to settle the long dispute over legal rights and money allotments between the two groups. During these discussions, two important Western Cherokee men died in Washington: John Looney, an Old Settler and veteran of the Creek wars, in mid-May; and on June 12 John Rogers, Jr., a leading chief of the Western Cherokees.[18] W. S. Coodey, now recovered, arrived with his lady, child, and servant to sit in with Samuel C. Stambaugh, legal representative for the Western Cherokee group.[19]

Jesse was undoubtedly pleased that his old friend Dutch, now a prominent Western Cherokee chief, was also in the city — as was Sam Houston, who now represented Texas as a U.S. senator. Houston had drawn much attention in New Orleans by wearing a Mexican serape about in public.[20] The *Alexandria Democrat* noted that twenty-five years earlier Houston, "one of the most remarkable men of the age," had been a house carpenter in Nashville.[21] As Houston helped to escort the Indians about the Capitol Building, they made signs of admiration at portraits of Andrew Jackson, President Polk, and other American dignitaries. When they came to a large portrait of Houston himself, the Indian tourists enjoyed a hearty laugh of surprise and appreciation. However, Houston's presence was not appreciated by all. Fearful of his influence with the Indians, Captain M. G. Sims, in charge of the capital escort of the delegation, refused to let the chiefs hold a private meeting with the Texan.[22]

On July 4 Houston was among the speakers delivering patriotic orations at a Georgetown fete. A rainy, soggy day forced the cancelation of parades and other outdoor events; but Georgetown University provided facilities, a sumptuous meal, and a band to go with the speeches and reading of the Declaration of Independence.[23]

By the last of July, Washington had begun to tire of its retinue of visitors from the Plains, even as new Indian delegations were arriving. Contrary to a newspaper story of July 24[24] that claimed that the Indians were continuing to flourish in Washington, Jesse Chisholm and his fellow prairie men were growing more and more weary of the civilized world. On July 17 the delegation had met again with President Polk, and Jesse and the other interpreters had informed him that some of the Indians were ill. All were discontent and had a strong desire to return home.[25] There was still another reason, as Jesse explained, why Santa Anna wished to leave. If a Comanche were absent from his tribe for over three months, he would be looked upon as being dead. All of his property and influence would be ceded to someone else. After that it was dangerous to return, for to do so would upset the new arrangement.[26]

Finally a bill was passed in Congress to appropriate $50,000 to pay for the treaty council and for return of the delegation to Texas. On July 24 they met for a last time with President Polk to take their leave. Polk presented them with silver medals of friendship as well as other gifts.[27]

It was August 30 before Chisholm and the Indian delegation reached Torrey's Trading House. The Lipans appeared at San Antonio, "decked off with the gewgaws bestowed upon them at the Capital" and very delighted with their visit. They had a great deal to say about the "mucho grande casa" they had seen there and scorned the local pueblos with "pugh! pugh!" They had also been impressed with the railroads, imitating the escape of steam from the engines with a "puff, puff" sound.[28]

But, as was generally the case, this visit to Washington failed to create much, if any, change among the Indian tribes themselves. The conflicts remained unresolved, and U.S. treaty promises remained unfulfilled. Even then some 10,000 Indians were swarming about Torrey's demanding the goods and presents promised them at Comanche Peak. With the situation growing more and more threatening, Chisholm, Shaw, and John Conner were asked by Neighbors to go out and help quiet the Indians.[29] When Sam Houston arrived back at Galveston in December, on his own authority he ordered Torrey to distribute some $5,000 to $10,000 in presents to the Indians. He also sent a ring, as a token of his good faith, and a cask of whiskey to keep the Indians pacified while he hurried back to Washington. He hoped to induce the U.S. government to live up to its word quickly and save the Texas frontier from an outbreak of hostility.[30]

Undoubtedly Jesse Chisholm was happy to return to the frontier that had been his life; but he was probably also pleased that now he had visited both sides of the continent and his eyes had seen both the Pacific and Atlantic oceans as well as the Gulf of Mexico. His service in the Indian affairs of Texas was almost done now. He would be called upon once more to help effect a treaty with the Comanches in that struggling new state, but his future would be mostly involved in the Indian conflicts and affairs north of the Red River.

Sometime prior to 1847, probably while he was away on one of his long sojourns afield, Jesse's wife Eliza died. When and of what we do not know. Further, records are unclear as to whether any children other than William were produced by the marriage during its ten-year span. It is known that in 1847, Jesse remarried, this time to another half-blooded Creek woman named Sahkahkee McQueen.[1] With his new wife, Jesse moved his home from the mouth of Little River up the Canadian to where the cold waters of a spring bubbled from a small bluff on the north bank. Here, at what became known as Chisholm Springs, two miles east of present-day Asher, Oklahoma, a daughter named Jennie was soon born.[2] In time, more children would follow.[3]

During his contacts with the prairie tribes, Jesse had taken part in the rescue of numerous captive children, some of whom were informally adopted into his family and eventually took the name of Chisholm. Two of them were particularly notable: Vincente, who in later life went by the name of George Chisholm; and Jackson Chisholm, a handsome, Caucasian-looking boy who after Jesse's death would marry Sahkahkee and become a well-known Indian Territory cattleman.

The taking of captives by Indian tribes on the Great Plains was not an uncommon practice. Women and children of the northern Mexican provinces and lower Texas were particularly vulnerable to raids by Comanches and others. The westward migration routes from the Rio Grande to the Platte River as well as the paths of settlers advancing with the American frontier were also virtually

A log cabin probably built by Jesse Chisholm still stood at the site of Chisholm Springs during the 1930s. *Courtesy of the Barker Texas History Center, The University of Texas at Austin.*

defenseless. Visits to Washington and treaties signed by their chiefs had little effect upon the Comanche war societies when they saw their hunting grounds being invaded and crossed by an ever-enlarging flow of emigrant wagon trains. In the face of increasing tensions, Chisholm and his Delaware friends continued to be the principal contacts between white civilization and the prairie tribes.

Western records are replete with accounts of persons who were held captive, later escaping or being rescued to tell their story in print. Traders, scouts, and exploring military expedition members often reported white captives in the camps they visited, and the government constantly received requests for its help in rescuing a family member. Some accounts peter out into inconclusiveness. In 1850, for example, it was reported from Little River that a white woman, "very fair and of a comely appearance," was living among the Comanches 150 miles to the west. She had told a trader that she was the sister of a Lieutenant Love or Lovett who had commanded a train out of Independence, Missouri, some three years earlier. Now married into the tribe, she was not completely unhappy. The men treated her well, she said, but the Comanche women often abused her. She was anxious to leave them and suggested that her freedom could be won with four or five good riding horses. We cannot determine her eventual fate; nothing more was reported concerning her.[4]

Rescuing Mexican and American children held captive by the Comanches and others, as Jesse Chisholm did in the period that followed the Treaty of Comanche Peak and his trip to Washington, was not an easy task. Often the attitude of the Indians was much the same as the attitude of whites toward the black slaves they held. The captives were valuable property, to be used or traded or sold as the owner saw fit; and the price of ransom grew as the desire to rescue intensified. Also, and not uncommonly, strong emotional bonds developed between the captive and his or her Indian family. These were particularly strong when capture resulted in marriage and childbearing, such as in the classic case of Cynthia Ann Parker. Because of this, it was generally less possible to rescue a girl than a boy captive. Even with boys, the situation was often made difficult by the reluctance of the captives to be rescued. Many of the children had been captured very young. Often they had been with their captors long enough that, knowing no other life, they refused to leave. Others, whose parents had been killed during a Comanche strike, had no family or home to which to return.

It was often possible to return the rescued American children to parents or relatives; but the Mexican captives presented another situation. Jesse Chisholm not only paid the sometimes high price to rescue the children but also offered those with no other refuge the shelter of his home and camp and a place among his family retinue.

The move to Chisholm Springs now made Jesse's residence the most westerly along the Canadian beyond Arkansas, Camp Holmes and Chouteau's trading post having ceased activity and neither being occupied except on occasion by bands of Kichais. That the area was still prey to roving bands of Indians had been bloodily illustrated in the spring of 1844. William Baxter, an employee of James Edwards, had resided in a cabin near Chisholm Springs with two slaves. Ominous signs of danger had caused the fearful Negroes to leave, and a short time later Baxter was murdered and his body and cabin burned. The perpetrators were believed to have been Osages.[5]

After Baxter was killed his hogs ran wild. The famished men of the James W. Abert expedition of 1845, returning eastward along the Canadian from a trek to the Rocky Mountains, killed one or two of the pigs while at the spring. The location was described by Abert as a fine spring whose crystal waters gushed from the side of a solid rock bluff.[6]

Even though he established a trading post at Council Grove on the North Canadian during the late 1850s, Jesse would continue to reside at Chisholm Springs until the Civil War. It is believed that he and his son William erected the sandstone structure that stands today over the still-flowing spring. The cold waters were directed through a trough inside the sandstone shed to provide a cooling trench for foodstuffs.[7] It is known that Jesse and his wife Sahkahkee had three slave cabins at Chisholm Springs in addition to their own home. Also he is said to have maintained a trading store of sorts there for the Indians of the region — Seminoles, Shawnees, Delawares, and Creeks as well as hunting parties of other tribes who happened by — while the loft of his home served as overnight shelter to visitors.

During the late 1840s, Jesse began to localize his trading operations in the country around the head of Little River, holding forth for a while at the old Chouteau post. Though his accounts are confusing as to time and place, Edward B. Johnson, son of Chickasaw Nation rancher Montford T. Johnson, stated that when he first saw the Chouteau Creek valley it was filled with Comanche Indians who had come there to trade with Chisholm. At that time, Johnson claimed, Chisholm's trading headquarters was located at old Camp Arbuckle.[8]

An indication of Chisholm's activity in this area is found in an incident in 1847 involving a captive American boy whom Jesse encountered in a Comanche camp. Two years before, the boy had been brought to Fort Gibson by Bill Conner. He had given his name as Gillis Doyle and said he had been taken prisoner four years earlier on the Colorado River while he and his father were out gathering rock. Gillis's health was good, though he appeared to be very ignorant, uncommunicative, and cowed otherwise. He spoke imperfect English, much preferring to communicate in the Comanche tongue.[9] Gillis was turned over to Cherokee agent Butler, who took him along on the Comanche Peak excursion. The boy often entertained the party with Comanche war dances.[10] During the extended wait at Comanche Peak, Gillis disappeared, and it was supposed that he had defected back to the Indians.

In May 1847 Little River trader Thomas A. Aird informed Seminole agent Marcellus Duval that Gillis had been seen at Kickapoo Town on the North Canadian. Duval with two other men immediately rode to the Kickapoo settlement to investigate, but they found no trace of the boy. Attempts to interview a very frightened Comanche woman and a Mexican girl, who had arrived among the Kickapoos a short time earlier, proved fruitless.[11] At Edwards's place, Duval talked with Jesse Chisholm, who had just returned from trading among the Comanches on the headwaters of Little River (in the vicinity of present-day Norman, Oklahoma). Chisholm acknowledged that he knew Gillis Doyle quite well from the Comanche Peak council and that he had, indeed, seen the boy not long before in a Comanche camp.

When Chisholm had attempted to renew his acquaintance with the boy, however, Gillis had pretended that he did not know the trader and that he could not even understand the English language. This took place in the presence of the Comanches, but that night Gillis came to Chisholm's camp alone. He said that he had acted as though he did not know the trader because he did not want the Comanches to suspect that he wished to return to the white settlements. He planned to escape, he said, without the Comanches knowing in what direction he went. He told Chisholm that during the treaty talks at Comanche Peak, he had gone to an Indian camp to buy some moccasins only to be recaptured and forced to go with the Indians. Since then he had been traded from band to band and master to master.

Gillis hoped to escape while the Comanches were near to the white settlement and asked Chisholm's advice on how to proceed. Chisholm gave the boy all the information he needed for finding his way to the Little River settlement. After leaving the Comanche camp for a couple of days and returning, Chisholm learned that Gillis had run away, taking a horse and a mule with him. Disappearing at the same time were a Comanche woman and a Mexican girl, age fifteen or sixteen, who had been captured when about four years of age. Both women were now living with Kickapoo men. Duval feared that Gillis, being from Texas, had been killed by the Kickapoos in retaliation for the murder of a Kickapoo by a band of Texans. The Kickapoos denied that they had seen or harmed the boy, but Duval was not so certain. Noticeably, Gillis disappears from the records at this point.

It was evidently during this same time period that Jesse Chisholm rescued Vincente, alias Caboon, alias George Chisholm.[12] In later life, the man would describe in detail to historian Joseph B. Thoburn how Jesse Chisholm freed him from the Comanches.[13]

Several years before, the Comanches had swooped down on the home of Vincente de Demencio (some give his family name as Huerus) near Parás, Mexico, murdered his parents, and taken him and his sister captive. Since that time he had become adapted to the Comanche nomadic way of life. He spoke their tongue well, understood their mores and beliefs, and enjoyed the excitement of the hunt and the idleness of camp life. Vincente could tolerate being a slave to a Comanche master, knowing that one day he would earn the right to be his own man within the tribe. But when his owner was killed

Women and children became easy pawns in the long struggle of cultures on the frontier. Jesse Chisholm redeemed many captive children, such as these two boys, from the Comanches and other Plains tribes. Chisholm also returned Indian children to their people. *Courtesy of the Smithsonian Institution National Anthropological Archives, Bureau of American Ethnology Collection.*

on a raid, the precariousness of his situation was revealed. Vincente was very nearly ceremoniously put to death along with the warrior's horse, according to Comanche custom.[14]

He was saved only when another warrior decided he was worth trading a horse for. This near encounter with death made Vincente realize that the next time he might not be so fortunate. One day the Delaware Black Beaver came to the Comanche camp to trade, and Vincente found a chance to talk to him privately. "I want to get away from Comanche," he told Black Beaver. "I want you to buy me."

But Black Beaver shook his head. "No, boy. Goods all traded. Indian no take buffalo robes back. No take horses back."

Vincente was dejected. "Then I have to run away and maybe so starve."

"No, boy," Black Beaver answered. "You wait, 'nother trader he come. He good man. He trade for you. He buy you."[15]

Several days later Vincente was sent by his master to look for a big mule and some horses that had strayed. They were very valuable to the Comanche warrior, and when Vincente could not find them he was afraid to return. He became cold and hungry, but he kept on with his search. He was atop a rise overlooking a long valley when his eye was struck by the glistening of an object far to the east. He headed for the place from which the reflection came and finally discovered a camp of wagons. It was the iron rim of a wagon wheel mirroring the sun's rays that had caught his eye.

The camp was that of a trader named Chisholm. The kindly faced man invited Vincente to warm himself by his fire and gave him food to eat. Then Chisholm sent some of his men out to locate the missing animals. When Vincente begged the trader to rescue him, Chisholm agreed that he would try when he came to the Comanche camp. As he had promised, Chisholm came to Vincente's Comanche camp, found the boy's master, and tried to buy him. But the man adamantly refused to sell him. Chisholm continued to insist, and the other stubbornly rejected his offers. Finally Chisholm told the Comanche that if he could not trade for Vincente he would not trade at all and go on to some other band.

It was a dangerous thing to do, and other warriors came up threateningly to join Vincente's master. But Chisholm stood firm, upping his trade offer. Before it was over he had proffered a horse and a stack of goods piled high on the ground — a blanket, some broadcloth, red flannel, knives, tobacco, a looking glass, beads, brass wire, and other items. At length the warrior gave in and accepted.

Afterward the Comanche instructed Vincente to steal some of Chisholm's horses and return to the band, but Vincente had no intention of doing that. He was free of his Comanche master, and he would never go back.

J esse Chisholm was not yet done with his trading excursions to Texas. He was still at it in 1849 when the discovery of gold in California ignited a great rush of white emigration across the central Plains, much of it being along the Canadian River trail blazed by Josiah Gregg ten years earlier. This southerly route offered grass for livestock much earlier in the season than did the northern routes. The flood of gold rushers along the Canadian River intensified the potential for conflict on the prairie beyond the Cross Timbers.

Emigrants massed at jumping-off places such as Fort Smith and Van Buren, Arkansas, during the winter of 1848/49. With the coming of spring, the flood of wagons across the Indian Territory began. At the time Chisholm had taken his wagons to the Red and Brazos river country to conduct trade with the Mescaleros and other Indians. There he was approached by the chief of a Southern Comanche band who had learned of the impending invasion. Ohhewekkee, a nephew of the now deceased Tabaqueena who had signed the Treaty of Camp Holmes, asked Chisholm to escort him to where he could talk with white authorities and their Indian allies about the matter. Jesse, "on account of what he considered important to our government," agreed to interrupt his trading activities in order to fulfil the Comanche's request and take them in.[1]

Bringing with him two redeemed Mexican children, a boy and a girl, Chisholm led the six-man Comanche party to Little River, where agent Duval maintained his Seminole subagency. Duval permitted the Indians to pitch their tents in his yard and provided for them as best he could. On the day following, a meeting was held under a brush shed at the Seminole agency among the Comanches, Duval, Chisholm, and Seminole chief Wild Cat. Ohhewekkee made the gift of a captive boy to the Seminole chief.[2]

Wild Cat, who had been a formidable foe of the U.S. Army during the Florida war, gave a strong peace talk to the Comanches, saying that his people had fought with the whites and found they made strong enemies as well as strong friends. Though the wily chief had his own secret plans at the time to escape the domination of the Americans by fleeing to Mexico, he advised the Comanches to take the road to peace that was open and smooth.

Ohhewekkee said that, though he was not a head chief at home, his words would be listened to when he returned. He insisted that his southern Comanches had never yet broken a treaty with the United States, that it was the northern Comanches who were attacking the wagon trains along the Santa Fe Trail.[3] He suggested that when white emigrants crossing the prairies met with Comanches, they hoist a white flag to signify they were friendly. Then the Comanches would meet and trade with them.

After several days with the Seminoles, Chisholm took the Indian delegation on to the Creek town of Tuckabatchee where more conferences were held with Creek leaders and Creek agent James Logan. Logan reported to Washington that the Indians had been brought to him by Chisholm, "a celebrated hunter." He stated also that he had convinced them that the United States was far superior to Mexico in military power. The Comanches acknowledged that they had heretofore not thought too highly of the Americans and complained that the whites and their Indian allies were destroying their buffalo. The Comanches wanted to know what recompense the United States was prepared to offer for the continuance of such aggression onto the Comanche hunting grounds. Logan promised he would convey their complaints and requests to the president of the United States.[4]

When Chisholm took the visitors back to Little River, they were anxious to return home. Agent Duval optimistically reported that the assurances made by the Comanches were "almost the equivalent to a treaty."[5]

While at Little River in March a visitor reported to the *Fort*

Smith Herald of meeting "Jess Chisholm, a Cherokee, who has been among the Camanches and speaks their language, and who informed Mr. S. that the Camanches wished to say to the whites that they desired to be friendly with them, and did not intend to molest them while on their journey, and they also, wanted the whites to meet them as friends."[6] Chisholm thus helped pave the way for the thousands of gold rushers who would cross the Plains in the months ahead.

Chisholm also rendered another vital service — offering advice and guidance to the inexperienced voyagers on the ocean of prairie between the Cross Timbers and the mountains of New Mexico. Chisholm and his Delaware associates were the resident experts in such matters as dealing with the prairie tribes whose languages they could speak, choosing places to camp, knowing how to find water during the dry seasons, and other vital prairie lore.

A frontiersman guiding a hunt west of Little River loquaciously expressed his opinion regarding the Canadian River trail, foreseeing Jesse's continued advancement into the area:

> Well, Colonel, (said one noble hunter) a hunter's life is a strange thing — one day you're swimming in fat, the next you have not even a joint to grease a lock. . . . If I had my way, I'd stick a fort right down here just between wind and water. . . . Oh, would it not be a fine place for a fort. How those traders would crowd about it to dip into the prairie trade — beaver, otter, deer, buffalo; and then for persons going to Santa Fe it would be as good as a hotel. All they have to do is keep up between these two rivers, they run strait to the very spot.[7]

In the spring of 1849 Captain Randolph B. Marcy arrived at Little River with a command of twenty-six 1st Dragoons and fifty 5th Infantry troops on his way to explore farther and develop a wagon route to New Mexico. While he was repairing wagons and purchasing cattle and feed for his trip, Marcy employed Jesse and Black Beaver to escort his troops as far as Chouteau's old trading post and possibly beyond.[8] From Little River, the pair and their entourage rode ahead, picking the trail and selecting campsites as they moved westward along the south bank of the Canadian River.

The Dragoons were trailed by the 5th Infantry soldiers, some walking and some hitching rides in the army supply wagons.

Following behind Marcy was the consolidated 479-member Fort Smith and California Emigrating Company with seventy-five wagons and a large number of horses and pack mules. The caravan struggled along the road made wet and muddy by incessant rains. Its progress was slowed by having to ferry wagons across streams and push them up hills, and complicated further by the lack of trail experience of the many easterners in the company. Traveling with this early gold rush company were wagons from the trading houses of Aird and Israel Vore that were then in business at the mouth of Little River.[9]

In their letters to relatives back home, the California-bound gold seekers complained of the inclement weather, of standing guard at night during terrible lightning storms, of wolves that prowled about the camp, and the hardships of the trail. Some had been shaken by the sight of the first "wild" Indians they had encountered when Seminole Chief Wild Cat and his war party suddenly appeared and approached their train. Most of the Indians wore little more than a blanket over their shoulders and rode bareback with only a piece of rope for a bridle. All were armed with bows and arrows and well supplied with whiskey. Wild Cat himself drew particular notice. The Seminole's neck, upper arms, and waist were decorated lavishly with silver ornaments, including a peace medal awarded him by the government.

The Seminoles caused them no trouble. When the rain ceased, the caravan went into camp just across the Canadian River from Jesse's place at Chisholm Springs. A happier mood prevailed as the forty-niners busied themselves with camp chores — making fires, cooking, repairing wagons, and tending to stock. Amid the hubbub of activity, an orchestra was improvised by two men, one playing the French horn and the other a handsaw and tent pin, while others joined in singing "The Girl I Left Behind Me." Still others loudly applauded a tall yarn someone had spun.[10]

Both Jesse and Black Beaver provided information regarding the southern route. That road broke away from the Canadian River at the Delaware Mountains by way of what was then known as the

Kickapoo Trail. It then led to the mouth of Mustang Creek, thence up that stream and struck off southwestward. The trail crossed the Red River between the mouths of the Little Washita (on the Texas side) and the Washita, then plunged across the great prairies of Texas to the Rio Grande.[11] Marcy would later return by that route with the guidance of Black Beaver, but for now he was primarily interested in mapping the Canadian River road to Santa Fe.

The rainstorms continued, and the trail along the south bank of the Canadian was a quagmire, causing hard going, ferrying flooded creeks and pushing wagons up hills. The group caught up with Marcy some twelve miles beyond Chouteau's post, where witnesses reported only traces of the trading house and of old Camp Holmes still evident.

Chisholm continued a short distance beyond Camp Holmes; but within sight of the Wichita Mountains he turned back, probably with the trading wagons of Aird and Vore, carrying a report from Lieutenant James H. Simpson to military superiors on the journey thus far.[12]

Jesse evidently did not remain at Little River very long after his return. In early June Marcellus Duval, reporting the arrival of some Kichais at his agency, said that he was without an interpreter because Jesse Chisholm had gone to Missouri.[13] In fact, Jesse was on his way there with a drove of Spanish mules. The hordes of California gold rushers would pay handsome prices for them at Independence and other points of embarkation from the States to cross the Plains. Jesse's mules were observed by a man in a New York company as they swam the Arkansas River near Van Buren, Arkansas:

> At first I thought the black dots [in the river] to be ducks, but now I saw that they were forty or fifty of the faithful mules. As they emerged from the water I saw all of them were very small and thin in flesh. As they struck dry ground they dropped down and commenced rolling in the dirt and grunting. After a little they would get on their feet, shake themselves and bray with seeming joy. Instead of being clothed with fat, their skin stuck to their bones like wet paper on a washboard, and their backs were covered with pack-saddle sores.

None of them would weigh over 700 pounds and some of them
not over 500 pounds. I was told the animals had just come in from
Santa Fe, New Mexico. I turned from them in disgust, little thinking I was making a great mistake, as was proved later on. These
animals belonged to one Chisholm, an Indian trader with the wild
Indians of the great plains and the Mexicans, a half breed, half
Cherokee and half white.[14]

The California rush was certainly the biggest but not the only
excitement taking place in the area during 1849. A gold or silver
rush on a much smaller scale took place in the Wichita Mountains
of the Indian Territory. That summer a sixty-one-man party of
Texans from Bonham traveled up the Red River. They met with a
large band of Wichitas who treated them well, though the Texans
noted the large number of horses with American and Spanish brands
among the tribe's herds. No important discoveries of precious metal
were made, and the rush soon fizzled out.[15]

It was reported that some three hundred Comanches — including Chief Santa Anna who had gone to Washington with Chisholm
— had died from cholera on the upper Arkansas River, undoubtedly
casualties of the California rush.[16] Chisholm remained active
among the tribes, nonetheless, working primarily among the central
and southern bands. In July 1850 Jesse and Black Beaver assisted
Abel Warren at Fort Smith in purchasing trade goods to the value
of several hundred dollars for a trading expedition among the prairie
tribes, the object being to garner some 5,000 to 6,000 mules that
could be sold to stock-needy California emigrants. Chisholm was in
charge of the three large, ox-drawn wagons that carried these trade
goods to the mouth of Cache Creek, where a trade was conducted
with the tribes there.[17]

These activities were not altogether appreciated by some who
argued that this trade provided arms and ammunition to the Indians, who employed them against whites on the Plains. In July the
Fort Smith Herald reported:

> ... several thousand dollars worth of goods had been purchased in
> that place for the Comanche and Apache trade by a Mr. Abel
> Warren, an old and experienced Comanche trader, that his object

was to purchase mules, and that this trader thought he would be able to return to that place this fall with five or six hundred mules to furnish California emigrants in the spring. . . . [T]hus it seems that the Comanches are to be furnished with supplies of warlike implements and encouraged to plunder our citizens to enrich Mr. Warren and the citizens of Fort Smith. . . . He is the same person who established the trading house on the north side of the Red River near the upper Cross Timbers, and so well known as the headquarters of the thieving band of Indians who plundered and laid waste our frontier a few years ago.[18]

Not only the Comanches caused trouble during this period; the prairies from the Red River south to the Rio Grande seethed with other Indian disturbances. Wild Cat, who had fled south to Mexico with a renegade band of Indians and escaped slaves, was terrorizing southwestern Texas, even raiding the Comanches. A big fight took place on Rush Creek near the Wichita Mountains between the Wichitas and the Tonkawas. Warren reported another battle between the Tonkawas and a combined force of Osages and Kichais, who accused the Tonkawas of killing and eating the son of their chief. On another occasion a party of Tonkawas took refuge in a Denton County, Texas, settlement from 160 enraged, war-painted Waco Indians. The Wacos charged that the Tonkawas had been subsisting on the flesh of their warriors.[19]

Jesse was involved in treaty making and captive rescuing again late in 1850 when he and John Conner were called upon by U.S. special Indian agent for Texas John H. Rollins to serve as scouts and interpreters — as well as persuaders — at a treaty council held December 10 on Spring Creek near the San Saba River. Writing to the commissioner of Indian affairs, Rollins noted that only four persons on the border were capable of acting as interpreters: Chisholm, who was on the Arkansas; Jack Harry, a Delaware who had recently died of cholera; Jim Shaw, who was serving as interpreter for Texas Indian agent Neighbors; and John Conner, who was working for a trading company in Texas.[20]

The treaty party assembled at Fort Martin Scott a mile east of Fredericksburg, Texas, Jesse Chisholm once more riding the long distance from his home on the Canadian to render his services. The treaty-making caravan of horsemen and wagons loaded with supplies and treaty goods moved northwestward across the Llano River to the San Saba. The party went into camp at the head spring of Spring Creek where there had been assembled a large encampment of Caddos, Lipans, Quapaws, Tawakonis, Wacos, and Comanches, who were again headed by Buffalo Hump.[21]

Rollins was then in such ill health from tuberculosis that he was carried to the site only for the purpose of signing the treaty. Most of the contact work was done by Jesse and Conner under the direction of agents Robert Neighbors and John S. Ford. Rollins died the following September.[22]

The agreements made at Spring Creek included those of trade, peace, and friendship of the Indians for whites as well as one another, the giving up of tribal criminals, the release of white and Negro prisoners (including runaway slaves), and total banishment of the whiskey trade. The United States agreed to establish trading houses, make presents, and furnish blacksmiths, schoolteachers, and preachers. For the first time, a territorial line was drawn. The Indians promised not to range below the military post line on the east side of the Colorado River or below a line running west from the headwaters of the Llano to the west side of the Colorado.[23]

Jesse and his party effected the rescue of eighteen captive children during this venture that lasted well into the summer of 1851. All but one were Mexican children; the exception was the son of a Texas family in Refugio County. Many other children refused to give up the hunter's life they had come to enjoy among the Comanches.[24]

This was the final act in Jesse Chisholm's long service to the cause of white-Indian relations in Texas, where now a series of new forts stretched southwestward along the trail he had once traveled to California and that Marcy had later surveyed. After the conclusion of the San Saba treaty Jesse returned to the Canadian River country, which was now being looked upon by the United States as a possible route for a transcontinental railroad that would help fulfil what many believed to be a manifest destiny of the American nation. Here, too, the services of experienced frontiersmen as guides, interpreters, and advisors would be much needed.

During the eighteenth century, the Comanches had come down from the north country and driven the Apaches southward to win control of the vast domain of buffalo-grazed grassland that was north and west Texas. Now white settlements were pushing back the Comanches to north of the Colorado River and even the Brazos. Comanche warriors still raided into southern Texas and across the Rio Grande to capture Mexican and American slaves and stock; but their hunting grounds and the limits of range for their nomadic home villages were being severely diminished. At the onset of the 1850s the Comanchería (essentially the land that is now western Oklahoma, north Texas, and the Panhandle) was an island of refuge for the prairie tribes, one in which Jesse Chisholm operated as a trader and an emissary for the advancing Americans and the Indian tribes east of the Cross Timbers.

To the north of the region, the Santa Fe Trail carried caravans of emigrants westward to Colorado, New Mexico, Arizona, and California, and behind them the migration of whites into northeastern Kansas. Southward from the coastal plains of Texas came an onrush of American and European settlers through Austin and San Antonio onto the Edwards Plateau and beyond.

The San Saba treaty of 1850 had done little to resolve the unrest on the Texas frontier. A number of factors were at work to intensify the already tumultuous conflict between the native tribes and the aggressive Texans. Chisholm's acquaintance, the Seminole leader Wild Cat, had gathered together a colony composed of Seminoles, Creeks, Cherokees, and a number of Negro slaves from the Indian

Territory and headed for Mexico. While Wild Cat was away from a camp south of the Canadian, the Negroes were captured by prairie Indians and held for ransom.[1] The slaves were later purchased by a party of Creek warriors, but Seminole Jim Bowlegs led a revolt against the Creeks to retake the slaves. Many of the Negroes were wounded. Some escaped only to be recaptured and killed by the Comanches after their dark skins had been scraped open to see what was under the surface.[2]

Wild Cat eventually made it to Mexico, where he was warmly received by Mexican officials as a potential force to repel the continuing incursions of Comanche raiders. In April 1851 some traders — Chisholm may have been one of them — reported rumors from the prairie that Wild Cat had been killed by the Comanches; but other accounts claimed that the rebellious Seminole, joined by Mexicans, was sweeping southwest Texas, stealing stock and driving the animals across the Rio Grande.[3]

The Comanches persisted as a threat against Texas settlements. Though the Comanche Nation was not at war, there was no restraining their young warriors. Early in the year General George M. Brooke, commanding U.S. forces in Texas, announced that he had given up efforts to conciliate the Comanches and that when spring came he planned to punish them for their depredations.[4]

In April Delaware Bill Conner warned that some 20,000 Comanches were congregated on the upper Red River preparing for war. Supposedly they were planning to attack the Pawnee Mahas, but Conner thought they would descend on the Texas frontier settlements.[5] A short while later trader George Barnard reported from his trading post on the Brazos that a large party of Comanches had visited there in June and denied that their warriors were guilty of depredations. They admitted, however, that the buffalo were extremely scarce, and it had become necessary to steal some horses and cattle to keep their people from starving.[6]

In May Colonel William J. Hardee had led a force of two hundred men from the Fredericksburg area to demand, as had been promised with the San Saba treaty, the surrender of Indians who had been committing outrages on the frontier. The party returned in late June with seventeen Mexican children whom they had rescued. There were also a number of other captives, now assimilated into Indian

Fort Arbuckle. Located south of what is now Oklahoma City, Fort Arbuckle was one of many military posts visited by Jesse Chisholm in his roles as trader and peacemaker. *Courtesy of the Archives and Manuscripts Division of the Oklahoma Historical Society.*

life, who had to be guarded to prevent them from absconding back to their adopted families.[7]

The Texas restriction of the prairie Indian and the developing activity along the Canadian River caused Chisholm to confine his operations more to the area that is now western Oklahoma. Quite likely he was present in the Cherokee Nation in 1851 when some $700,000 was paid out to the Cherokee Old Settlers for lands and improvements given up in Arkansas.[8] During this period Chisholm was involved in a trading partnership with Little River trader Israel Vore and four other men to sell supplies to travelers crossing the Plains.[9] Vore once wrote of a visit that he had made to the Wichitas accompanied by Jesse Chisholm. Vore carried with him a Bible, which he presented through Chisholm to Wichita Chief Arshar-rewah. Just who read it to the chief is not known.[10]

Jesse was provided a new base of operations that year when Captain Randolph Marcy moved his command from Camp Arbuckle near present-day Byars, Oklahoma, to an oak-covered hillside over-looking Wild Horse Creek seven miles west of what is now Davis, Oklahoma, and established Fort Arbuckle.

Marcy had made a reconnaissance from Fort Gibson to the Brazos in 1851, escorting Generals Matthew Arbuckle and William

G. Belknap. Their purpose was to create a line of military posts on the trace that Chisholm and his party had cut across Texas in 1839.[11] Marcy, whose account of his New Mexico journey had proved him to be an alert and capable reporter, conducted another interesting exploration of the Red River to its source deep in the Palo Duro Canyon of the Texas Panhandle in 1852, invading the very heart of the Comanchería. Marcy was guided by Black Beaver and other Delaware scouts.

Even while this was taking place, Chisholm was called on to perform an important favor for the Wichita Indians. Their principal chief, Towakka, had learned that the U.S. government had sold the Choctaw and Chickasaw nations of Mississippi all of the land between the Canadian and Red rivers to the border of the Texas Panhandle. This included the land south of the Washita that the Wichitas had occupied for over a century or, as the Wichitas put it, for the last four generations. Towakka requested that Chisholm escort his younger brother, Chief Toshuhquash (White Tail, a signer of the Treaty of Comanche Peak), to Fort Smith and interpret for him in making an appeal to U.S. officials about the matter.[12] Jesse did so, the two men arriving at Fort Smith in July 1852. Jesse translated for Toshuhquash in making his plea. In his letter to Thomas G. Drew, superintendent of Indian affairs, the Wichita chief requested a meeting with officials to work out a just resolution. He asked in particular for farming equipment, seeds, livestock, and money in payment for the Wichitas' land. He also requested that someone be sent to teach his people how to cultivate the ground so they could feed and clothe themselves.

Eventually, in a new treaty made by the United States with the Choctaws and Chickasaws, agreements were reached whereby the Wichitas and other prairie bands would be permitted to reside on a leased district south of the Washita River.[13] The government, however, did nothing to relieve the severe distress of the tribe.

By the end of 1852, Fort Belknap and a number of other posts — Phantom Hill, Chadbourne, Mason, Turrett, McKavett, and Clark — had been established in western and central Texas.[14] The movement of white settlers northward had already resulted in the founding of Dallas in 1841 and Gainesville on the Red River in 1848,[15] themselves significant entrenchments into the land of the Comanches, Kiowas, and Wichitas.

Texas officials were still determined to rid their state of Indians. In the spring of 1853 Jesse Chisholm's friend John Conner was hired to accumulate all of the remnant Indian bands considered foreign to Texas — the Delawares, Shawnees, Quapaws, Cherokees, and Seminoles — on the headwaters of the Llano River. He was then to escort them north of the Red River whence they had come.[16] With the exception of a few of the Delawares, the removal was mostly done by that fall.[17]

At the same time agent Neighbors and Marcy, guided by Black Beaver, were exploring the headwaters of the Brazos and Big Wichita to locate reservation areas for the Ionies, Caddos, Kichais, Tawakonis, and Penateka Comanches. Sites were selected near Fort Belknap, one for the Comanches and another for the other tribes. These agencies became known as the Upper and Lower Brazos Reserves.[18]

Chisholm was also rendering his services as a contact and mediator for the eastern tribes, who were still seeking an accommodation with the prairie Indians. In the spring of 1853 the Cherokees and Creeks dispatched "some of their most intelligent men" to inform the Comanches and others that it was their desire to establish a lasting friendship and to "open with them an intercourse that would tend to civilize and improve their condition."[19] Jesse was the principal member of the party that traveled up the North Canadian to where it was formed by the juncture of Wolf and Beaver creeks. There he met with the Comanches and others to arrange for a grand council of some thirteen tribes to be held at the Salt Plains in June 1853. When the council was held, Jesse acted as head interpreter and mediator for some fifteen hundred Indians. He attempted to persuade the Comanches and their allies that, with Texas now a part of the United States, the Plains tribes would have to give up their captive-holding practices.[20]

This all-Indian meeting immediately preceded a U.S. treaty-making venture conducted in July by Thomas Fitzpatrick, Indian agent for the Upper Arkansas. He met with the tribes just to the north of the Salt Plains at the abandoned site of Fort Atkinson on the Santa Fe Trail. Many of the same Indians who had been present at Chisholm's North Canadian meeting attended the Arkansas council.

Jesse had no sooner arrived back on the Canadian than he was contacted by a messenger from Lieutenant Amiel Whipple, whose expedition was then moving westward along the river. Chisholm's relationship with the Whipple survey is fortunate, for from it we learn much of him. The various journals of the expedition kept by Whipple, by Lieutenant David S. Stanley, and by Baldwin Möll-hausen, a German artist who traveled with them, all speak of Chisholm at length.[21]

The survey had been approved by Congress, along with two other such transcontinental explorations, and put into action by Secretary of War Jefferson Davis in a search for the most feasible route to the Pacific Ocean. Consisting of U.S. troops, botanists, physicians, naturalists, topographers, surveyors, and others, the Whipple party departed Fort Smith in mid-July 1853 to locate a southern route along the 35th parallel.

At Skullyville, site of the Choctaw Agency, three wagons and teams were hired from Abel Warren, who joined the exploring caravan himself. The expedition proceeded down the Arkansas to the Canadian and then down that river past Edwards's post to Beaversville. They were guided by Delaware John Bushman, whom Whipple had hired on a temporary basis. Upon reaching the Cross Timbers, Bushman refused to continue on, saying: "Maybe you find no water; maybe you all die."[22]

Whipple paused at Beaversville (old Camp Arbuckle, where Black Beaver then lived) to shoe his mules and repair his wagons. He strongly desired to secure a good guide to take him across the arid, Comanche-held plains to New Mexico. Black Beaver, who was too ill to go with him, warned against both Indian hostility and the lack of water caused by the recent severe drought.

Accordingly, Whipple sent for Jesse Chisholm, who had been recommended to him as the "great Comanche interpreter and famed guide," and was "the guide I have long sought to get."[23] Whipple was so determined to persuade Chisholm to accept the job that he invited the frontier half blood to his dinner table and "treated him like a gentleman." He even indulged in flattery. Further, the officer offered to pay Chisholm higher wages than guides in the area had ever

received before, in addition to provisions. He argued that it was
nonsense for Chisholm to worry about the Indians. He could easily
return with the mail carriers to San Antonio and safely home from
there. But Jesse shook his head and said that he had decided not to
go.

Whipple, a Massachusetts graduate of West Point, took himself
and his assignment seriously. He had great hopes that his survey of
a railroad route across the North American continent would be the
one chosen out of the three being made by the U.S. Topographical
Corps. Chisholm's rejection of his offer caused Whipple to flare in
anger. With much indignation he declared that he was annoyed and
offended that anyone as intelligent as Chisholm would show so much
apathy concerning the survey he was making, that a railroad would
be more beneficial to the frontier than the largest gold mine in the
world. He even went so far as to express his surprise at the stupidity
that Chisholm and others showed on the matter.

Jesse remained unperturbed. Likely he was thinking with some
humor that the prairie Indians probably felt considerably different
about a railroad being built through their lands. But he patiently
offered to send Whipple a Mexican boy who had lived a long time
among the Comanches, who spoke their tongue, and knew the Plains
well. The next morning, a Mexican teenager appeared at Whipple's
and said that his name was Vincente and that he would serve as
guide for the expedition. Whipple hired him at $25 a month plus
transportation home. Though not entirely satisfied, Whipple was
anxious to get on with his expedition.

Despite his temporary upset with Chisholm for not going along,
Whipple had much good to say about the frontiersman in his daily
record of the journey:

> He is a man of considerable wealth, and extensively engaged in
> trade. In the prosecution of his regular business, he could realize
> twice the amount the government would be willing to pay for his
> services. His determination [not to go] is to be regretted the more
> from the influence he possesses with the wild tribes westward. He
> is a man of excellent judgment, and has travelled much among the
> western savages. At the great Indian council, held about six weeks
> since, he was selected as the general interpreter of all. . . . He has
> traded with, and has been much among, the Comanches, and

understands not only their language, but their manners, customs, and ceremonies, probably better than anyone not belonging to their tribe.[24]

Chisholm, according to Whipple, spoke numerous tongues, including Cherokee, English, Spanish, Creek, Kiowa, Kichai, Delaware, Shawnee, Chickasaw, and Choctaw. Nor was the Comanche language excluded, for Whipple extracted a vocabulary of words of that nation from Chisholm as they traveled together for a ways. The officer also learned much Indian lore from him.

Chisholm said that though his wife's people, the Creeks, were becoming less strict in their ancestral rites, they still kept the tribal fire burning. They also maintained their ancient custom of having one family of the tribe set apart for priesthood. Chisholm described the Creek ritual of preparing a boy of that family to become a priest, or medicine man.

The Cherokees, Chisholm said, had from time immemorial baptized their children when they were three days old, believing it was necessary for the child to live. The tribe also practiced the custom of offering sacrifice in the form of the burnt heart or entrails of a deer or other animal. They believed in a God and rewards in an afterlife but not in the devil and punishment. He said they believed that the misdeeds of men were punished during their lifetime by sickness, poverty, and even death.

Chisholm expressed a high opinion for the good sense and mental ability of the Comanches. He said that they, too, believed in a Great Spirit. If God were on their side, they would win in a battle. If they lost, they believed it was because they were being punished for their sins. The tribe held yearly gatherings to light their sacred fires. They would build a large number of huts in which they would fast and purify themselves for seven days. No one would speak or pray during their stay, though occasionally someone would rise and dance until exhausted, then sit down again in silence. The Comanches, Chisholm noted, were superstitious about the number seven. The tribe had seven clans, the seventh son is a prodigy, and seven in anything was considered good.[25]

Jesse's continued activity in rescuing captives from the prairie tribes is indicated in the Whipple reports. Vincente was but one of several Mexican youngsters who is listed as having been rescued from Comanche slavery by Jesse Chisholm and now belonging to his family group. Others included Mazimo, Guadalupe, Cedra Canales, Mariana Fransito, and two other unnamed girls.[26] Though Vincente was reckoned to be sixteen or seventeen years of age, he was "not larger than a well-developed lad of eleven."[27] He had been with Chisholm for six years, and he said he had been treated kindly during that time. His sister was even yet with the Comanches, being married to a warrior.[28] By agreement and preference, Vincente stated, he was to live with Chisholm until he reached the age of twenty-one; then he could go wherever he pleased.[29] "Vincente was a long time with his captors," Whipple noted, "and speaks the Comanche tongue perfectly. He is a bright, active, intelligent lad, and Chisholm is very fond of him."[30]

The former captive accompanied the Whipple expedition as it moved westward along the Canadian River, being of special value to the party when it encountered a village of Kiowa Indians in the Texas Panhandle. When confronted by a band of warriors with their bows strung, Vincente rode forward waving a white flag that was tied to his rifle barrel, and made peaceful contact. Though normally a carefree soul who was often out chasing buffalo when Whipple needed him, Vincente was highly incensed when he witnessed the Kiowa men directing the smoke of their pipes toward the sun. He claimed that they were sorcerers who were trying to cast an evil spell on the surveying party.[31]

During 1854 and 1855 Chisholm's trading arena was invaded by white gold-seeking parties. The notion there was gold on the Plains had not been forgotten. In June 1854, 278 Arkansas men with eighty teams, plus about one hundred Cherokees and still another group of whites, traveled west up the Red Fork (Cimarron River) of the Arkansas looking for a new El Dorado. The men searched the river until it became only a creek, then turned south to the Canadian and on to the Wichita Mountains, eventually returning without finding a trace of gold.[32] Another gold rush swept the Wichita Mountains during the summer of 1855 when a Missouri company explored the area without success.[33]

Chisholm was still making his trading excursions into Texas, as evidenced by a report of Indian agent Robert Neighbors.[34] Neighbors knew Chisholm well, having gone to Washington with him in 1846 and assisted at the San Saba treaty in 1850. Now, as superintendent of the Texas Indian agencies on the Brazos, he noted: "There has been a very extensive trade carried on during the summer. It can be proven by Indians here, that at one time Jesse Chisholm and other traders introduced and traded to those bands [Comanches] 75 rifles, ammunition, etc., that have since been used in depredating on our frontier."[35]

The matter of armament, as in all warring conflicts, was a crucial one in the struggle for supremacy on the Plains. It had been only when the Texas Rangers were equipped with the seven-shot revolver that they were able to fight from horseback more effectively than the Comanches using bows and arrows. Opposition was strong among most whites against arming the Indians with modern weapons. There was the counterargument, however, that the government depended upon the Indians to feed themselves. In the face of persistent depletion of the buffalo by whites as well as Indian hunters, it was necessary for the tribes to have guns with which they could kill the wild game their people needed for food. Jesse Chisholm, who was so close to the Comanches and understanding of their situation, would be expected to sympathize with the latter view.

For years the Comanches had ruled the prairies of the great Southwest, aggressively raiding deep into Texas and across the Rio Grande into Mexico. But now their Comanchería sanctuary, and with it Chisholm's operating area, had been encircled. By the late 1850s the status of the Comanches and other tribes of the southern Plains had become more and more defensive. Both the Texans and the U.S. military were laying plans to strike into the Indians' home sanctuary.

B y 1858 Chisholm was operating his Indian trade in a wide area of western Oklahoma from the Salt Plains on the Cimarron to the Wichita Mountains — an Indian empery of rolling, shortgrassed prairie cut by eastward-flowing water courses. Buttes and sand hills, the most prominent of which were the Antelope Hills, spotted the region. Known to early travelers as the Boundary Mounds, the Antelope Hills protruded above the sagebrush prairie on the south bank of the Canadian just east of the 100th parallel, which divided the Indian Territory and the Texas Panhandle. The flat-topped buttes also marked a favorite resort for Indian bands. Buffalo herds were always in the area. Channels of clear, cool water meandered along the Canadian's wide bed of gleaming white sand. There was ample firewood available along its banks as well as grassy fields for the tribal horse and mule herds.

Still another significant attribute of the hills lay in the view they offered of the surrounding landscape — a much-appreciated opportunity for Indian tribes who lived in constant danger of enemy attack. From this elevated vantage point, the prairie panorama was visible for miles in every direction. To the north, where the Canadian made its wide loop around the Antelope Hills, the cottonwood and willow-lined Little Robe and Commission creeks snaked in from the northwest. Twenty-five miles to the north was Wolf Creek, its course draining northeastward from the Panhandle plateau to join with Beaver Creek and form the North Canadian. Southward, running parallel to the Canadian, was the steep-cut, ocher-banked Washita, its surrounding countryside dotted with unique, reddish knolls. Off

The Antelope Hills. On the boundary of Indian Territory and the Texas Panhandle, these well-watered and game-rich sand hills were a favorite gathering place for Indians and traders. *Photograph by Stan Hoig.*

to the west was the rugged, ravine-slashed tableland of the Texas Panhandle; to the east the Canadian snaked on through sandy, scrub oak country toward the Cross Timbers.

Chisholm brought his wagons to the migratory tribal camps, spreading his blankets before the tepees of friendly chiefs and conducting trade with the villagers. Warriors came with pelts, ponies, and mules, and women came with beadworked robes and soft, tanned deerskins to barter for the much-desired goods that Chisholm brought from the world of the white man. He was always warmly welcomed by the chiefs and the tribespeople.

There were times, though, when the warriors were angry with the whites; then it was dangerous for any outsider to enter this Indian fortress that is now western Oklahoma.

By now Chisholm had established a trading post on the North Canadian at the edge of the buffalo prairie; just when is not clear, though some say it was in 1868. James Mead indicated that Chisholm had maintained a trading establishment at Council Grove (now in west Oklahoma City) for many years and had constructed buildings and corrals there.[1]

It is believed that Chisholm also operated a saltworks northwest of Council Grove in Blaine County, Oklahoma.[2] Early maps of the region show a wagon trail from Chouteau's post on Chouteau Creek, passing through the site of Council Grove to the head of Salt Creek. There a saltwater spring issued forth from a rocky gorge and drained northeastward into the Cimarron. The product likely served Jesse as an Indian trade item, being carted to Fort Gibson and Fort Smith as well as to Texas (probably at Preston) and sold commercially.

Edward B. Johnson, whose father Montford Johnson operated a ranch just across the Canadian River about a mile from Chisholm's Council Grove location, states that Phil A. Smith was in charge of the trading post. Richard Cuttle was in charge of Chisholm's teams, taking furs, hides, and other items to market and returning with merchandise.[3]

There is indication, too, that Chisholm may have established temporary trading posts well beyond Council Grove. One of these, according to Henry Donnell, who traded with Chisholm at the time, was on the North Canadian just east of the head of Salt Creek. This is supported by the statement of a military officer who referred to "Chisholm's Upper Ranche" in reporting an incident between a surveying party and Indians on the North Canadian a few miles below Salt Creek.[4] The other possible trading post was mentioned by a newspaper correspondent who accompanied agent Jesse Leavenworth on a trip to the Cimarron River to meet with the Comanches and Kiowas in 1867. In his account of the event, the reporter noted that George Bent was with Dutch Bill Greiffenstein at "Chisholm's old post on Wolf Creek, fifteen miles from the [North] Canadian and 200 miles from the Arkansas."[5] This would be between Fargo and Gage, Oklahoma, possibly at the mouth of Little Wolf Creek.

At the start of 1858, the prairie Indian retreat of western Oklahoma was still virtually untouched by the white man, a haven of safety nestled between the forces of American advance in Kansas and Texas. But now war would come to this land, changing its character forever. Attacks would be launched by Texas Rangers, civilian posses, and mounted Dragoons of the U.S. Army against the

Comanches and other tribes whose camps Jesse Chisholm frequented as a trader. He would barely escape harm from these onslaughts himself, and even his special relationship and privilege of entry into the Indian camps would be endangered by the wrath of tribesmen who sought revenge for the deaths of relatives and friends.

In 1857 agent Neighbors had reported that the sixteen hundred Indians on the Brazos reservations were living quietly in newly erected huts and wigwams, cultivating wheat and corn.[6] While Neighbors was lauded for his efforts by some, there were many on the Texas frontier who held an intense hatred for the Indians and wished them all either destroyed or removed from the state altogether. They were partially rewarded when word came that Wild Cat and his entire band had succumbed to smallpox.[7]

Early in 1858 Jesse Chisholm and a small party of Cherokees, outfitted for a trading venture, departed the Salt Plains and headed south to contact the prairie tribes. Twenty-three days later, probably in Texas, they met a large number of Comanches, Kiowas, Wacos, and Wichitas who treated them in a very friendly fashion and did a large trade. The Indians claimed that a party of Mexicans and a group of Mormons — who in 1846 had located in the Cross Timbers of the Washita[8] — had been among them distributing presents. The Mormons had encouraged the prairie tribes to unite and stand against the encroachment of the United States. When other whites reached Utah, the Mormons insisted, they would spread out and drive the Indians from their homes.[9]

From Fort Arbuckle the newly appointed and first Indian agent for the Wichitas, Colonel Alexander H. McKissick, reported on April 15, 1858:

> Jesse Chisholm, a half breed Cherokee well known to yourself as a brave and resolute man, and well acquainted with the feelings and habits of all the tribes West, has just abandoned and returned from an expedition that he fitted out to trade with the Comanches. He informs me that there is no doubt but that the Comanches & other prairie tribes are evilly disposed; and believes that the Mormons have been tampering with them, that they speak of a "great chief" who is able to destroy the people of the whole United States, and who can be no other than Brigham Young.[10]

Jesse Chisholm was fortunate in leaving the Comanche camp just when he did. Had he stayed just a few days longer he might well have been caught in a surprise attack by a force of 102 Texas Rangers and 113 Brazos Reserve Indians under Captain John Ford, whom he had served during the San Saba treaty of 1850.[11] Mostly the Indians were Tonkawas, but there were also Anadarkos, Caddos, Kichais, Wacos, Delawares, and Shawnees in the group.

Having departed Camp Runnels on the Brazos on April 22, 1858, Ford had headed north. Crossing the Red River, he had picked up a travois trail and followed it on northward to the Antelope Hills, where his scouts reported a Comanche buffalo hunt under way nearby. Secluding his command for the night, Ford launched an attack early the following morning, May 12, against a large Comanche camp located just across the Canadian River on Little Robe Creek. Ten years later, in November 1868, General George Armstrong Custer would pass by this same spot on his way to attack the Cheyennes on the Washita River.

Ford's attack resulted in the capture of a number of women and children and some three hundred horses and mules. The number of Comanche dead was not known precisely, but the Rangers and their Indian allies reportedly took seventy-six scalps. All of the lodges of the village were burned and camp paraphernalia destroyed.

Later, when the fighting was done, the village burned, and captives taken, it would be discovered that one of the Indian victims was the Comanche Chief Pohebits Quasho, or Iron Jacket. The Comanche had worn a coat of Spanish mail beneath his buffalo robe, making him difficult to bring down. Only when a bullet had rammed up beneath a metal scale had Iron Jacket been felled. It was not the only time in the history of Indian warfare that a relic of the Spanish conquistadores had come to light.[12]

Another expedition against the Indians of the western Indian Territory was conducted the following July by Chickasaw agent Douglas Cooper. The military-minded Cooper led a force of "woods Indians" — Chickasaws, Choctaws, and Cherokees — from Fort Arbuckle with Black Beaver as a guide. During the excursion, the party encountered American surveyors A. H. Jones and H.M.C. Brown, who were then bravely working their way toward the 100th meridian separating the Indian Territory and the Texas Panhandle.

Cooper's group also came across a wagon trace believed to have been made by Mormons. Failing to locate any Indians, Cooper returned to Fort Arbuckle with his horses badly jaded and his followers weary.[13]

There was another well-attended council held at the Salt Plains that August, and it is probable that Jesse Chisholm was present. At the Indian get-together, Chief Pahhauca made an effort to form a combined force of all Comanche bands with the Osages, Kiowas, and others. He wished to make a coordinated attack against Texas to avenge their defeat at the hands of Ford.[14] The effort came to naught.

Other events were at work that would shape the fate of the region. Thus far the warring against the Comanches had been conducted by the Texans. But during the summer of 1858 four troops of the U.S. 2d Cavalry Battalion under Major Earl Van Dorn were issued orders to pursue the Comanches north of the Red River. Accordingly, Van Dorn led his battalion, guided by Caddo and Tonkawa scouts, across the Red to west of the Wichita Mountains. There he established Camp Radziminski on Otter Creek.[15]

At the same time, another arm of the United States in the form of an Indian commission arrived at Fort Arbuckle with the aim of suing for peace with the Comanches. The Wichita Indians, then residing and farming peacefully in the Leased District on Rush Creek, were sent out to the Comanche camps to use their influence in persuading the Comanches to come in for peace talks. The chiefs finally consented to do so despite their anger over the Ford attack, and in September a large body of Comanches, including families, headed for Fort Arbuckle. They stopped on their way for a green corn feast with their Wichita friends.

While they were encamped at the Wichita village, the Comanches were discovered by scouts from Van Dorn's command. Van Dorn immediately placed his troops on the long, seventy-five-mile, thirty-six-hour march for the Wichita village. He arrived in the early hours of morning to find the encampment asleep and posted his men for a daybreak attack. In the onslaught that ensued, fifty-six Comanches were killed and 120 lodges destroyed. Lieutenant Cornelius Van Camp was killed by a Comanche arrow through the heart, four other troopers also lay dead, and eleven suffered wounds.[16] The hapless Wichitas lost most of their valuable robes and blankets, and much of their food stores in the raid. They were reported to be dying at a rate of two to four a day.[17] Van Dorn's action was severely criticized by men such as Albert Pike of Arkansas.

The Indian Territory frontier was in this state of disruption when the Beale Wagon Road Survey expedition departed Fort Smith on October 28, 1858, on its way along the Canadian River route to New Mexico — an adventure in which Jesse Chisholm played a part and which provides us with another insight concerning the frontiersman.

Though the Van Dorn massacre of the Comanche peace caravan caused him much concern, Lieutenant Edward F. Beale had no intention of aborting his mission of crossing the Plains. But, as Whipple had five years earlier, he knew the need for a good, experienced guide. As he started his wagon train westward toward the mouth of the Canadian River, Beale sent his brother George to Fort Arbuckle to recruit either Jesse Chisholm or Black Beaver. George returned, however, to report that both had declined to serve, saying that the infuriated Comanches would likely burn off every blade of grass before them until they had no animals left and would be obliged to turn back on foot.[18]

Beale was undeterred, continuing down the Canadian past North Fork Town at the mouth of the North Canadian and on beyond the Little River settlement. On November 12 the caravan passed the home of Jesse Chisholm, noting its location on the north side of the river not far from where a spring fed into a large pond fringed with trees and bushes a mile south of the north-bank road. Here they found parked several stagecoaches under R. Frank Green, who had been awarded a government contract to deliver mail via the Canadian route to New Mexico. Because of the Van Dorn affair, Green had held up for nearly a month waiting for Beale, who could give him escort.[19]

Passing Chouteau's old post, the expedition emerged from the Cross Timbers onto the prairie, now taking the California gold rush trail along the south bank of the Canadian. They soon spotted their first buffalo, a bull, and began taking greater precaution because, as Beale commented, "[W]hen buffalo are on one side of the hill, an Indian is on the other."[20] Beale held up his order of march to await the military escort of a Dragoon company under Lieutenant Enoch

Steen as a six-inch snow that had fallen on November 19 slowly
melted away. At noon on November 26, finally, the Dragoons arrived,
towing two pieces of artillery and "making our little party of one
hundred and thirty men," plus others, a more formidable force.[21] It
was probably at this time, too, that Jesse Chisholm and a Shawnee
friend named Little Axe joined the survey. Just what persuaded
Chisholm to change his mind is not indicated in the records of the
expedition.

Passing Rock Mary — a butte so named by the Marcy expedition
of 1849 — and its companion protrusions, which Beale dubbed
Steen's Buttes, the party cut southwestward to the Washita with the
Wichita Mountains in sight far off to the south. Beale noted in his
journal: "From this point onward we have no guide, as Mr. Chisholm
who has been with us knows the country no further; yet his judgment
is so mature that I shall endeavor to persuade him to accompany us
all the way to Anton Chico."[22] Apparently the officer meant that
Jesse had not yet ventured into the Texas Panhandle country.
However, Beale did persuade him to continue on for a way; the last
mention of the Cherokee trader comes from just west of the Antelope
Hills after Beale had returned to the Canadian River course. Here
the officer named a small Texas creek for Chisholm.[23]

From there on, the records of the expedition do not mention
Chisholm again, though Little Axe is listed on numerous occasions
as a hunter for the American explorers, even into New Mexico. It
appears likely that Jesse was again simply doing the favor of
providing a good guide in lieu of serving himself and that he turned
back a short distance beyond the Antelope Hills.

During the following summer a small portion of the Beale party
under civil engineer J. R. Crump returned to North Fork Town by
way of the Canadian route. Crump made the 850-mile return journey from New Mexico in the company of a mail wagon. Near the
Antelope Hills he encountered a herd of cattle being trail-driven
from the Creek country to New Mexico. The first settlement encountered on his return, Crump noted, was Jesse Chisholm's house on
the Canadian. This indicates that during that summer of 1859 Jesse
Chisholm was likely still maintaining residence at Chisholm
Springs even though he was conducting his Indian trade at Council
Grove.[24]

Other clashes between U.S. troops and the Comanches occurred during 1859. In February a command of fifty soldiers and fifty Wichita guides embarked on a scouting expedition west from Fort Arbuckle. Within twenty miles of the post they encountered a large party of Comanche warriors, and a skirmish ensued. Two Comanches were killed and two soldiers wounded before the Indians withdrew.[25] When word reached Arbuckle that the Comanches were coming to take the fort, fifty troops under Captain Eugene A. Carr were sent from Fort Leavenworth to give support. Another fight took place between troops under Lieutenant David S. Stanley, 1st Cavalry, and the Comanches, with eight Indians reportedly killed and several wounded. The troops lost one man, and two more were slightly wounded in the fracas.[26]

Following his successful attack on the Comanches at the Wichita village, Van Dorn had returned to his home in Mississippi to recuperate from his wounds, returning the following spring to Camp Radziminski, where a bored garrison yearned for action. Joined by Captain Edmund Kirby Smith and Lieutenant Fitzhugh Lee, both destined soon to become generals for the Confederate States of America, Van Dorn led another military expedition northward into southern Kansas. In early May he located and attacked a Comanche village near Crooked Creek. Forty-nine of the Indians were killed and thirty-six taken prisoner. One trooper was lost, while Lieutenant Lee suffered an arrow driven through a lung.[27]

Still other events that would have a direct bearing upon Jesse Chisholm's world in the Indian Territory were taking place in Texas. Despite the insistence of Neighbors that his Brazos Reserve charges were peaceful and dedicated to farming, these Indians caught much of the blame for depredations and were the target of intense hatred by the victimized Texans.[28] Late in 1858 a group of settlers who called themselves the Erath County Rangers went on an Indian-hunting foray, located a camp of friendly reservation Indians under Choctaw Tom, and fell upon it during the night. Seven Indians, including three women, were murdered while asleep in their blankets. Neighbors kept the other Indians from retaliating, but near-panic swept the Texas settlements, which feared reprisals. Texas Governor Hardin Runnels attempted to have the Erath Rangers arrested, but a white grand jury refused to indict the participants in the attack.[29]

At Gainesville, a company of civilian rangers was enlisted for three months' service to combat the Comanches, while another group — taking up the Revolutionary War vigilante title of Regulators — was organized to chastise the Indians for thefts of stock and other acts.

Contributing to the turmoil, also, was a campaign of hatred spewed out by John R. Baylor. Baylor, whose army surgeon father had been on the 1826 gold-seeking excursion with Jesse, had left the Fort Gibson area under a cloud of suspicion in 1844 with a $200 reward on his head for complicity in the murder of a Creek man by Baylor's brother-in-law.[30] A personal feud had erupted in the Indian service between the younger Baylor, who had been dismissed as agent for the Comanches of the Upper Brazos Reserve, and Neighbors. Baylor became involved in the publication of an intensely racist newspaper called *The White Man* and by print and speech began stirring up dissension among the settlers from his ranch on the Clear Fork.

To this point there had been little actual conflict between the Indians of the Brazos Reserve and the whites of the region. But with the murder of Choctaw Tom's people and the agitation by Baylor, the Texas frontier flamed with hatred, fear, and violence.

In the meantime the federal government had followed Neighbors's recommendation and negotiated a treaty with the Choctaws and Chickasaws. By it a large tract of land north of the Red River near the Wichita Mountains would be leased for the permanent settlement of the Wichitas and other smaller tribes. No action had yet been taken to move any tribes onto the area; but Neighbors, now realizing the serious plight of his Brazos Reserve Indians, recommended that they be removed from Texas to the Leased District. Baylor and his followers were by no means satisfied with a solution that did not contain bloody vengeance, and they set about to organize an armed force for the purpose of annihilating the reserve bands.[31]

Gathering together some 280 men of a self-styled Frontier Army of Defense, Baylor advanced onto the Lower Brazos Reserve. There he was faced down by Captain J. B. Plummer, who headed a unit of U.S. 1st Infantry assigned to protect the Indians. But as Baylor's rabble army retreated, one of his crew murdered an eighty-year-old Indian man. The warriors of the reservation responded by attacking the invaders, killing three and wounding several more. Baylor fell back to the village of Fort Belknap where he sent out a call for 1,000 volunteers to join in wiping out the reservation tribes.[32] Many responded, but after a while the aggregation of Texans wearied of oratory that produced no action and began departing for home.

Now came the approval from Washington, D.C., for Neighbors to remove his Indian charges from the Brazos to the Leased District. First it would be necessary to select a site for an agency post. On June 30 Neighbors arrived at Fort Arbuckle with headmen of the Brazos Reserve bands and met with Indian Superintendent Elias Rector from Fort Smith. With Rector were Albert Pike, well-known Arkansas lawyer and poet, his two sons, and Cush Quesenbury.[33] The search for a location for the new agency was made under the military escort of Major William H. Emory, commandant of Fort Arbuckle. Chickasaw agent Douglas Cooper had a preference for a location on Bluff Creek, but Rector voiced strong opposition to it, citing creeks that overflowed and stagnant pools of water that he felt helped spread disease among the Indians. He chose instead a site near the Washita River.[34]

At a council on July 1, Neighbors and Rector assured the chiefs that they would be residing on land owned by the United States and would therefore receive the full protection of the government from all harm there. The chiefs expressed satisfaction with the new country and agreed to move from their native Texas.[35]

On August 1, 1859, the Upper Brazos Agency was closed and, without time even for the Indians to gather up much of their livestock, the exodus began. Neighbors assured the Indians that the government would compensate them in full for their loss of property. The caravan of wagons, Mexican carts, army ambulances, cattle, horses, dogs, and 1,051 Indians moved northward toward the Red River under the escort of Lieutenant George H. Thomas. At Steen's Crossing of the Red River just east of the mouth of the Big Wichita, the Upper Brazos group was joined by 370 Comanches of the Lower Reserve. The latter were led by their new agent Matthew Leeper

Robert S. Neighbors was gunned down for his role in protecting Indians in Texas from attacks by white settlers. *Courtesy of the Barker Texas History Center, The University of Texas at Austin.*

and escorted by Captain C. C. Gilbert. The combined parties then continued on to the Washita where the new agency was established on a small creek named for Leeper.[36]

Also at this time the Wichitas, who had remained close to Fort Arbuckle since the Van Dorn attack in fear of Comanche reprisals against them, were relocated. Chisholm took part in this moving operation, hiring out a wagon, team, and driver from July 21 to August 18 at $4 a day for the twenty-nine days.[37]

After much delay in the resettlement, Neighbors turned his Indian wards over to the new Wichita agent Samuel A. Blaine and returned to Texas. Leeper and a small party accompanied him. En route they met with a group of Kiowas who attempted to steal their horses, severely wounding Leeper in the process.[38] Only a short time after returning to Texas, Neighbors was ambushed and killed with a double-barreled shotgun by a man named Edward Cornett on the streets of Belknap.[39]

On October 1 Major Emory arrived at the new Washita River agency with units of the 1st Cavalry and 1st Infantry to establish Fort Cobb three miles from the agency. The new post would serve as a protector for the agency Indians and as a factor of intimidation for the tribes still residing on the prairie. Much of the contact with the tribes would be through Chisholm, one of the few outsiders still accepted inside the Comanche camps.

In May 1860 Indian Superintendent Elias Rector reported that he had just received word from Fort Cobb that the Comanches and Kiowas were encamped on the Canadian River near the Antelope Hills some eight or nine hundred strong. They had made it known to their trader, Chisholm, that they wished to make peace and live among their brother Comanches in the Leased District.[40]

Soon, however, the turmoil and conflict surrounding the Comanche Indians and other tribes of the area, as well as the life of Jesse Chisholm, would be drastically affected by other forces of history that would cause a momentous upheaval on the frontier as well as in the rest of the nation — the American Civil War was about to begin.

W hen the American Civil War erupted and ignited the
passions of men within the Indian Territory as elsewhere
through the country, there were few men more split in
loyalty than Jesse Chisholm. Born and reared within the already
badly divided Cherokee Nation, ingrained with the culture of the
slave-holding South, and long associated with Indian Department
and military figures, he had many friends, Indian and white, in both
the Union and Confederate camps. Further, Jesse held high influence among both the eastern tribes and the buffalo-hunting peoples
who roamed the prairies between the Arkansas and Red rivers, all
of whom were caught squarely between Unionist and secessionist
allegiance. Chisholm held no antagonism for either side. His enemy
was the war itself, the venomous conflict of hate and distrust that
placed him in a difficult position between embattled friends in whose
hearts there was no middle ground.

Both Jesse and his wife Sahkahkee are listed on the 1860 census
of the Creek Nation as being owners of slaves.[1] Within Chisholm's
multiracial entourage, however, it was largely a matter of everyone
carrying out his assigned duties. The great respect and confidence
that Jesse later afforded Negro employee George Ransom is clear
indication that he was far from being the slave abuser that his father
had been.

The Indians from the South themselves were badly split by the
war. John Ross, the mixed-blood leader of the Cherokees who held
fifty-one slaves and owned eleven slave houses in 1860,[2] tried at first
to maintain a neutral position between North and South and found

it an impossibility. On the side of the Confederates were the Cherokee half bloods, who formed a chapter of a southern society known
as the Knights of the Golden Circle. The group's principal object was
defending and perpetuating slavery. The Cherokee full bloods responded with a secret organization of their own, known as the Pins
from the emblems they wore on their hunting shirts. Their support
of the Union was evidenced when they prevented an attempt by a
rebel sympathizer to hoist a Confederate flag at Webbers Falls.[3]

Similarly, the Creeks, into whom Chisholm had twice married
and with whom he had strong ties of friendship, were as badly split
as the Cherokees, the Upper Creeks being largely pro-South and the
Lower Creeks favoring the Union. Chief Rolly McIntosh and his
brother Chilly, who together held over one hundred slaves,[4] were
engaged already with the full-blooded Creek leader Opothle Yahola
in a lethal feud that would also divide their loyalties in the war. The
McIntoshes took the side of the South, while Opothle Yahola fa-
vored the Union. The enmity between the men was of long standing,
evolving from the 1824 assassination of William McIntosh, father
of the two Creek chiefs, over the sale of Creek lands in the East.
The McIntoshes harbored no doubt that Opothle Yahola had been
involved.[5]

To the west, the Comanches, Wichitas, and the Texas refugee
tribes of the Leased District — Indians with whom Jesse Chisholm
had a long and trustful relationship and who looked to him for
guidance — were entrapped by the abrupt withdrawal of Union
forces in the spring of 1861. Ties to their home range now made them
dependent upon their most dreaded enemies, the Confederate Texans, for military protection, food, and other subsistence.

And there were Jesse's white friends — men such as the New
England–born, scholarly Arkansawyer Albert Pike; journalist William Quesenbury; and Chisholm's old trading partner Israel Vore.
As early as 1832 Pike had joined a small group of trappers and
hunters that traversed the wild, unexplored country between Arkansas and New Mexico, earning his credentials as an explorer of
the Southwest.[6] Though Pike had at one time penned a verse that
scorned secession, he had taken up the cause of the Confederacy to
carry its banner among the Indians of the Territory.

Fort Cobb, Indian Territory, 1859. This small outpost served as a trading center and refuge for the Leased District tribes when the Civil War erupted. *Courtesy of the Archives and Manuscripts Division of the Oklahoma Historical Society.*

Events had moved quickly within the Territory following the beginning of hostilities at Fort Sumter. Federal officials had quickly seen that the meager forces and equipment would be lost to the Texas Confederates if they were not withdrawn. Accordingly, Lieutenant Colonel William Emory was ordered to lead the Fort Smith garrison to salvage the fighting men and military hardware of the territorial forts. Upon reaching Fort Washita, Emory learned that an attack by Texas forces was imminent. Gathering in the Union contingent there, Emory headed for Fort Arbuckle. He was hotly pursued by the Texans, who had occupied Fort Washita immediately behind him.[7]

En route to Arbuckle, Emory was overtaken by Lieutenant William W. Avery, who carried orders for the command to repair to Fort Leavenworth after its sweep of the Indian Territory.[8] Taking on the Fort Arbuckle troops and materiel, Emory moved on west up the Canadian where he joined the Fort Cobb garrison near present-day Minco, Oklahoma, on May 1. Among the Cobb refugees was Jesse's old friend Black Beaver, who had been advised by the post commander to forget his fine log house with its large front porch and two fireplaces, his forty-one and a half acres of fenced land, and his four hundred head of cattle and leave. Black Beaver later told a newspaper writer that the commandant had told him to "[L]et [his] cattle go to hell and save [his] scalp, and he thought Indian better do it."[9] Black Beaver joined the exodus of Union military personnel, whom he and a Kickapoo named Possum guided to Kansas. Their route went directly north of the abandoned Kansas settlement of El Dorado.[10]

The Emory-led troops arrived in Emporia, Kansas, on the evening of May 24, their mile-long train reported as consisting of six hundred horses, five hundred mules, and ninety wagons. Despite the fact that they had to leave most of their dress clothes behind, the soldiers went to town to meet the local women and find drinking material. They were sorely disappointed to find that Emporia was the one totally dry town west of the Mississippi.

In Lawrence citizens crowded the streets and waved from every balcony and window as the caravan straggled through.[11] The editor of the *Lawrence Republican* reported on June 13, 1861: "Yesterday we met on the streets of Lawrence, Black Beaver, who for several years has lived amongst the Choctaws. He says he was driven off because he was a Yankee Indian. . . . In the language of the Indian, 'bad white man and fool red man talk about seceding and raise Texas flag, and swear he scalp Yankee Indian.' "

There is no indication that the caravan of 759 military men and 150 civilians — officers' wives, children, teamsters, and others — had passed by Chisholm's place at Council Grove, but it was later said that the traces of the heavily loaded army wagons were followed four years afterward by Jesse in breaking what would become known as the Chisholm Trail. The route was referred to as Beaver's Trail by Creek leaders.[12]

Even as the Union forces were retreating in May, a large group of Creek Indians under Opothle Yahola was touring the various tribes to the west to propose a confederacy of neutrality in accordance with the wishes of John Ross. After visiting the Seminoles at their council house in present-day Pottawatomie County, Oklahoma, they rode to old Camp Arbuckle, learning there of the departure of Black Beaver with the Union forces. The Creeks continued on to a Kickapoo camp near what is now Lexington, Oklahoma, before extending their tour as far west as the Antelope Hills. Following a council with the Comanches, the Creeks went to the Salt Plains, where they met with the Kiowas. On their return to their own country, they stopped at Chisholm's trading post at Council Grove to discuss the situation with him.[13]

Just what Chisholm's advice to Opothle Yahola and his followers was is not known. There can be little question that he was sympathetic to their situation. Yet, the facts are that Jesse himself was initially drawn to the service of the South. Likely this was because of his affiliation with the prairie tribes, whom the war had thrust under the control of the rebels.

Confederate and Union officials vied strongly for the loyalty and support of the Indian Territory tribes. Secretary of Interior William P. Dole had avowed that the U.S. government would not permit the "smallest interference with their tribal or domestic institutions" by "unscrupulous and evil men."[14] Edwin H. Carruth, U.S. Indian agent, wrote to Tusaquach, chief of the Wichitas, promising: "The Texans have killed the Wichitas; we will punish the Texans."[15] But even as Union officials were issuing promises that they had little potential of fulfilling, the Confederacy was moving through now-Brigadier General Albert Pike to make treaties of wardship with the tribes of the Territory.

Accompanied by Quesenbury — who had been appointed as the C.S.A. agent for the Creeks — and a few others, Pike left Fort Smith with two wagons in late May and moved up the Arkansas River to Tahlequah flying a specially designed flag. The standard contained eleven white stars for the states of the Confederacy in a circle against a field of blue. Inside the circle were four smaller stars for the Choctaws, Chickasaws, Creeks, and Seminoles with a fifth one to be added when "we deem it fit to treat with the Cherokees."[16]

After failing to persuade John Ross away from his neutral stance, Pike traveled on to North Fork Town where he held a council with the Creeks, Choctaws, and Chickasaws and signed treaties with each.[17] From North Fork Town, Pike continued on to the Seminole Agency not far from Chisholm Springs. After concluding a treaty with that similarly split nation on August 1, he met with some fifty reserve Comanches, Wichitas, and Kichais brought there by Chisholm and Elias Rector, once a U.S. marshal in Arkansas and

Indian superintendent. Rector now held the rank of major in the Confederate Army and, for the recently declared Confederate States, the title of superintendent of Indian affairs.[18]

After signing the pact with the Seminoles, Pike moved on westward to the Wichita Agency, accompanied by Rector, Wichita agent Leeper, Jesse Chisholm, and a protective escort of Creeks and Seminoles. There, with the assistance of Chisholm, Pike distributed presents and held councils with the prairie bands — Comanches, Wichitas, Caddos, Hadachos, Wacos, Tawakonis, Anadarkos, Tonkawas, Ionies, Kichais, Shawnees, and Delawares. Treaties were signed with these tribes, though the Kickapoos, still holding to their intense hatred for the Texans, refused to join in. Jesse Chisholm signed the agreements as a witness, having served as a principal interpreter. [19] The Wichitas would later claim that their three chiefs were prisoners of the rebels, that they had signed the Pike treaty only under coercion, and that one of their chiefs who refused to sign had been killed.[20]

Ross eventually gave in to pressures from other Cherokees and agreed to negotiate with the Confederacy. Pike arranged for a council to be held at Tahlequah in October, this time able to get Ross — whom Opothle Yahola described as "a man lying on his belly, watching the opportunity to turn over"[21] — to sign a treaty. Jesse Chisholm was also present, having gone out and brought in some of the Comanche leaders.[22]

There was much concern and hostility among the secessionist Indians over the matter of the Creeks and Seminoles who had remained loyal to the Union. Reluctant to fight the Creek loyalists, the Cherokees sent a delegation to talk with them in October. The Cherokees learned that the Creeks headed by Opothle Yahola had divided into three groups. One group had returned home to butcher hogs and gather up their food supplies, clothing, and whatever other possessions they could carry. Another had already headed northward with some Seminoles and a large number of slaves to whom they promised their freedom. A third group had gone to Chisholm's place at Council Grove to seek his counsel once again on their course of action.[23]

A force of rebel Cherokees, Creeks, Seminoles, and Texans under now-Colonel Douglas Cooper pursued the loyal Creeks. On November 19 near the juncture of the Cimarron and Arkansas rivers, they found Opothle Yahola and his men waiting, stripped to the waist in the winter air, prepared to do battle. The loyalists repelled the rebels in a battle that was known as the Red Fork fight, then crossed the Arkansas and resumed their flight. The rebels pursued, and an indecisive engagement was fought on December 9 at Bird Creek, the rebels again being repulsed.

But on the twenty-sixth following, supported by forces under Colonel James McIntosh and the Cherokee Stand Watie, Cooper rendered a severe blow to the retreating refugees, killing or capturing a large number of women and children and scattering the remainder throughout the countryside where they were exposed to the snow and cold. In this engagement, known as the Battle of Round Mountain, Opothle Yahola's people suffered heavy losses in life as well as food, clothing, and personal goods.[24]

The Creek, Seminole, and Negro refugees arrived at what was called Fort Roe on the Verdigris River of Kansas in a most destitute condition. Their plight was described by a Union official:

> Many of their ponies died from starvation. The women and children suffered severely from frozen limbs, as did also the men. Women gave birth to their offspring upon the naked snow without shelter or covering. . . . Not a comfortable tent was to be seen. Such coverings as I saw were made in the rudest manner being composed of pieces of cloth, old quilts, handkerchiefs, aprons, &c., stretched upon sticks, and so limited were many of them in size that they were scarcely sufficient to cover the emaciated and dying forms beneath them. Under such a shelter I found in the last stages of consumption the daughter of Hoipoeithleyohola.[25]

Eventually the refugees would be moved to a camp near Emporia, the first of many refugee Indians who would wait out the Civil War, suffering hunger, disease, and severe cold of winter. Opothle Yahola himself perished there in the spring of 1863.[26]

Both George (Vincente) Chisholm and Chisholm's daughter Jennie said that in 1861 Jesse Chisholm called the loyal Indians of the Territory together at Chisholm Springs and led them to the site of present-day Wichita.[27] However, these accounts must be questioned. Opothle Yahola's retreat departed from near North Fork Town, and records clearly show that the Creeks did not go to the Wichita area. Also, records indicate that Jesse remained within the Territory well into 1862. There is strong evidence that at the time of Opothle Yahola's flight Chisholm was still serving as an emissary to the western tribes for the rebels.

In a letter to Chisholm from Fort Smith in December 1861, Rector wrote: "I wish you to go out immediately and see the bands of Comanches that are encamped above Fort Cobb and tell them that it is the wish of their great father at Richmond that they come in at once and settle on the reserve. . . . I want them to send four or five of their Chiefs and head men to Genl. Pike's headquarters, near Fort Gibson where he and myself will meet them and talk with them and give them a great many presents."[28] A bill of purchase from trader John Shirley at Fort Cobb dated January 25, 1862, shows that Chisholm procured $267.88 in goods as presents — vermilion, indigo, tobacco, blankets, knives, shawls, wool hats, silk handkerchiefs — for the chiefs of the various prairie bands. A $40 navy-issue six-shooter was purchased as a special present for Toshaway, second chief of the Comanches.[29] Vouchers signed by Chisholm in February 1862, acknowledging payment of $450 for his services in collecting and conducting a delegation of Comanches and other bands to Pike's headquarters, indicate that he fulfilled Rector's request. And a letter from a C.S.A. agency official at the Wichita Agency to Charles B. Johnson, Texas rancher and beef contractor, on May 6, 1862, requested instructions on how to settle up Jesse Chisholm's account for goods and beef that he had furnished.[30]

Pike left Little Rock in late February with $265,927.50 in specie, mostly gold and silver, for advance payments to the Cherokees, Choctaws, Chickasaws, Creeks, and others. Rector had been sent on ahead from Fort Smith to meet Chisholm and treat with the Comanches at Fort Gibson.[31] Buffalo Hump stated his allegiance to the South, declaring in a letter to John Jumper of the Seminoles that "our brothers, the Texans, and the Indians are away fighting the cold weather people. We do not intend to go North to fight them but if they come down here, we will all unite to drive them away."[32]

However, agent Leeper at the Wichita Agency soon discovered

that being ward to the wild-natured Comanches was more than he had bargained for. He reported: "They have destroyed pretty much all of the poultry belonging to Dr. Shirley, have shot arrows into his milk cows, killed several of the beeves belonging to the contractor. They are in the habit of shooting beeves full of arrows in the beef pen before they are issued, killing some of them and rendering others unable to be driven to the different Indian encampments."[33] When interpreter Horace P. Jones tried to admonish Chief Buffalo Hump on the matter, the old man "abused him in unmeasured terms."[34] The young Comanches habitually held war and scalp dances, bragging of their agility in stealing horses and taking scalps and of the rapturous embraces bestowed upon them by the young Comanche women. Three of their warriors attempted to invade the bedroom of Dr. Shirley's wife but desisted after a scuffle with the trader.

The ledger for Shirley's trading post indicates that Chisholm was an occasional customer there as late as August 18, 1862.[35] If he had not yet departed for Kansas by late October 1862, it is almost certain that he would have left the area following a bloody raid made upon the Wichita Agency by a group of refugee Indians from Kansas. This incident made it virtually impossible for the Reserve Indians to remain in the Indian Territory. It evidently did the same for Jesse Chisholm, who was so closely associated with them.

The Indians of the Wichita Reserve had become more than uneasy in their new relationship with the Texans, and they soon became strongly disenchanted with Leeper. The situation was further disturbed by others, such as the Delawares, who were encouraging the reserve Indians to desert the Confederates.[36] The Delawares, Jesse's close friends, had been quick to declare themselves on the side of the North. In Kansas, Black Beaver had stated his intention to attend a meeting that John Ross had called at the Burnt Timbers on the Canadian, saying he was determined to go even if he risked being killed.[37] And in September 1861 the Delawares had issued a resolution signed by their head chiefs, John Conner and Anderson Sarcoxie, calling upon all of the tribes in the region to stand with the Union. They further sent fifty warriors who were mustered into the U.S. service at Fort Leavenworth.[38]

Matters came to such a state by August 1862 that a large

number of the agency wards did leave the Wichita Reserve. Rumors were soon heard that some of the Indians who had gone to Kansas from the Territory were planning to send down a war party to attack the agency. Leeper, forewarned, hastily departed.[39]

The rumors were true enough. A well-armed group of seventy Delawares and twenty-six Shawnees arrived on the Washita River and began to infiltrate the bands still living just outside the reserve area. An exception among the disaffected were the Tonkawas, whom all of the other tribes despised because of their affiliation with the Texans and their cannibalistic habits. Stories that the Tonkawas had killed a Caddo boy and were about to feast on him touched off the bloody attack of October 23.[40] Just after dark on that evening, the force of allied Kansas refugees and Leased District residents entered the agency, murdered four white men who worked there (Leeper was mistakenly thought to have been one of them), placed their bodies in the agency buildings, and burned the structures. The Tonkawas, who were camped nearby, disappeared into the night. However, on the following morning they were discovered hiding in a clump of trees, surrounded, and brutally massacred, their bows and arrows being small defense against the rifles and pistols of their foes. Out of some 390 Tonkawas only about 150 managed to reach the safety of Fort Arbuckle to the east.[41]

Word came that a large unit of Texans and Creeks under Chilly McIntosh was on the march for Fort Cobb. The Wichitas and others had no choice now but to flee northward to Union-controlled Kansas. This they did, taking their people and possessions on a month's march some three hundred miles to Walnut Creek below El Dorado. The refugees carried with them a large number of scalps and, wrapped in a rebel flag, papers belonging to the Wichita Agency and the Tonkawa chief who had been killed. Some of the papers were signed by Sam Houston. The Wichitas and others from the Leased District suffered through the winter in Kansas desperately short of food, shelter, and clothing.[42]

Where Jesse Chisholm was at this time is unknown. On December 16, 1862, a C.S.A. officer at Fort Smith wrote to contractor Johnson stating: "The General [Hindman] has appointed Mr. Jesse Chisholm acting agent for Reserve Indians and I forward you herewith a letter for him concerning his appointment and instructions

Jesse and his son William are believed to have built this sandstone shed over the spring at Chisholm Springs. *Courtesy of the Archives and Manuscripts Division of the Oklahoma Historical Society.*

which you will please to *forward* to him *as soon as possible.*" [43] Likely Chisholm had already departed for Kansas with the Reserve Indians and never even knew of the appointment. A Confederate report states that both Chisholm and Black Beaver were among the Indians on the Arkansas River by the fall of 1863.[44] Just where is not clear.

Indications are that Jesse had not yet arrived at the mouth of the Little Arkansas. Trader James Mead later told of visiting the area in the spring of 1863, and there was "not a living soul in all the country."[45] Further, Union Indian agent H. W. Martin was at the location in June of that same year, attempting to arrange a council with the Indians there, and he made no mention of Chisholm's presence.[46] According to Mead, it was in the fall of 1864 that Jesse brought his family to the area and built comfortable cabins, corrals, and sheds in the south end of a hackberry grove near a spring on what came to be known as Chisholm Creek. Camped about his place was a large retinue of his children and adoptees and their families.[47]

The sturdy shed stands today much as it looked when historian T. U. Taylor *(left)* visited it. *Courtesy of the Barker Texas History Center, The University of Texas at Austin.*

During this same period, the suffering Wichitas, Wacos, and Kichais moved their villages to the mouth of the Little Arkansas, while the Caddos, Delawares, and Absentee Shawnees located ten miles to the east on Dry Creek.[48] This gave them closer access to the buffalo-hunting grounds just west of the Arkansas River, though they were at considerable risk of being attacked by the aggressive Cheyennes, who now considered this to be their hunting territory.[49]

Chisholm maintained his close association with the fragmented bands of Indians still remaining in the western portion of the Indian Territory. He was present inside the Territory during the spring of 1864 at a council between the Comanches and Kiowas and some northern officers and representatives of the Union-favoring Indians.[50] The Union men brought a large consignment of guns and ammunition, which they offered to the two tribes if they would make war on the southern Indians. They were to kill all the men and boys, take the women and children prisoner, and drive off the cattle, horses, and mules. The Comanches and Kiowas would have to give up their white prisoners, but they could keep the Indian women along with the horses and mules. The cattle would be purchased from them.[51]

Chisholm, who served as interpreter, prevented this, advising the Comanches and Kiowas not to listen to the "bad talk" of the northern men. He said that he opposed making war on the Indians to the south as they were all his friends. His talk obviously influenced the Comanche chief who spoke last and agreed fully with Chisholm, saying that he thought those Indians who spoke for war "had been drinking strong water," for he did not think that sober men would propose making war on their friends.[52] The Comanche told the northern officers they could keep their guns and ammunition, that his people would continue to live on the prairie and use their bows and arrows to kill the buffalo. He said that while he had made a treaty with Pike, he was holding one hand out to the North and one to the South.

The strength of Chisholm's influence was expressed by a Waco chief who declared: "Chisholm heap, heap big chief — Comanches, Kiowas, Apaches and Arapahos."[53] Jesse's opposition to the northern plan caused some to express doubts of his loyalty to the Union. Still, his services as an interpreter and liaison with the Indians were of much value to both the North and the Indians.

Jesse's unique talents were put to use in a meeting with the Wichita, Caddo, Waco, Kichai, Anadarko, and Ionie refugees on the White Water River of Kansas. With his advice and assistance, the Indian leaders wrote a letter to northern officials promising they would resist any attempts by other tribes to get them to war on the United States; they also made a plea to President Lincoln in which they described their pathetic condition:

> This great war has driven us from our own country and from our homes, and we cannot raise corn and provisions for our women and children, and a great many people have been sick this year, with the small pox, and a good many of them have died and left widows and orphan children, and many of our people are sick now. From this cause many of our hunters could not go out to hunt the Buffalo for food, and to buy clothing for their families, as they could when in their own country.
>
> We have always been told by our White Fathers that they would help us when we needed help, and we need it now very much. And

we hope you will tell your Agent to give us bread for our women
and children and clothing for them before the next snow falls. We
hope our white fathers will not forget their red children when they
are suffering.[54]

Now would begin efforts to reactivate the tribal structures that
had been so badly disrupted by the war and renew attempts by the
federal government to bring peace to the frontier. As he had for so
many years, Jesse Chisholm would play a key role in the process.

There is no record that it actually happened — that some men of the frontier met around a campfire one night, drank whiskey, and told stories of their experiences in the West. But they were all there with Jesse Chisholm at the mouth of the Little Arkansas: the most famous frontiersman of all, Colonel Kit Carson; the renowned William Bent of Bent's Fort on the Arkansas; and John Simpson Smith, who had spent nearly thirty years among the Blackfeet and Cheyennes. Also, there were a number of Kansas Indian traders such as Dutch Bill Greiffenstein, James Mead, Charles W. Whittaker, Judge A. F. Greenway, and Buffalo Bill Mathewson; Dr. John Shirley, up from his trading post in the Indian Territory; agent Jesse Leavenworth; Generals William S. Harney, reputed as an old Indian fighter, and John B. Sanborn; the much-experienced Indian Bureau official Thomas Murphy; and others.

Not since the Treaty of Fort Laramie in 1851 had so many notable men of the West met together. It can only be surmised that these men spent a sociable yarn-spinning session together one night during the treaty council. Likely it would have been little, squint-eyed Dutch Bill (later to be known as the father of the city of Wichita, which came to exist at this site) who graciously uncorked a jug of whiskey and treated the campfire gathering.

And it may well have been the stocky, ruddy-faced Kit Carson, flaxen hair falling to his shoulders, who started the tales, humorously recounting his favorite story about the time he had been chased up a tree by a grizzly bear. Old John Smith probably told of his adventures when he escaped the Blackfeet by floating down the

Missouri River in a buffalo-hide bullboat, swigging whiskey and laudanum to ease the pain of a toothache. The hard-drinking Greenway, brother to the Osage agent, could have amused the crowd with the story of how in 1852 he had accompanied an Osage war party to the Little Arkansas, losing his hat, his buffalo gun, and his desire ever to do it again. And without a doubt, General Harney could be counted on for stories from his many years of frontier experience, including his part in the Atkinson expedition, which explored its way up the Missouri River in 1825.

Maybe even Jesse joined in; certainly he had plenty of interesting adventures of his own to tell about. But probably he sat back and said nothing as usual, playing the host. After all, this was his home here at the mouth of the Little Arkansas. Some called it a trading post and others referred to it as Chisholm's Ranch. Mostly he used it as a home for his family, a base for his trading excursions into the Territory, and a holding point for cattle that raiding parties of Caddos and other refugee tribes brought back from the unattended grazing lands of the Leased District and adjacent areas.

The practice of foraying into the Territory, rustling cattle from the prewar Indian herds, had become epidemic all along the line of the Kansas–Indian Territory border during the war. "Our Southern frontier is swarming with these speculators," wrote the editor of the *Emporia News* on August 6, 1864. "And one report is that 12,000 head of cattle have passed north this summer. We are informed that they are being driven out of the Indian country and Texas, in droves of thousands by Indians from the plains, and that white men pay them for doing it."

Wichita agent Milo Gookins complained about this "illicit and immoral traffic" and said that the loyalist Indians were threatening to replenish their herds after the war by raiding into Kansas.[1] Charges were made by Kansas newspapers that a conspiracy existed among prominent Kansas businessmen, high-ranking military officers, and both Indian and white cattle thieves concerning the contraband beeves.[2] It was counterargued that the cattle were fair game, being unclaimed as they were and many belonging to the disloyal Indians of the Territory. In the West it was partly a matter of refugee tribes going after stock that had been theirs before the war began, though herds in Texas were often victimized as well.

A roadside marker commemorates Chisholm's home at Chisholm
Springs near Asher, Oklahoma. *Photograph by Stan Hoig.*

Rightly or wrongly, Chisholm played a temporary role in this, acting more or less as an agent for Enoch C. Stevens, who was connected in business with the Sac and Fox Indian Agency in eastern Kansas. According to James Mead, who was located at nearby Towanda at the time, Chisholm collected a herd of some 3,000 head of cattle, which he held in his corral or grazed on the site of present-day west Wichita.[3] Some of these animals were sent to fill government annuity contracts in New Mexico, while others were driven to the Sac and Fox Agency to feed the hungry wards there.[4] But this trade in Indian Territory cattle evidently came to an end for Chisholm when Stevens drowned while attempting to cross a swollen stream near the agency in his buggy.[5]

Jesse Chisholm is known to have been inside the Territory during 1864. It is possible, even probable, that he then first used the route that would eventually become the initial leg of the famous Chisholm Cattle Trail. According to a statement made by George (Vincente) Chisholm to historian Thoburn, the first trip was made by his father over the trail during the spring of 1865.[6]

Most historians have relied on James R. Mead's memory for information concerning the initiation of the Chisholm Trail. But Mead's recollections are contradictory, sometimes placing the event in the fall of 1864 and at other times in the spring of 1865 or 1866. Mead also indicates in later accounts that he was along on the historic trip, while in earlier versions he gives no indication that was the case. In an 1890 paper delivered to a Kansas historical group, Mead stated that in December 1865 Chisholm purchased trade goods from him, and that in the following January the Cherokee trader loaded his wagons and made his first trip back to Council Grove. He was supposedly accompanied by trader Henry Donnell,[7] who stopped at the Red Fork of the Arkansas to trade with the Osages. By this account, Chisholm conducted a lucrative trade and returned later that spring, his wagons heavy with buffalo robes and peltry. He made camp near Mead's trading post on the Walnut.

"I am owing you," Chisholm reportedly told Mead. "I have no money, but have buffalo robes, wolf skins, beaver, buckskins. You can take your pick from them."[8] Mead decided on the wolf and coyote skins, each of which was legal tender for a dollar on the frontier; and Chisholm counted out 3,000 of them. Mead claimed that on this trip

Chisholm followed the most direct and practicable route, and that this was the first wagon train to pass over "the great trail which by common consent was given the name of Chisholm from the man who located it."[9]

In a 1907 account, Mead placed the first trip as early as the fall of 1864, stating:

> Jesse Chisholm loaded some wagons with the usual hunter's and trader's outfit — coffee, tobacco, sugar, blankets, etc. — and with his usual retinue of followers and employees, started south to mark out a trail to his old ranch at Council Grove on the North Canadian. . . . I accompanied him on this trip with some of my own teams. Chisholm and his Indians knew the country well, were expert plainsmen and selected the best possible route. . . . As we progressed southward, we soon mapped out a plain road and we named the streams from some incident or occurrence that would happen in the locality.[10]

In still another word on the subject, Mead wrote that Chisholm brought four hundred head of cattle from his Council Grove post, and he, Mead, purchased them at $16 a head. On another occasion Mead declared: "Mr. Chisholm's teams and my own were the first which ever passed over that route and marked out what afterward became known as the Chisholm Trail."[11]

Whether the gentlemanly Mead suffered the natural failings of memory or responded to the human impulse to place oneself even closer to a historical event than was actually the case will probably remain conjectural. Nonetheless, Mead was a principal actor on the Kansas and Indian Territory frontier and later contributed much to its recorded history. His trading activities were noted by the *Emporia News* on August 13, 1864, when the paper reported that J. R. Mead of Towanda had passed through town that week with several large loads of hides and furs, mostly buffalo robes, bound for Leavenworth. Mead said that he had traded for them west of the Arkansas.

Still, it is clear that Jesse Chisholm was active inside the Territory even during 1864, as a trader and as one involved in both Confederate and Union relations with the Indians there. In traveling between his ranch on Chisholm Creek and Council Grove on the North Canadian, Chisholm could hardly have avoided use of the trace that was the most direct between the two points and the one that ultimately became a part of the great Texas cattle trail to Kansas.

As of October 1864 Jesse Chisholm was in the employ of the newly appointed Comanche-Kiowa agent Jesse Leavenworth, son of General Henry Leavenworth for whom Jesse had served as a guide in 1834. Working principally as an emissary to the Comanches and Kiowas, Chisholm is known to have gone into the Territory for Leavenworth on occasion, probably spending the winter of 1864/65 there in contact with those tribes. Likely he was doing some trading on his own, also, the trapping and hunting season for peltry being from October through February when the animal pelts were in their best condition. Further evidence that Chisholm was in the Indian Territory on or about February 11, 1865, is revealed by a statement he witnessed regarding an argument between a Shawnee and a Caddo over a stolen horse.[12]

On February 15, 1865, Chisholm wrote to Jesse Leavenworth from a Kiowa camp on the Chikaskia River to report that the Kiowas, Arapahos, Plains Apaches, and Wichitas had gathered and were willing to make peace as soon as the U.S. Army ceased fighting them. The Indians wanted Leavenworth to write to Washington and have all army troops informed of the peace so as not to be deceived as the Cheyennes had been at Sand Creek. Chisholm said he had distributed presents to the Indians as he had been instructed by Leavenworth's black aide George Ransom. "I have furnished a good many of my own goods and got some of C. Roth as there was not enough of yours to go around and give them all a taste to satisfy them."[13]

An attempt was made in early 1865 by the Confederates to enlist the help of the Indian tribes of the Territory to apply pressure against the Union forces in Kansas.[14] Chisholm's old trading partner Israel Vore, now a Confederate major and Creek agent, reported that he had word the Indians were thirsting for revenge against the Kansas frontier. Vore sent couriers out to all of the major tribes of the Indian Territory promising them tobacco and wampum if they attended a grand council at Chisholm's Council Grove ranch.[15]

Out of a wish to minimize the Texas presence, efforts were made to reactivate Albert Pike to head the delegation. Pike, who had been

Agent Jesse Leavenworth. Leavenworth, like many others, depended heavily on Jesse Chisholm to bring the Indians in to talk peace. *Courtesy of the Archives and Manuscripts Division of the Oklahoma Historical Society.*

through some bad times with other Confederate leaders, declined to serve. Instead, Vore was dispatched to escort Brigadier General James W. Throckmorton to conduct a preliminary meeting at Chisholm's Council Grove location. It was agreed there with representatives of the various tribes that a meeting would be held on May 26 at a cottonwood grove on the Canadian River two miles east of present-day Verden, Oklahoma. The site was given the title Camp Napoleon.[16]

Among the over 6,000 Indians in attendance were those from both the eastern and prairie tribes. At this time the Indians were told that the whites had made peace, the war was over, and the Indians could no longer expect any help from the South.[17] The Comanches and Kiowas agreed they would no longer war on the North, but the Cheyennes and Arapahos, still smarting from the massacre of their village at Sand Creek by Colonel John M. Chivington on November 29, 1864, held back.

George Ransom, who had been dispatched by Leavenworth to go into the Territory and bring the Indians to the Arkansas for consultation, returned from the North Fork of the Red River to report that a grand council lasting nearly a month had been held. A Caddo chief had sent word to Jesse Chisholm that all the Indians wanted peace except the Cheyennes, who were still for "war to the knife."[18]

Sergeant H. J. Tibbits, who visited the mouth of the Little Arkansas for Brigadier General James H. Ford, commanding the District of the Upper Arkansas, reported in late June: "I told Chisholm that you wanted to employ him, and that you wanted that he should go to the Indians and see what they were going to do. Chisholm started Tuesday morning the 27th, and says that he wishes you not to send any parties south of the Arkansas River till his return, for it may endanger his life. Chisholm will report to you in person as soon as he returns."[19] Leavenworth wrote to Ford at the same time to say that Chisholm had left with a party of Caddos who claimed that many of the refugee Indians had left Kansas and gone to the Wichita Mountains.[20] These were mostly the young warriors, however. The home camps of the refugee Indians were destined to remain in Kansas for another two years of privation, sickness, and decimation before the government could get them returned to their reserve.

Many northern men were suspicious of Leavenworth's dealings with the Indians and some doubted Jesse Chisholm's loyalty. A scout for Brigadier General Ford, Sam Peppard, wrote:

> I have learned from good authority that there is a Cherokee half-breed, by the name of Chishem, claiming to be a refugee from the Cherokee Nation, who has been trading with those hostile tribes all winter. I inquired of the settlers if he was a loyal man, and all that knew him said he is not a loyal man, and Major Gookins doubts his loyalty. He (Chishem) is the man who issued the goods to them for Colonel Leavenworth — those tribes, namely, Kiowas, Apaches, and Arapahoes — then left the next day. Chishem is the man that Colonel Leavenworth received information from that the hostile Indians wished to make a treaty of peace.[21]

Chisholm contacted the Comanches, Kiowas, and Plains Apaches inside the Indian Territory and persuaded them to come north to meet with representatives sent out from Washington. On July 14 Chisholm wrote to Leavenworth from a camp near Fort Arbuckle. "I have the honor to inform you that I have seen Ten Bears, Comanche Chief, and he has agreed to bring all the chiefs to council in the course of 20 or 35 days at which time you may expect to meet me with them at Bluff Creek near the mound of rocks on the hill."[22] Ten Bears was a close friend of Chisholm. The Comanche chief had been to Washington, D.C., with a delegation in 1863 and had had an audience with President Abraham Lincoln.[23] Missing the sight of one eye, Ten Bears wore a pair of steel-rimmed spectacles that gave him a unique, Ben Franklin–like appearance among the other Indians.

Advance parties of the Kiowas and Plains Apaches arrived at the mouth of the Little Arkansas on August 2, saying they were anxious for peace. Chisholm was still with the Comanches, who wanted more assurances of safety before they came up. At the same time, Jesse's adopted Mexican son Jackson brought another message from the trader, written at the trading house of Dutch Bill Greiffenstein at Cow Creek just below present-day Wichita. Dated August 1, 1865, it read: "I am here with 125 Indians and nothing for them to eat. What shall I do with them? Fetch [them] over in

Satanta. The Kiowa war leader was one of many Plains Indians who knew Jesse Chisholm well. *Courtesy of the Western History Collections, University of Oklahoma.*

the morning or not? Please let me know by Jackson. Yours, etc., J. Chisholm."[24]

Eight days later the frontiersman arrived at Leavenworth's camp with a large entourage of Indians in tow, including the families and lodges that the chiefs had brought, trusting Chisholm's word that they would be safe.[25] The Cheyennes, however, were still too angry and distrustful of whites to join the other tribes. Only Black Kettle, the Cheyenne principal chief who was still in bad grace with the Cheyenne Dog Soldier war society over the Sand Creek affair, dared to attend the preliminary meeting to arrange for a treaty council, doing so with much trepidation. Black Kettle was accompanied by the half-blooded sons of William Bent, George and Charlie Bent.[26]

Soon after the arrival of the Indians, Major General Sanborn joined them with his staff. A council was then held to make the arrangements for a postwar treaty venture with all of the tribes of the mid-Plains. Once again Jesse Chisholm rendered his abilities as an interpreter and advisor to both the Indians and the whites at the meeting.[27]

In September 1865 an important meeting of the tribes of the Indian Territory with representatives of the United States was held at Fort Smith. Agent Gookins was there, as were some Comanches, but Chisholm was busy elsewhere in the service of Leavenworth.[28] Despite the negative report made by scout Peppard, General Ford attempted to hire Chisholm away from Leavenworth to serve him as a military scout, offering $10 a day with no loss of time. This compared to the $7 paid by the Indian Bureau, but, as the agent stated, "Chisholm refused all offers and devoted himself diligently with me . . ."[29] Leavenworth was highly appreciative of Chisholm's dedication, writing to superiors: "Mr. Chisholm, a half-Cherokee and a man of good character and who has always lived with or near the Comanche Indians, has rendered me, and the Government, the greatest service in bringing about peace on the frontier."[30]

It was agreed at Sanborn's meeting with the Indians that a grand council would be held on October 4 at Bluff Creek, forty miles to the south, though this would eventually be changed back to the mouth of the Little Arkansas. It was determined that this council would attempt to utilize the expertise of some of the most Indian-experienced men in the West — in particular Kit Carson and William Bent — to bring about a solution to the Indian problem of the mid-Plains.

The Treaty of the Little Arkansas was far more notable for who attended the affair than for what it actually accomplished. It was, indeed, one of the grandest accumulations of frontier dignitaries, white and Indian, since the Treaty of Fort Laramie in 1851. In addition to the notable white men in attendance, the council featured a number of important Indian figures, including such well-known leaders as Black Kettle and Little Robe of the Cheyennes; Little Raven, Storm, and Big Mouth of the Arapahos; Poor Bear and Iron Shirt of the Plains Apaches; Little Mountain and Satank of the Kiowas; and Lone Wolf, Iron Mountain, Buffalo Hump, and Ten Bears of the Comanches.[31] When all parties had finally been assembled, the area that would later be encompassed by the city of Wichita, Kansas, was engulfed in a collection of tepees, Sibley tents, grass huts of the Wichitas, horses, mules, wagons, commissioners, agents, soldiers, teamsters, traders, and thousands of Indians.

Of major interest to the commission was the halting of Indian attacks on the Santa Fe Trail transportation. In return for promises of annuity goods and other assistance, the Comanches, Kiowas, and Plains Apaches were asked to cede their claim to all lands north of the Canadian River, though they would be permitted to make their periodic visits to the Salt Plains.

Chisholm served as interpreter in council with the Kiowas, disproving the claim that no person not born into the tribe had ever yet learned to speak the tongue of that tribe. Through Chisholm, Kiowa Head Chief Tohawson, or Little Mountain, pointed out that the Great Father was always promising to do something but never did.[32] He also declared the Kiowa proprietorship of the buffalo range: "The Kiowas own from Fort Laramie and the north fork of the Platte to Texas, and always owned it. That [includes] all the branches, creeks, rivers and ponds that you see; all the deer and buffalo, wolves and turtles, all belong to him — were given to him by the Great Spirit. White men did not give it to him."[33]

The matter of white captives held by the Comanches and Kiowas was broached by the commissioners. Eagle Drinking, a Comanche, admitted to holding some white captives, but he pointed out that seven years before, Major Van Dorn had captured some of his people, who were still being held prisoner by the whites. The Kiowas agreed to send for their captives, and a party with an army ambulance was sent south in an attempt to obtain release of the whites from tribal members who had no wish to make peace. The rescue party returned with five captives: Mrs. Caroline McDonald, age twenty-six, of Fredericksburg, Texas; her daughter, one-year-old Rebecca; a nephew, seven-year-old James Taylor; a niece, Dorcas Taylor, three years old; and James Burrow, age seven, of Georgetown, Texas.[34]

During the council a Negro man from Texas rode into camp and said that he had recently given seven ponies to redeem his wife and two children from the Comanches, but the Indians had reneged on releasing two others who were supposed to be a part of the trade: a woman of about forty years and her four-year-old granddaughter. The woman was the widow of a Union man who had been hanged in Texas during the war for refusing to join the rebels.[35]

Talks were also held with the Reserve Indians. Still extremely destitute and impoverished — four of their members had died of starvation only recently — the tribes expressed their strong desire to be sent back to their homeland in the Indian Territory. The treaty commission recommended that an agency be reestablished for them at the abandoned Fort Cobb.

By now the weather had turned windy and cold, and the trouser-clad and bare-legged orators alike were compelled to cut short their speech making. On the morning of October 18, the camp arose to discover that the first frost had come and that the water in the buckets had frozen to nearly a half inch in thickness. A number of the men complained of having slept cold that night. But this was the final day. All the tribes had been dealt with except the Osages. When the commissioners talked with them that afternoon, the Osage chiefs were asked to relinquish that part of their reservation west of the Arkansas River, for a price. The Osages declined emphatically, saying that they had sold parts of their land twice before and had seen nothing from it as yet. "Heap talk, no money," they said and rode off.

On the following morning, having temporarily pacified the warring tribes, but with much less concern shown to the pathetic reserve tribes who had stayed loyal to the North during the war, the commissioners packed up their gear and headed homeward for the comforts of hearth and featherbed where there would be, as a commission scribe put it, "[n]o broken slumbers, no aching bones, weary of their contact with solid earth."[36]

Events would soon prove the Treaty of the Little Arkansas to have been a futile attempt to solve the Indian problem on the Plains. But for now, the winter fur season was coming on, and Jesse Chisholm turned back to his basic occupation as an Indian trader. In doing so, he initiated a new trading route between the Indian Territory and Leavenworth, Kansas.

Smoke drifted skyward from the cross-pole tops of Indian lodges along the wooded sand hills of the North Canadian River. Warm spring days had dressed the cottonwood, blackjack, elm, and tamarack with new leaves. The greening meadows along the river were filled with Comanche, Kiowa, Cheyenne, and Arapaho pony herds. The bands had come here to meet, sing, dance, and celebrate their tribal rituals. They were here, also, to conduct trade with Jesse Chisholm and other traders from Kansas who brought them the white man's merchandise. This site on the north bank of the river, just before it turns abruptly from an easterly to a southerly course (west of Longdale, Oklahoma), was a choice camping spot. It featured a good spring surrounded by a large grove of trees. A year later, in the spring of 1869, the site would gain identity as Sheridan's Roost, when General Phil Sheridan chanced by en route from Fort Sill to Camp Supply and killed sixty-three wild turkeys in a day of shooting.[1]

Jesse had been here since early in the year, hoping to get the best of the season's furs and robes, and by now his supplies had begun to run low. His bacon and flour were entirely gone. Even the Indians were short of buffalo meat and the tallow that they ate as the white man ate bread. Jesse, who shared the Indians' appreciation for bear meat and honey, one day longingly expressed his desire for such a meal. He was overheard by an Indian woman. Wishing to please him, she brought forth a small brass kettle in which was stored some bear grease. Jesse ate heartily of it, not realizing that the metal pot had contaminated the grease. It would be his last meal.

Jesse had only recently seen his fourth grandchild, a girl named Mary, born to his thirty-one-year-old son William. He knew his time was coming to an end. In his lodge one night he had mused on his life to James Mead, speaking with pride of his long service to the cause of peace, and justifiably so. Even at the age of sixty, when the Treaty of the Little Arkansas failed, he had continued to travel far across the prairie on horseback to settle differences between the Indian and the white man.

The Treaty of the Little Arkansas had not achieved the principal result desired by the whites: the removal of the Plains tribes from Kansas. White settlers, land developers, railroad interests — all strongly supported the U.S. government's wish to eliminate the Indian barrier to the settlement of Kansas and to promote the advance of American national destiny across the continent. However, the warring Dog Soldiers of the Cheyennes, in league with the Arapahos and Sioux, still controlled the buffalo range of western Kansas, while Comanche and Kiowa warriors continued to endanger transportation and emigration on the Santa Fe Trail.

During 1866 and 1867 new efforts would be made to remove the Indians from Kansas, even as had been done in Texas. Government plans were already under way for the transfer of all of the reservation Indians from eastern Kansas to the Indian Territory. This involved the Pottawatomie, Kickapoo, Shawnee, Delaware, Kaw, Sac and Fox, and Osage tribes. Efforts were also being made to return the refugee tribes to the Territory.

The angry debate as to how to deal with the Plains Indians continued between proponents of punitive military action and those of pacification. For now the latter would win out with the promotion of another grandiose peace council designed to remove the tribes from the path of American progress by treaty.

During this same period an important development affecting the status of Indian-white relations in the region took place. It would also affect the life and place in history of Jesse Chisholm. The Civil War years had produced an abundance of longhorn cattle on the vast grazing lands of Texas, and Texas stockmen were seeking markets for their herds. The steel line later called the Kansas Pacific (eventually a branch of the first transcontinental railroad, the Union Pacific) was being built across the central Plains, offering the opportunity of reaching the lucrative eastern markets from Kansas railheads.

Efforts by Texas cattlemen to utilize northern shipping points before the war had been stymied in Missouri and Kansas by fear of contamination from the dreaded Texas fever. Texas beef droves had been barred by angry citizens. State laws were passed prohibiting passage of Texas cattle beyond the Indian Territory, where the herds were often grazed for fattening. But, in February 1867, Kansas enacted a law that, while banning Texas herds from the eastern trail routes, legalized the crossing of Kansas lands to the west of Saline County.[2] Seizing on this new situation, entrepreneur Joseph G. McCoy established cattle-shipping pens at the railhead of Abilene, Kansas, and launched a promotional campaign to bring Texas droves there.

The old Shawnee Cattle Trail across eastern Indian Territory from Fort Gibson up the Arkansas River to Wichita now became obsolete as Texas ranchers sought a more direct route to Kansas. As a result there began in the early fall of 1867 a flood of Texas cattle across the Indian Territory to the mouth of the Little Arkansas and on northward to the Union Pacific railheads, Abilene being the first. Suddenly the home range of the prairie tribes was being invaded by a new type of American, the Texas trail drover and cowman who followed a new trail to Kansas across the very center of the Indians' domain.

A portion of this new cattle trail followed a route from the North Canadian to the mouth of the Little Arkansas, a route that had already commonly become known as Chisholm's Trail. That title had been used by Philip McCusker, a former soldier who became well known as a Comanche interpreter, in a letter to Indian Superintendent Thomas Murphy on November 15, 1867 — evidence that the trail was named for Chisholm prior to its eminence as a road for Texas beef.[3] It is doubtful, despite the claims of some, that Jesse Chisholm ever drove a herd of cattle over this road that became a part of the great Chisholm Cattle Trail.[4] George Chisholm later insisted that Jesse made no cattle trail. It is clear, though, that Chisholm made many trips over the route on horseback and by wagon for more than two years before the advent of the first trail herd over it in the summer of 1867.

Artist A. R. Ward sketched Texas long-horned cattle on an early drive to Kansas along the trace that became famous as the Chisholm Trail. From *Harper's Illustrated Weekly,* October 19, 1867.

In January 1866, for the first time, Jesse Chisholm was listed as a registered Indian trader. His name appears along with that of William Mathewson on the government rolls as a trader with the firm of Edwin H. Durfee of Leavenworth.[5] His need for a sponsor indicates that Chisholm's finances had suffered badly during the Civil War. Durfee, a New Yorker who had come west to become a very active importer and wholesaler in Indian goods, ran his own steamboats on the upper Missouri and was expanding southwestward through Indian contact men such as Chisholm, Mathewson, Mead, Whittaker, and others.

The Durfee Company store in downtown Leavenworth featured a large assortment of western and Indian paraphernalia — Indian blankets of all colors and sizes, beaded bridles, vermilion, wampum, furs, buffalo robes, and many other items of the frontier — which it offered to its customers. Several buffalo calves, a pet antelope, two fawns, a black bear cub that was led about on a string, bales of peltry and buffalo hides, and a huge pile of elk horns made the store a curiosity to citizens and visitors alike.[6]

At Leavenworth's request, Durfee was given the sole trading rights to the Leased District area. Other traders on the frontier resented this intensely, and strong charges were made as to a conspiracy among Leavenworth, Durfee, and Mathewson to cheat the Indians.[7] It was claimed that, instead of being freely issued, the Indians' own annuity goods, assigned to them by treaty, were being traded to them for robes, peltries, horses, and mules. No such accusations were made against Jesse Chisholm. Chisholm's employment with Durfee indicates that after the Treaty of the Little Arkansas had been concluded in mid-October 1865, Jesse took his wagons to Leavenworth and loaded them with trade goods supplied by Durfee. From Council Grove, he made trips westward to the camps of the Kiowas and Comanches as well as to those of the Cheyennes and Arapahos. Portions of these last two tribes had taken up residence in northwestern Indian Territory following the treacherous attack on them at Sand Creek in 1864.

Chisholm was back at the Little Arkansas Wichita Agency in May 1866 to give witness in regard to a Shawnee-Caddo stolen-horse incident.[8] It is probable that at the same time he was conducting trading operations at Council Grove, a probability supported by an incident near Emporia, Kansas, as reported in the *Emporia News* of November 24, 1866.

Emporia was the most forward settlement of size in southern Kansas when it was visited by Captain Henry Brandley, a state representative from Chase County, in the fall of 1866. Brandley told of having encountered a small train of heavily loaded wagons, belonging to some traders from the Canadian River in the Indian Territory, that had just delivered a load of furs to Leavenworth. The owner, who was located on the Canadian, told Brandley that trade goods could be purchased cheaply enough at Leavenworth to justify taking wagons there rather than to Fort Smith, a market one hundred miles closer. He offered his opinion that, if a road were opened via El Dorado to Leavenworth, it could be quite profitable to all concerned by the trade it would develop between Kansas and the upper Canadian. Brandley did not identify his informant; however, the trader's Canadian location and the fact of his having previously traded at Fort Smith make it virtually certain that it was Jesse Chisholm, on his way back from Leavenworth with trade goods.

Chisholm had been followed to the mouth of the Little Arkansas by other traders such as James Mead. In December Mead, who was also operating a trading post on Pond Creek just inside the Territory, reported a large train of furs and pelts that passed through his settlement at Towanda.[9] This could well have been Chisholm's train.

Though trading activities occupied Chisholm during the winter and early spring, the summer of 1867 once again called him into the service of peace on the frontier. He was in attendance as a delegate to a meeting of the National Creek Council at its grounds near present-day Okmulgee, Oklahoma, on July 4.[10] While there he acted as an interpreter in settling a dispute between the Creeks and Caddos, witnessing an agreement on paper whereby the Creeks would pay $1,000 indemnity for a Caddo who had been killed by a Creek, another $500 for a Caddo who had been wounded, and another payment for property taken from the Caddos by the Creeks.[11]

From Okmulgee, Chisholm traveled on to Fort Gibson where he reported to authorities regarding the condition of the Indians on the western prairies. Large numbers of Cheyennes and Arapahos were in the vicinity of Fort Cobb, he said, and with them were numerous white captives.[12] The Seminole agent requested that Jesse return to the area and see if he could secure the release of some of the prisoners. The white captives were a strong reflection that the Treaty of the Little Arkansas had failed to end the conflict on the Plains. The Dog Soldiers of the Cheyennes, in particular, had been unwilling to follow the path of peace accepted for their nation by Black Kettle and other chiefs. They had been avenging Sand Creek with raids against frontier settlements and transportation in Kansas, Nebraska, and Colorado Territory.

Increased agitation by Kansas citizens and the military for punishment of the Indians, however, had been temporarily restrained by the inability of the postwar frontier army to chastise effectively the nomads of the prairies. Generals Alfred Sully, Winfield S. Hancock, and George Custer each failed badly in his attempts to catch and punish the fleet-mounted warriors of western Kansas.

There were those in government and elsewhere who insisted to Congress and President Andrew Johnson that a peaceful settlement of the Indian problem could still be found. Another attempt to effect a successful and lasting peace treaty with the tribes was approved, and steps were initiated for a commission to visit the Plains and meet with the Indians.

On July 20, 1867, a preliminary meeting between agent Leavenworth and the Comanches, Apaches, Kiowas, Arapahos, and Wichitas was held at the mouth of the Little Arkansas. Chisholm was also in attendance, along with James Mead, George Bent, and William Greiffenstein.[13] George Bent later described how the men seated themselves in a circle near the Wichita camp, smoked, and discussed a proposed new treaty council. Not far away an old Wichita couple, both with long gray hair, wailed in mourning for the loss of their son who had been killed recently by a Cheyenne war party when returning from Texas with stolen horses.[14]

The secretary of interior had arranged for the purchase of a herd of 425 cattle from Robert H. Taylor of Bonham, Texas. The secretary naively intended the cattle to be issued to the Comanches and Kiowas for "domestic use" — evidently for milking — as an approach to an agrarian existence. Taylor sublet the contract to James Daugherty and a drover named J. H. Haynes. Though miffed at having the secretary go around him in the matter, Leavenworth dispatched Mathewson to receive them. He also hired Mathewson and Greiffenstein to deliver into the Territory the annuity goods already promised the Comanches and Kiowas under the 1865 treaty. The agent further employed Mathewson to deliver two Texas boys, who had been rescued from the Indians, to Fort Arbuckle, where they would be met by friends.[15]

As directed, Mathewson went to the Shawnee Crossing of the Canadian River, near the Leased District, and received the cattle from Haynes. They were then turned over to George Ransom, who, after being brought to the Plains by Leavenworth in 1865, had gone to work for Jesse Chisholm. Jesse had developed a very high regard for the man's reliability and integrity. During the spring and summer of 1867, he had entrusted Ransom to take his mule-drawn wagon trains of furs and peltries, their worth usually estimated at over $20,000, from the Leased District to Leavenworth, Kansas.[16] Ransom was to hold the Taylor herd until told what to do with it. In the absence of further orders, he and other Negro herders grazed the cattle all the following winter on the Canadian near Chouteau Creek.[17]

In early September agent Leavenworth crossed the Arkansas and prepared to head for the Salt Plains for a conference with the Indians. At that time he reported that "two herds of cattle, numbering some fifteen hundred, have just arrived here from Texas, and the herders report seeing very few Indians."[18] It is not known who owned the herds reported by Leavenworth. Possibly one of them belonged to Colonel O. W. Wheeler and his partners, who promoter McCoy said were the first to bring Texas cattle over the Chisholm Cattle Trail.[19]

Superintendent of Indian Affairs Thomas Murphy, as well as a newspaper correspondent, was with Leavenworth as they crossed the Chikaskia — where they witnessed one of the great buffalo herds that blackened the prairie for miles in all directions — then rode on southward to the Salt Fork of the Arkansas.[20] There the two men met with the Comanches, under Ten Bears, and the Kiowas, whose head chief, Tohawson, had died since the 1865 council. Chisholm was not present, and McCusker, then a trader for Mead, handled the interpreting duties in making arrangements for the new treaty effort.

The party was joined at the Salt Fork by Mathewson, who was on his way back to the Little Arkansas from his mission to Fort Arbuckle. From him Leavenworth and Murphy learned of a tragic episode that had recently taken place along the Chisholm road. The affair involved the refugee tribes, whom the government had been unsuccessful in moving south, despite the efforts of the Wichita agent Henry Shanklin. Excessive rain, illness, and government red tape had delayed their departure from the mouth of the Little Arkansas for nearly two years.

During the summer of 1867, a cholera epidemic that was sweeping across Kansas struck the camps of the refugee tribes. Despite this, in August 1867 a contingent of 313 Absentee Shawnees, ninety-two Caddos, fifty-eight Delawares, and eight Ionies departed for the Leased District under the direction of special agent J. J. Chollar and commissary officer Charles F. Garrett.[21] These Indians left the Little Arkansas in apparent good health, having thus far escaped the cholera outbreak. On Chisholm's trail south, however, they were stricken by the dreaded disease, with devastating results. While encamped on Ephraim Creek some fifty of the Shawnees and forty-seven of the Caddos perished. When Mathewson had passed the site on his way back from Fort Arbuckle he had seen the victims lying dead "like rotten sheep" along the way.[22] The stream was later renamed Skeleton Creek in memory of this disaster.

The Wichitas, Wacos, Tawakonis, and Kichais, who left the Little Arkansas the following November, encountered a calamity of another kind. These people were forced to abandon much of their annuity foodstuffs and clothing and leave their dying tribal members to the mercy of wolves. They were loaded into ten decrepit wagons that had been hired out from local settlers and started south. While encamped on the Ninnescah River, they could see prairie fires burning in all directions. The Indians were not concerned at first, but during the night the wind changed to northerly, and a sudden gale brought the fire racing in upon the camp. The Indians made every effort to save their most valued possessions, their horses, but in spite of their exertions some 131 head of saddle horses, mares, and colts were lost, with many others badly burned and doomed to perish later. McCusker, who was with them, reported the incident to Superintendent Murphy: "I travelled with them one day's march, and really it was a pitiful sight to see the women and children, old men and old women trudging along on foot, most of them barefooted and nearly naked . . . "[23]

Jesse Chisholm was very ill during the October council at Medicine Lodge Creek. Perhaps he suffered from cholera, for he certainly had ample opportunity to contract it from the refugee Indians. Though Commissioner of Indian Affairs Alfred Taylor later wrote that Chisholm was present at the Medicine Lodge council, there is no evidence that the trader played any significant role in the council proceedings. Chisholm's name is conspicuously absent from the mountains of copy that was dispatched to eastern newspapers by the large corps of journalists who covered the event in great detail. The names of Philip McCusker and Charles Whittaker appear on the Comanche-Kiowa-Apache treaty documents as interpreters and witnesses.[24]

By the Treaty of Medicine Lodge, the Comanches, Kiowas, and Plains Apaches agreed to reside upon a reservation area in the

Jesse Chisholm was ill during the Medicine Lodge Council in October 1867, depicted here by J. Howland. From *Harper's Illustrated Weekly,* November 16, 1867.

vicinity of the Wichita Mountains just to the south of the Leased District. The Cheyennes and Arapahos accepted a reservation along the Salt Fork (of the Arkansas) in north-central Indian Territory, though apparently the Cheyenne Dog Soldiers did not realize the treaty stipulation or had no intention of settling there.[25]

It was clear to Chisholm that the postwar reconstruction had altered the status of things. Southern Kansas would soon be settled by whites. His place and heart were with the dwindling frontier that yet existed inside the Indian Territory.

Chisholm was still weak from his illness when, following the Treaty of Medicine Lodge, he arrived in Leavenworth to procure more trade goods from Durfee and Company for the coming winter's trade. It was during this trip to the town and while he was yet recovering that Chisholm visited the photographic studio of E. E. Henry and had made the one image of himself that remains for us today.[26] The picture, James Mead said, was taken "in his soiled and travel-worn clothes, just as he came in town with his train from the plains, and after he was much broken in health from a long spell of sickness. The picture conveys a poor idea of the man when in his prime."[27]

Chisholm spent several days in Leavenworth during the same period that other plainsmen of note were there, James Mead, William Mathewson, and Dutch Bill Greiffenstein being among them. Brevet Major General George Custer was present, too, impatiently waiting for his court-martial hearing on charges of deserting his post at Fort Wallace. Still another name soon to be of note in the region for his efforts to open the Indian Territory to settlement was that of Captain David L. Payne, who was just back from far southwestern Kansas where he had served in a futile search for Indians to fight.[28] Both Custer and Payne would play leading roles in the arena of the Indian Territory behind Jesse Chisholm.

Chisholm's presence was noted on November 17, 1867, by the *Leavenworth Daily Conservative*, which reported: "Durfee & Co. started old Jesse Chisholm to the southern Cheyenne country, in Northern Texas, with twenty-two wagons, containing $25,000 worth of goods." With the Leased District Indians now back in the Territory, Chisholm moved permanently back to the Council Grove site where he planted one hundred acres in corn and began construction of a log ranchhouse and trading post.[29] Following the Treaty of Medicine Lodge, Montford Johnson had become interested in the idea of opening a cattle ranch to the west of Council Grove between the two Canadian rivers. He had mentioned the notion to Chisholm, who discussed the idea with the Cheyennes and Arapahos who had been assigned to the area. They told Jesse that they would not bother Johnson so long as he did not employ white men, especially Texans.[30]

Neil R. Johnson described a buffalo-hunting expedition that took place just after Jesse's return from Medicine Lodge. Jesse headed a party of hunters that included Johnson's grandfather. Chisholm's teamster, Bill Cuttle, and William Chisholm drove wagons in which to bring back the hides and meat. Jesse led the party up the South Canadian some eight miles, camping the first night in a walnut grove at the mouth of a small stream. The next morning they rode up a draw, following its course until a small herd of buffalo was spotted grazing unsuspectingly on a flat. Jesse reconnoitered on foot, then returned to lead a mounted charge upon the herd. The hunters all made successful kills. Then the dead buffalo were skinned, their tongues, humps, and several sides of ribs cut away. These were laid upon the hides until the wagons arrived to carry the cargo back to camp. In the afternoon the meat was cut into long, thin strips and hung out on rawhide ropes to sun-dry.[31] This would be one of Jesse's last buffalo hunts. Not only his day but that of the great herds was soon to end as professional white hunters invaded the prairie. But there would be one final peacemaking mission for Jesse to perform.

In the spring of 1868 Chisholm was holding trade with the Indians at their consolidated encampment on the North Canadian.[32] Word reached Jesse that a band of hostile Comanche, Kiowa, and Cheyenne warriors had encountered a group of white surveyors, led by William Rankin, some twenty miles below on the river. The Indians had surrounded the white men, threatening them with death if they continued. Rankin had offered presents and tried to explain that he and his crew were surveying the Creek lands in accordance with their 1866 treaty. However, he could not pacify the warriors. Having learned that "Jesse Chisholm, an intelligent and highly influencial half breed Cherokee who has an extensive rancho and trading house," was in camp just upriver, Rankin sent a desperate plea for help.[33]

Jesse responded to Rankin's call and came to the assistance of the beleaguered surveyors. He remonstrated with the band against interfering with the surveyors, pointing out that they were working in the employ of the United States. If the men were harmed, he said, the government would consider it an act of hostility by their nations. But the prairie tribes had long since learned that the presence of surveyors inevitably meant a loss of their land. Even Chisholm's influence could not overcome the Indians' angry determination to halt Rankin and his crew. The badly scared surveyors were forced to flee to the safety of the Seminole Agency.[34]

Chisholm had been joined at the North Canadian camp by Mead, Greiffenstein, and other Kansas traders since the previous December. Mead twice departed the great encampment of Indians and traders, returning to Kansas during the winter and early spring for more goods. On the last occasion he arrived back at the trading grounds to find the site strangely deserted except for a huge flock of

A commemorative stone and engraved granite slab mark the presumed gravesite of Jesse Chisholm on the North Canadian River near Geary, Oklahoma. *Photograph by Stan Hoig.*

migratory wild geese. Gone were the hundreds of conical lodges with their cross-pole tops, the teeming crowds of tribespeople, the meat-drying racks, the trader's wagons, and the great horse herds that had spotted the landscape. Mead's experienced eye could read the signs of a hasty and excited exodus. Mystified, he headed his teams on down the North Fork toward Chisholm's place at Council Grove. After a few miles, he discovered a small enclosure fenced with freshly cut poles. Inside was a rock-covered mound with a board at its head into which, according to Mead's 1890 account, had been inscribed:

"JESSIE CHISHOLM, Died, March 4th, 1868."[35]

Mead's memory was faulty on the date, however. The Chisholm family Bible lists Jesse's date of death as being "4th April 1868,"[36] and this is supported by newspaper accounts that indicate that Greiffenstein arrived in Kansas in late April to report the death of his friend to Edwin H. Durfee at Leavenworth.[37]

After finding Chisholm's grave, Mead continued on down the

North Canadian to Council Grove, where he found Greiffenstein, Whittaker, and other traders assembled. From them he heard the story of how Jesse had eaten from the pot of bear grease, how he had died from it, and how they had given him a proper burial.[38] Mead and Greiffenstein were joined by Greenway, and they all agreed that they should hold a wake in the memory of their departed friend. It was Mead who later wrote Chisholm's eulogy in the *Wichita Eagle* of May 23, 1890: "He was by nature noble, chivalrous and brave. An arbitrator among the wild tribes of the plains and territory, beloved and respected by all."

Mead also related a discussion he had had with Chisholm. "A few days before his [Chisholm's] unexpected and sudden death, in the course of a conversation he said: 'I know little about the Bible and churches, but the good God who sent me here, gave me the knowledge of right and wrong. I have never wronged anyone in my life. I have been a peacemaker among my brethren. No man ever went from my camp hungry or naked, and I am ready and willing to go to the home of the Great Spirit just as I am, whenever he calls for me.' "[39]

Even Mead, perhaps, did not know the full role that Jesse Chisholm and his forebears had played in the march of American history from Tennessee through Arkansas, the Indian Territory, Texas, and Kansas, or know the full extent to which Jesse's shadow had fallen across the major events and personalities of the times in which he lived. Yet there can be little challenge to the claim that the immortality that was brought to Jesse Chisholm by the chance application of his name to the great cattle trail from Texas to Kansas — the significant initial link in the advance of the white man across the homeland of the Comanches and Wichitas — was a fitting commemoration for one who had done so much in the cause of peace on the Plains and who in himself was a bridge between the distant worlds of the white man and the Indian.

Notes

Guide to Abbreviations

AMD-OHS. Archives and Manuscript Division, Oklahoma Historical Society

BTHC-UT. Barker Texas History Center, University of Texas

LIB-OHS. Library, Oklahoma Historical Society

OIA. U.S. Office of Indian Affairs

NA. National Archives

SCD-UA. Special Collections Department, University of Arkansas

WHC-UO. Western History Collection, University of Oklahoma

Prologue

1. J. S. Murrow to J. F. Weaver, December 13, 1911, Chisholm File, Joseph B. Thoburn Collection, AMD-OHS.
2. James Mead to J. B. Thoburn, July 29, 1908, ibid.
3. James R. Mead, "Reminiscences of Frontier Life," Mead Collection, Kansas State Historical Society, Wichita.

Chapter 1. The Chisholms and the Cherokees

1. *Leavenworth Daily Conservative,* May 8, 1868.
2. An affidavit by John Chisholm, Jesse's brother, on January 25, 1842 (First Cherokee Commission, Folder 1106, NA), establishes that Jesse's mother was not Martha Rogers, as has long been claimed, but rather a full-blooded Cherokee woman named Corn Tassel. While unfortunately no identity was given for her other than as the sister of a minor Arkansas chief named Corn Tassel, the name clearly indicates a bloodline connection to the famous principal chief. It is not clear if she and her brother were first- or second-generation descendants.

    All claims that Martha Rogers was Jesse's mother stem from misinterpretation of statements by Narcissa Owen in her *Memoirs of Narcissa Owen, 1831–1907,* 104. She refers to "Ignatius, who married Martha Rogers" and who "had a son named Jesse." This is not to say that Martha was Jesse's mother. Owen does state that Jesse had a sister named Martha, but she would have had to be a half sister.
3. William Tatham, who interpreted Old Tassel's talk at the Treaty of Long Island in July 1777, described the chief as a "stout, mild, and decided man, rather comely than otherwise, who, through a long and useful life in his own country, was never

known to stoop to a falsehood." John P. Brown, *Old Frontiers, the Story of the Cherokee Indians,* 167 fn. 12.

4. "Corn Tassle Talk," *Calendar of Virginia State Papers* IV, 306.

5. Sam'l C. Williams, ed., "Tatham's Characters Among the North American Indians," *Tennessee Historical Magazine* VII, 3 (October 1921):176–78 (emphasis in original).

6. J.G.M. Ramsey, *Annals of Tennessee, 1797–1884,* 419–20.

7. Frederick Jackson Turner, "Documents on the Blount Conspiracy, 1795–1797," *American Historical Review* X (1904–1905):574–601.

8. Samuel Cole Williams, *History of the Lost State of Franklin,* 30.

9. *Territorial Papers of the United States,* comp. and ed., Clarence Edwin Carter, IV, 67.

10. Kate White, "John Chisholm, a Soldier of Fortune," *East Tennessee Historical Society Publications* I (1929):61.

11. John Chisholm's slave-dealing activities are clearly established in a letter he wrote to the governor of Kentucky, Isaac Shelby, indicating he would deliver "the Negroes, according to promise," and that he intended to carry on the business extensively. John Chisholm to Governor Shelby, January 24, 1795, Draper Collection, II, 53, WHC-UO.

12. Mary U. Rothrock, *A History of Knox County, Tennessee,* 396–98. There may well have been other children. James Chisholm, who resided within a mile of the Hiwassee blockhouse, was identified as Ignatius's brother by Doublehead. James Chisholm to Meigs, undated but received July 5, 1803, and Doublehead to Meigs, June 24, 1803; Records of the Cherokee Agency in Tennessee (hereafter Records, Cherokee Agency), 1803–1804, NA.

13. "Impeachment of William Blount," in *Annals of Congress, Debates and Proceedings,* 4th–5th Congress, 2383, 2386.

14. Rothrock, *History of Knox County,* 396–97; Isabel Thompson, "The Blount Conspiracy," *East Tennessee Historical Publications* II (1930):6–7.

15. Chisholm to John McKee, March 17, 1797, *Annals of Congress,* 4th–5th Congress, 2347.

16. Turner, "Documents on the Blount Conspiracy," 595–605.

17. *New American State Papers* III, 190–92. This simple ploy may not have fooled his enemies, but it did much to confuse history. Chisholm's ruse was so successful that even Cherokee agent Return J. Meigs, in testifying to Chisholm's character, stated that John D. Chisholm was "like some other people [who] were duped by Mr. Chisholm who projected an attack on the Spanish Territory." Return J. Meigs to General Armstrong, June 24, 1814, Records, Cherokee Agency, 1816–1818, NA.

An examination of original documents in the National Archives leaves little doubt that the signature of John Chisholm (Chisolm) on the 1791 Treaty of Holston, on the confession statement signed in London in 1797, on many letters from John D. Chisholm in the Cherokee Agency file, as well as on two petitions from early Arkansas (cited in *Territorial Papers* XIV, 42, 528), and on the Cherokee treaty of 1817 are unmistakably by the same hand.

18. *American State Papers,* Class II, Indian Affairs, 704.

19. Details of Doublehead's murder in Records, Cherokee Agency, 1801–1835, NA, give good support to the eyewitness account in J.F.H. Claiborne, *Life and Times of Gen. Sam. Dale, the Mississippi Partisan,* 45–49.

20. Chisholm to Meigs, March 18, 1809, and Meigs to Chisholm, March 1809, Records, Cherokee Agency, 1808–1809, NA. The Cherokee chief's name is spelled various ways throughout historical records. Both he and Doublehead were signers of the Treaty of Holston in 1791, and both had met with President Jefferson at Washington, D.C., in 1806. Charles J. Kappler, comp. and ed., *Indian Treaties, 1778–1883,* 32; McMinn to secretary of war, January 10, 1818, Records, Cherokee Agency, 1817–1821, NA.

21. Tahlonteskee to Meigs, June 23, 1810, and June 17, 1811, Records, Cherokee Agency, 1810–1812, NA.

22. John D. Chisholm, June 28, 1812, ibid.

23. Knox County Court Minutes I, entry for February 4, 1797, and II, entry for April 13, 1802, Knox County Archives, Knoxville.

24. Texas Census Records, Cherokee County, 1850, NA.

25. Russell to Hempstead, November 1, 1813, in *Territorial Papers* XIV, 720–21.

26. A story in the November 17, 1867, *Leavenworth Daily Conservative,* undoubtedly based on an interview with Chisholm, indicates that Jesse was born in Tennessee and had been in the West sixty years (generally speaking).

27. Russell to Hempstead, in *Territorial Papers* XIV, 720–21. John D. Chisholm was witness to Lovely's will; *Wills and Administration of Arkansas County, Ark., 1814–19.*

28. Russell to Hempstead, in *Territorial Papers* XIV, 720–21.

29. Meigs to Armstrong, June 24, 1814, and John D. Chisholm to Meigs, July 22, 1814, Records, Cherokee Agency, 1813–1815, NA.

30. Clark to Lovely, May 2, 1816, in *Territorial Papers* XV, 134–35.

31. Grant Foreman, *Indians and Pioneers,* 46.

32. Ibid., 43–44, citing Jackson, McMinn, and Meriwether to secretary of war, July 9, 1817, Jackson Papers, 6559.

33. *Niles' Weekly Register* (Baltimore), September 27, 1817, 80.

34. Foreman, *Indians and Pioneers,* 58, citing William Clark to G. C. Sibley, November 11, 1817; Thomas Nuttall, *Nuttall's Journal of Travels into the Arkansas Territory During the Year 1819,* 192n.

35. Chisholm's death is indicated in a letter from Grubbs to Meigs, October 29, 1818, Records, Cherokee Agency, 1816–1818.

36. Nuttall, *Journal of Travels,* 174–75.

37. *Senate Executive Document No. 512,* 23d Cong., 1st sess., "Emigration of Indians," 133–42.

38. Cherokee chiefs to Calhoun, February 27, 1825, and ensuing correspondence, Correspondence of the Office of Indian Affairs (Central Office) and Related Records, Letters Received, Cherokee Agency West (hereafter Letters Received, Cherokee Agency West), 1824–1831, NA.

39. James D. Horan, *The McKenney-Hall Portrait Gallery of American Indians,* 266.

40. *Arkansas Gazette* (Little Rock), July 2, 1828.

Chapter 2. Frontier Fever

1. *Arkansas Intelligencer* (Van Buren), May 19, 1849.

2. Louise Barry, "Kansas Before 1854: A Revised Annals," *Kansas Historical Quarterly* XXIX, 1 (Spring 1963):59.

3. Nuttall, *Journal of Travels,* 109.

4. The Fort Gibson Post Returns for October 1826, AMD-OHS, list Assistant Surgeon J. W. Baylor as being absent since September 11 with an exploring party in the vicinity of the Salt Mountains. This would have been on the Cimarron in present-day Woodward County, Oklahoma. The entry indicates how little was known of the region north and west of Fort Gibson at the time.

5. *Wichita Eagle,* May 23, 1890.

6. *Senate Executive Document No. 512,* 23d Cong., 1st sess., "Emigration of Indians."

7. George Chisholm affidavits, Fourth Cherokee Commission, 1181, Record Group 75, NA.

8. Nelson Chisholm was murdered and robbed between Fort Gibson and Fort Smith during the spring of 1846; *Cherokee Advocate* (Tahlequah, Cherokee Nation), March 19, 1846. See Stan Hoig, "The Genealogy of Jesse Chisholm," *Chronicles of Oklahoma* LXVII, 2 (Summer 1989):194–205.

9. The application of the names Tiana and Talihina to Houston's Cherokee mate have no substance in fact. See Stan Hoig, "Diana, Tiana or Talihina, The Myth and Mystery of Sam Houston's Cherokee Wife," *Chronicles of Oklahoma* LXIV, 2 (Summer 1986):53–59, for a discussion of this subject.

10. Before coming west in 1817, Jolly had lived on Hiwassee Island, then known as Jolly's Island of the Tennessee River. Sam Houston had gone there in 1809. Diana Rogers is said to have been Jolly's niece. See Thomas M. N. Lewis and Madeline Kneberg, *Hiwassee Island, An Archaeological Account of Four Tennessee Indian Peoples,* 18.

11. Grant Foreman, *Advancing the Frontier,* 38. In a May 30, 1843, letter to John Rogers, Jr., who was either the brother, father, or uncle of Diana Rogers, thanking him for an offer of help in solving the Texas Indian problem, Houston referred to "our early and long friendship." "You have known me since I was a small boy," Houston recalled. Other than wishing Rogers and his family well, Houston gave no indication of his personal relations with the Rogers family. See Amelia W.

Williams and Eugene C. Barker, *The Writings of Sam Houston, 1793–1863* III, 399.

12. *Arkansas Gazette* (Little Rock), November 25, 1828.

13. Mary Whatley Clarke, in *Chief Bowles and the Texas Cherokees*, 11–15, states that Bowles came west prior to 1800. Cherokee Agency correspondence indicates, however, that Bowles did not apply for a passport to come west until January 1810, and it was after that date that he and his group accompanied Tahlonteskee's party. See Meigs letter, January 10, 1810, and Bowles letter, January 26, 1810, Correspondence and Miscellaneous Records, Cherokee Agency East, 1801–1835, NA.

14. Carolyn Thomas Foreman, "Dutch, the Cherokee," *Chronicles of Oklahoma* XXVII, 3 (Autumn 1949): 252–67.

15. Stephen F. Austin to Cherokee chiefs, April 24 and May 8, 1826, in Malcom D. McLean, comp. and ed., *Papers Concerning Robertson's Colony in Texas, 1823 through September 1826* II, 543–46, 565–66.

16. Carolyn Thomas Foreman, annot., "The Cherokee War Path," *Chronicles of Oklahoma* IX, 3 (September 1931):233 n. 2.

17. Houston to Col. Matthew Arbuckle, July 8, 1829, in Williams and Barker, *Writings of Sam Houston* I, 136–38.

18. Foreman, "Cherokee War Path," 239.

19. John Henry Brown, *Indian Wars and Pioneers of Texas,* 10–13.

20. *Arkansas Advocate* (Little Rock), April 17, 1835.

21. Claim presented by Dutch to the United States on March 19, 1833, Letters Received, Cherokee Agency West, 1840, NA.

22. Grant Foreman, *Indian Removal,* 72; Carolyn Thomas Foreman, "Report of Captain John Stuart," *Chronicles of Oklahoma* V, 1 (September 1927):333–47.

Chapter 3. Beyond the Cross Timbers

1. Report of Lt. Dawson to Gen. Arbuckle, printed in the *Arkansas Advocate* (Little Rock), March 9 and 16, 1831.

2. *Missouri Republican* (St. Louis), June 15, 1826.

3. Washington Irving, *A Tour of the Prairies,* 1–22.

4. Grant Foreman, *Pioneer Days in the Early Southwest,* 103–4.

5. Otis E. Young, "The United States Mounted Ranger Battalion, 1832–33," *Mississippi Valley Historical Review* XLI, 4 (December 1954):468–69. Sam Houston, who was then making his first trip into Texas, was asked to help rescue Abbay. He met with a Comanche chief at Mexía and was told that it was probably the Pawnees who had taken him. See Williams and Barker, *Writings of Sam Houston* I, 279–80.

6. Foreman, *Pioneer Days,* 116–19.

7. George Shirk, "Peace on the Plains," *Chronicles of Oklahoma* XXVIII, 1 (Spring 1950):6. Arbuckle was greatly insulted at being replaced by Leavenworth, who diplomatically declined an invitation to a dinner, replete with military band and the firing of howitzers, thrown for Arbuckle before he left for Virginia on furlough; *Arkansas Gazette* (Little Rock), July 1, 1834.

8. Irving, *Tour of the Prairies,* 12–14.

9. George Catlin, *Letters and Notes on the Manners, Customs, and Conditions of the North American Indians* II, 72–75.

10. James Hildreth, *Dragoon Campaigns to the Rocky Mountains,* 104–5.

11. *Senate Executive Document No. 1,* 23d Cong., 2d sess., "Colonel Henry Dodge's Journal," 74–75 (hereafter "Dodge's Journal"). See also accounts in the *Arkansas Gazette* (Little Rock), September 9, 1834, by Colonel S. C. Stambaugh and in the *Arkansas Advocate* (Little Rock), October 31, 1834, reprinted from the *Kentucky Gazette* and quite possibly written by Kentuckian Lieutenant Jefferson Davis.

12. Fred S. Perrine, ed., "The Journal of Hugh Evans," *Chronicles of Oklahoma* III, 3 (September 1925): 184.

13. "Dodge's Journal," 76–77.

14. Catlin, *North American Indians,* 84–85.

15. Ibid., 64; "Dodge's Journal," 79.

16. "A Fragment of History," *Chronicles of Oklahoma* XIII, 4 (December 1935):483; Perrine, "Journal of Hugh Evans," 193; "Dodge's Journal," 82; Catlin, *North American Indians,* 70.

17. "Dodge's Journal," 87.

18. Foreman, *Advancing the Frontier,* 26.

19. "Dodge's Journal," 87.

20. Ibid.; Letters Received by Adjutant General's Office (Main Series), 1834, NA.

21. Catlin, *North American Indians,* 76–77.

22. Ibid., 79.

23. Ibid., 80.

24. *Army and Navy Chronicle* (Washington, D.C.), August 27 and November 5, 1835.

25. Foreman, *Advancing the Frontier,* 131–34.

26. Owen, *Memoirs,* 45, 123; Emmet Starr, *Cherokees West, 1794–1839,* 123–24. Narcissa Owen was not entirely correct when she stated that her father, Thomas Chisholm, was the last hereditary chief of the Western Cherokees. He did not gain his post by heredity but by election, and his father, John D. Chisholm, was never a chief.

27. *The Times* (Little Rock), March 7, 1835, reported that the Comanches and Wacos had already been in to trade. The fort was almost finished, and the men were preparing to plant corn, put in a garden, and build some boats in which to haul their furs downriver.

Chapter 4. The Canadian River Advance

1. Thomas James, *Three Years Among the Mexicans and the Indians; Arkansas Gazette* (Little Rock), July 22, 1823. For an account of the James expedition and its arrival in Santa Fe see the *Missouri Republican* (St. Louis), August 27, 1823.

2. Grant Foreman, ed., "The Journal of the Proceedings at Our First Treaty with the Wild Indians, 1835," *Chronicles of Oklahoma* XIV, 4 (December 1936): 394.

3. Harold W. Jones, ed., "The Diary of the Assistant Surgeon Leonard McPhail," *Chronicles of Oklahoma* XVIII, 3 (September 1940):285.

4. General Matthew Arbuckle to Mason, May 18, 1835, Fort Gibson Letter Book, 1834–1836, AMD-OHS.

5. *Daily National Intelligencer* (Washington, D.C.), September 18, 1835.

6. Josiah Gregg, *Commerce of the Prairies,* 17–19.

7. *Niles' Weekly Register* (Baltimore), October 17, 1835.

8. Jones, "Diary of McPhail," 288.

9. *Army and Navy Chronicle* (Washington, D.C.), October 1, 1835.

10. Foreman, "First Treaty," 406.

11. Stokes to Arbuckle, September 23, 1835, in Lewis Cass Papers, Box C-32, WHC-UO.

12. Return of Creeks Vaccinated by Doctor George L. Weed in the Creek Nation in July 1832, Letters Received, Creek Agency West, 1826–1836, NA.

13. Edwards's Trading Post file, Grant Foreman Collection, AMD-OHS; Grant Foreman, ed. and annot., *A Traveler in Indian Territory, the Journal of Ethan Allen Hitchcock,* 156.

14. T. U. Taylor, "In the Land of the Chisholms," *Frontier Times* XV, 11 (August 1938):499.

15. Roll of Claims Against Osages Presented to Major William Armstrong, January 11, 1839, to February 1, 1842, Correspondence of the Office of Indian Affairs (Central Office) and Related Records, Letters Received, Western Superintendency (hereafter Letters Received, Western Superintendency), 1842–1845, NA.

16. J. S. Murrow to Joseph B. Thoburn, December 13, 1911, Chisholm File, Joseph B. Thoburn Collection, AMD-OHS. Murrow performed the wedding ceremony for Jesse's son William and Julia McLish.

17. P. L. Chouteau to Stokes, April 19, 1836, and A. P. Chouteau to C. A. Harris, November 25, 1837, Lewis Cass Papers, Box C-32, WHC-UO.

18. George Bird Grinnell, *The Fighting Cheyennes,* 45–49.

19. A. P. Chouteau account of Wolf Creek battle, June 28, 1838, Letters Received, Western Superintendency, 1837–1839, NA; debate in Senate, published in the *Daily National Intelligencer* (Washington, D.C.), April 16, 1839.

20. Foreman, *Traveler, Journal of Hitchcock,* 156.

21. Statement of goods and provisions furnished Comanches and Kiowas who lately visited Choctaw Agency on way to Washington, in ibid.; George Chisholm to Gov.

P. M. Butler, January 20, 1843, Letters Received, Western Superintendency, 1842–1843, NA.

22. William Armstrong, letter of June 8, 1839, Letters Received, Western Superintendency, NA.

23. Grant Foreman, *Marcy and the Gold Seekers,* 4–5; Foreman, *Advancing the Frontier,* 219.

24. Baldwin Möllhausen, *Diary of a Journey from the Mississippi to the Coasts of the Pacific with a U.S. Government Expedition,* 93.

25. Aurora Hunt, *Major General James Henry Carleton, 1814–1873,* 49–50; statement of Jesse Chisholm, September 17, 1845, Special Files Office of Indian Affairs (hereafter OIA Special Files), 35–57, NA.

26. Herbert Eugene Bolton, *Texas in the Middle Eighteenth Century,* 87–89, 93.

27. Statement of George Brinton, September 19, 1845, and James Logan to commissioner of Indian affairs, September 28, 1845; OIA Special Files, 35–47, NA; Joseph W. Robertson to James S. Mayfield, April 7, 1841, in *Senate Executive Document No. 14,* III, 32d Cong., 1st sess., 57–58. It was claimed that Edwards's place became a clearinghouse of sorts for rescued children; Grant Foreman Collection, AMD-OHS. It is not unlikely that captive slave children passed through Edwards's post since it was the most forward point on the Canadian River frontier, but this appears to be an overstatement of the situation.

28. Bill of Sale by Jesse Chisholm to Lucinda Edwards, January 24, 1841, OIA Special Files, 5, NA.

29. Clarke, *Chief Bowles,* 110.

30. Joseph W. Robertson to James S. Mayfield, April 7, 1841, in James H. Winfrey and James M. Day, eds., *Indian Papers of Texas and the Southwest, 1860–1916,* I, 122–23; *Senate Executive Document No. 14,* 32d Cong., 2d sess., III, 57–58.

31. Foreman, *Traveler, Journal of Hitchcock,* 156.

32. Ibid.

33. Report of John Drew to P. M. Butler, January 3, 1843, Letters Received, Cherokee Agency, 1843, NA.

34. The list of eighty-eight names in John Drew's company includes (Albert) Finney Chisholm, son of Thomas Chisholm. Albert Finney Chisholm died at Fort Gibson in 1862. See Grant Foreman Collection, Box 4, Archives-Manuscripts, AMD-OHS.

35. John Ross to P. M. Butler, December 11, 1842, Letters Received, Cherokee Agency, 1843, NA.

36. John Drew to P. M. Butler, January 3, 1843, ibid.

37. Edwards's Trading Post file, Grant Foreman Collection, AMD-OHS. In its February 5 and 12, 1897, issues, the *Fort Smith Elevator* published a highly prejudiced and false account of this frontier episode, stating that several of the recaptured slaves were hanged.

Chapter 5. Serving Sam Houston

1. Rupert Norval Richardson, *The Comanche Barrier to South Plains Settlement*, 110–12.

2. Winfrey and Day, *Indian Papers of Texas* II, 135–36.

3. Richardson, *Comanche Barrier*, 117–18.

4. Houston to Indian Commission, March 29, 1843, in Williams and Barker, *Writings of Sam Houston* III, 436–38.

5. Jesse was assisted by Luis Sánchez, Jim Shaw, Red Horse, and Jim Second-eye. Second-eye was the head war chief of the Delawares. His Indian name, Rokanoowho, meant the Long Traveler and was given to him because he had journeyed to such far-off places as Santa Fe, the Navaho villages, California, and Oregon.

6. W. P. Webb, "The Last Treaty of the Republic of Texas," *The Southwestern Historical Quarterly* XXV, 3 (January 1922):155.

7. Rupert Norval Richardson, *Frontier of Northwest Texas, 1846 to 1876*, 54. The three Torrey brothers, John, David, and Thomas, were all active in the Indian trade. John established the company that first began operation at New Braunfels, and died in 1893 after a career in business and farming. James was with the ill-fated Santa Fe expedition; following his release from a Mexican prison, he was active on the frontier until he died of illness at Bird's Fort in 1843. David, who was closely associated with Houston, was killed by a band of Apache and Comanche Indians near Presidio, Texas, in 1849. See Walter Prescott Webb, ed., *The Handbook of Texas* II, 790–91.

8. Winfrey and Day, *Indian Papers of Texas* II, 163. Terrell served as Texas secretary of state under President David G. Burnett and was later attorney general of Texas. He died in 1846.

9. *Arkansas Intelligencer* (Van Buren), June 24, 1843.

10. Winfrey and Day, *Indian Papers of Texas* II, 163.

11. Ibid., 150–51.

12. *Portraits of North American Indians . . . Painted by J. M. Stanley*, 50.

13. Jesse Chisholm was paid $245 for his services in connection with the Tehuacana Creek treaty; Winfrey and Day, *Indian Papers of Texas* II, 181–82.

14. Ibid., 153–54.

15. Ibid., 255. Eldridge would later become paymaster for the U.S. Navy and would be with Commodore Oliver Perry's expedition that opened Japan to world trade.

16. Ibid., 251–75.

17. Ibid., 242–46. Bird and his settlers were ordered away from the site in favor of the Peters Colony, which had legal title to the land, but the fort continued to be used from time to time. It later became known as Birdville. See Richardson, *Frontier of Northwest Texas*, 45–46.

18. Resolution of Old Settlers, September 14, 1843, Letters Received, Cherokee Agency, 1844, NA.

19. List of Tribes Attending Tahlequah Conference, Letters Received, Cherokee Agency, 1843, NA. Carolyn Thomas Foreman, "Pierce Mason Butler," *Chronicles of Oklahoma* XXX, 1 (Spring 1952):14.

20. David I. Bushnell, Jr., "John Mix Stanley, Artist-Explorer," *Smithsonian Annual Report, 1924,* 508.

21. *Portraits by Stanley,* 46.

22. Ibid., 44.

23. Bushnell, "John Mix Stanley," 510.

24. *Portraits by Stanley,* 9–13.

25. W. H. Clift, "Warren's Trading Post," *Chronicles of Oklahoma* II, 2 (June 1924):128–40.

26. H. G. Catlett to W. Medill, May 12, 1849, Correspondence of the Office of Indian Affairs (Central Office) and Related Records, Letters Received, Texas Agency (hereafter Letters Received, Texas Agency), 1847–1852, NA.

27. B. W. Alberty affidavit, Cherokee files, vol. 469, 107, AMD-OHS.

28. Winfrey and Day, *Indian Papers of Texas* II, 64; *Arkansas Intelligencer* (Van Buren), December 30, 1843, and January 6, 1844; *Portraits by Stanley,* 53.

29. *Arkansas Intelligencer* (Van Buren), December 30, 1844.

30. *Portraits by Stanley,* 53–55.

31. *Arkansas Intelligencer* (Van Buren), January 6, 1844.

32. Winfrey and Day, *Indian Papers of Texas* II, 23–24.

33. Ibid., 64–66.

34. Ibid., 59–61.

35. Ibid., 66.

36. Ibid., 25.

37. Williams and Barker, *Writings of Sam Houston* IV, 329.

38. Winfrey and Day, *Indian Papers of Texas* II, 62–72; Thomas G. Western to Benjamin Shoat, June 15, 1844, Record Book, Texas Bureau of Indian Affairs, Texas State Archives.

39. Winfrey and Day, *Indian Papers of Texas* II, 119–21.

40. Ibid.

41. Jonnie Wallis, *Sixty Years on the Brazos, the Life and Letters of John Washington Lockhart,* 98. While Lockhart's retrospective account is faulty in many ways, it is apparent that he was present at this meeting between Houston and the Indians.

42. Webb, "Last Treaty," 155–56.

43. Ibid., 157. Chisholm was paid $250 for his services in searching for the Comanches from October 12 to November 11, 1844, plus $94.75 for supplies as of December 9, 1844; ibid., 141, 148.

44. Ibid., 231–32.

45. Ibid., 157–69; Anna Muckleroy, "The Indian Policy of the Republic of Texas," *The Southwestern Historical Quarterly* XXVI, 3 (January 1923):196–99.

Chapter 6. In Search of Sequoyah

1. Brown, *Old Frontiers,* 478.
2. Grant Foreman, *Sequoyah,* 3–8.
3. P. M. Butler to T. Hartley Crawford, September 12, 1844, Letters Received, Cherokee Agency, 1844, in reference to letter from William M. Duval, August 8, 1844.
4. *Cherokee Advocate* (Tahlequah, Cherokee Nation), February 13, 1845.
5. *Arkansas Intelligencer* (Van Buren), March 29, 1845.
6. Ibid., May 3, 1845.
7. *Arkansas Intelligencer* (Van Buren), May 24, 1845.
8. Foreman, *Sequoyah,* 71.
9. *Cherokee Advocate* (Tahlequah, Cherokee Nation), June 26, 1845.
10. *Arkansas Intelligencer* (Van Buren), February 22 and March 15, 1845.
11. *Cherokee Advocate* (Tahlequah, Cherokee Nation), June 19 and August 21, 1845.
12. Ibid., May 29, 1845.
13. Clift, "Warren's Trading Post," 135.
14. Lee David Benton, "An Odyssey into Texas," *Chronicles of Oklahoma* LX, 2 (Summer 1982):116–17.
15. William Minor Quesenbury Diary, 1845–1861, SCD-UA; original held in Duke University Library.
16. Ibid.
17. Ibid.

Chapter 7. Council at Comanche Peak

1. Richardson, *Comanche Barrier,* 140.
2. *Cherokee Advocate* (Tahlequah, Cherokee Nation), July 2, 1846.
3. *Report of Messrs. Butler and Lewis,* September 13, 1845, 4–5.
4. *Cherokee Advocate* (Tahlequah, Cherokee Nation), May 28, 1846.
5. "The Journal of Elijah Hicks," *Chronicles of Oklahoma* XIII, 1 (March 1935):69; *Arkansas Intelligencer* (Van Buren), January 24 and February 7, 1846.
6. *Report of Butler and Lewis,* 3–4.
7. "Journal of Elijah Hicks," 70–72.
8. *Cherokee Advocate* (Tahlequah, Cherokee Nation), July 2, 1846.
9. *Report of Butler and Lewis,* 5–6.

10. Richardson, *Frontier of Northwest Texas,* 57. Barnard, who was also taken prisoner as a member of the Santa Fe Expedition, worked for the Torreys and was responsible for locating the post at Tehuacana Creek. He later operated a store and stone mill near the Comanche Peak site. See Webb, *Handbook of Texas* I, 111.

11. Benton, "Odyssey," 124–25.

12. "Journal of Elijah Hicks," 80.

13. Ibid., 82–83.

14. Ibid., 79–84.

15. Ibid., 84–85.

16. Ibid., 90–92.

17. Ibid., 92–95.

18. Ibid., 93–94.

19. Ibid., 94.

20. Ibid.; *Daily National Intelligencer* (Washington, D.C.), May 23, 1846.

21. "Journal of Elijah Hicks," 94.

22. Ibid., 96.

23. *New Orleans Picayune,* May 22, 1846.

24. "Journal of Elijah Hicks," 96–97.

25. Neighbors to Medill, July 21, 1846, Robert S. Neighbors Papers, BTHC-UT.

26. *Report of Butler and Lewis,* 13; *Baltimore Sun,* July 10, 1846.

27. "Journal of Elijah Hicks," 95.

28. Ibid., 89.

29. Ibid., 92.

30. *Report of Butler and Lewis,* 17–19.

31. *New Orleans Picayune,* May 22 and 23, 1846.

32. Ibid., June 20, 1846.

33. "Journal of Elijah Hicks," 97–98.

34. Ibid., 98.

35. Ibid.

36. Kappler, *Indian Treaties,* 554–57.

37. "Journal of Elijah Hicks," 99.

38. Ibid., 98.

39. Ibid., 99.

Chapter 8. A Visit to Washington

1. *Baltimore Sun,* June 27, 1846. The commission purchased a bay horse from Jesse

Chisholm for $35 to provide transportation for a Cherokee from Torrey's Trading House; voucher, P. M. Butler, May 20, 1846, NA.

2. *Alexandria Gazette & Virginia Register,* June 13 and 17, 1840, citing *New Orleans Topic.*

3. Butler to Medill, June 28, 1846, Letters Received, 1838–1848, Office of Indian Affairs Letter Books (hereafter OIA Letter Books) I, BTHC-UT.

4. *Baltimore Sun,* June 27, 1846, citing *Cumberland* (Maryland) *Civilian.*

5. *Daily National Intelligencer* (Washington, D.C.), June 29, 1846.

6. Ibid., June 16, 1846.

7. Turner, "Documents on the Blount Conspiracy," 602.

8. Owen, *Memoirs,* 50.

9. *Daily National Intelligencer* (Washington, D.C.), June 29, 1846.

10. Milo Milton Quaife, ed., *The Diary of James K. Polk* II, 3–4, 30, 46.

11. Ibid.

12. Ibid.

13. *Alexandria Gazette & Virginia Register,* July 25, 1846.

14. *Cherokee Advocate* (Tahlequah, Cherokee Nation), August 6, 1846.

15. *Columbian Fountain* (Washington, D.C.), July 24, 1846.

16. Ibid., July 27, 1846.

17. Ibid., June 30, 1846.

18. *New Orleans Picayune,* May 26 and June 21, 1846.

19. Ibid., June 19, 1846.

20. *Cherokee Advocate* (Tahlequah, Cherokee Nation), April 2, 1846.

21. *Columbian Fountain,* August 13, 1846, citing *Alexandria Democrat.*

22. *Alexandria Gazette,* July 3 and 4, 1846; *Cherokee Advocate* (Tahlequah, Cherokee Nation), August 6, 1846; Sims to Medill, July 16, 1846, OIA Letter Books I, BTHC-UT.

23. *Daily National Intelligencer* (Washington, D.C.), July 8, 1846.

24. *New York Herald,* July 24, 1846.

25. Quaife, *Diary of Polk* II, 29; Moty Kinnard to OIA, July 7, 1846, OIA Letter Book No. I, BTHC-UT.

26. *Arkansas Intelligencer* (Van Buren), August 22, 1846.

27. Quaife, *Diary of Polk,* 46; Sims to Medill, July 9, 1846, in OIA Letter Books I; *New York Herald,* July 24, 1846.

28. *Daily National Intelligencer* (Washington, D.C.), September 21, 1846.

29. J. A. Briggs to Medill, August 31, 1846, OIA Letter Books I, BTHC-UT.

30. Ibid., December 9, 1846; Williams and Barker, *Writings of Sam Houston* VIII, 40–41.

Chapter 9. Comanche Captives

1. T. U. Taylor, *Jesse Chisholm*, 47, 132–33.
2. Ibid., 29.
3. These included Frank Chisholm, born about 1855; Mary Chisholm, born about 1860; and Lucinda Chisholm, date of birth unknown. See Hoig, "Genealogy of Jesse Chisholm," 194–205.
4. *Washington* (Arkansas) *Telegraph*, August 14, 1850.
5. Report of Creek chiefs, May 11, 1844, Letters Received, Western Superintendency, 1844–1845, NA.
6. John Galvin, ed., *Lieutenant James W. Abert's March*, 61; François des Montaignes (Isaac Cooper), *The Plains*, 159.
7. Taylor, *Jesse Chisholm*, 132–34, 147–48, 151. It is evident that the sandstone shed, located on private property two miles east of Asher, Oklahoma, has been repaired on occasion over the years, but it is very likely the same basic structure as originally erected by Chisholm and his son William prior to the Civil War. Photos taken by T. U. Taylor on his visit to the place in the summer of 1930 show two log cabins that are no longer there. A marker was placed on State Highway 39 by the Pottawatomie County Historical Society in October 1838. See "Chisholm Spring Trading Post," *Chronicles of Oklahoma* XLIV, 2 (Summer 1966):204–5.
8. Howard F. Van Zandt, "The History of Camp Holmes and Chouteau's Trading Post," *Chronicles of Oklahoma* XIII, 3 (September 1935):328.
9. Foreman, *Advancing the Frontier*, 174–75.
10. "Journal of Elijah Hicks," 70; *Arkansas Intelligencer* (Van Buren), June 14, 1845.
11. M. Duval to W. L. Marcy, May 20, 1847, Correspondence of the Office of Indian Affairs (Central Office) and Related Records, Letters Received, Seminole Agency (hereafter Letters Received, Seminole Agency), 1846–1855, NA.
12. Mrs. Jennie Chisholm Davis to J. B. Thoburn, September 5, 1911, and Davis to Thoburn, undated, Chisholm file, Joseph B. Thoburn Collection, AMD-OHS.
13. Joseph B. Thoburn and Muriel Wright, "The Story of the Mexican Captive," in their *Oklahoma, a History of the State and Its People* II, 823–24.
14. Ibid. See Documented Life of Vincente de Huersus, Vincente Chisholm File, AMD-OHS.
15. Thoburn and Wright, "Mexican Captive," 823–24.

Chapter 10. On the Gold Rush Trail

1. M. Duval to Medill, March 25, 1849, Letters Received, Texas Agency, 1847–1852, NA.
2. Ibid. One Mexican boy who was brought in at this time "by some Cherokees" was sold to a blacksmith for $100.

3. *Fort Smith Herald,* May 2, 1849.

4. James Logan to Samuel M. Rutherford, April 11, 1849, Letters Received, Western Superintendency, 1849–1851, NA.

5. M. Duval to Samuel M. Rutherford, March 9, 1849, ibid.; Foreman, *Advancing the Frontier,* 246, citing Duval to Medill, March 25, 1849.

6. *Fort Smith Herald,* March 28, 1849.

7. Ibid.

8. Ibid., June 2, 1849.

9. Ibid., June 6, 1849. Alexander, George, and Thomas Aird were licensed traders with the Seminoles; Thomas Aird operated as clerk at the Little River post. See Records of the Southern Superintendency, 1854–1857, NA.

10. Mrs. Jennie Chisholm Davis to J. B. Thoburn, September 5, 1911, and Davis to Thoburn, undated, Chisholm file, Joseph B. Thoburn Papers, AMD-OHS.

11. Robert H. Dott, "Lieutenant Simpson's California Road Through Oklahoma," *Chronicles of Oklahoma* XXXVIII, 2 (Summer 1960):175.

12. Ibid., 161.

13. M. Duval to Medill, June 4, 1849, Letters Received, Seminole Agency, 1824–1876, NA.

14. Foreman, *Marcy and the Gold Seekers,* 34.

15. *Choctaw Telegraph* (Doaksville), July 19, August 20, and October 11, 1849.

16. Ibid., August 30, 1849.

17. Foreman, *Marcy and the Gold Seekers,* 166, citing *Fort Smith Herald,* July 13, 1850.

18. Newspaper clipping from *Fort Smith Herald,* July 1849, Letters Received, Texas Agency, 1847–1852, NA.

19. *Washington* (Arkansas) *Telegraph,* August 14 and 16, May 14 and 21, and June 11, 1851.

20. Articles of Treaty between Judge John H. Rollins and Comanches, Lipans, Etc., on December 10, 1850, Letters Received, Texas Agency, 1847–1852, NA. See also Winfrey and Day, *Indian Papers of Texas* III, 130–36.

21. Winfrey and Day, *Indian Papers of Texas* III, 130–36.

22. Williams and Barker, *Writings of Sam Houston* V, 345 n. 3.

23. Winfrey and Day, *Indian Papers of Texas* III, 130–36.

24. *Washington* (Arkansas) *Telegraph,* July 16, 1851.

Chapter 11. Diminishing Frontier

1. Edwin C. McReynolds, *The Seminoles,* 262–63.

2. Ibid.

3. *Fort Smith Herald,* March 21, 1851; *Daily National Intelligencer* (Washington, D.C.), January 8, April 9, and August 23, 1851.

4. *Daily National Intelligencer* (Washington, D.C.), March 10 and 31, 1851.

5. *Fort Smith Herald,* March 21, 1851.

6. *Daily National Intelligencer* (Washington, D.C.), July 2, 1851.

7. Ibid., May 15 and July 4, 1851.

8. Ibid., October 30 and November 10, 1851.

9. Israel G. Vore, who had previously managed a store at Pheasant Bluff on the Arkansas River, entered into partnership with Thomas A. Aird as early as 1849. He had fortunately been away from home in 1843 when his merchant father and his mother were murdered, robbed, and their home burned by the three Starr brothers. See Carolyn Thomas Foreman, "Israel Vore and the Levering Manual Labor School," *Chronicles of Oklahoma* XXV, 3 (Autumn 1947):198–200.

10. Ibid., 205.

11. Grant Foreman, *Adventure on the Red River,* ix–x; *Daily National Intelligencer* (Washington, D.C.), May 22, 1851.

12. Toshuhquash to Drew, July 19, 1852, Thompson Kenny Papers, AMD-OHS. White Tail had signed the Treaty of Comanche Peak and had been with the delegation that had later visited Washington with Chisholm; *Baltimore Sun,* June 27, 1846.

13. Berlin B. Chapman, "Establishment of the Wichita Reservation," *Chronicles of Oklahoma* XI, 4 (December 1933):1045–56.

14. *Daily National Intelligencer* (Washington, D.C.), June 26, and December 10 and 24, 1851.

15. Richardson, *Frontier of Northwest Texas,* 44, 104.

16. *Daily National Intelligencer* (Washington, D.C.), May 10, 1853; S. G. Simmons to Jefferson Davis, November 12, 1853, Letters Received, Texas Agency, 1853–1854, NA; Charles E. Mix to Thomas S. Drew, May 26, 1853, Correspondence of the Office of Indian Affairs (Central Office) and Related Records, Letters Received, Southern Superintendency (hereafter Letters Received., Southern Superintendency), 1853, NA.

17. *Daily National Intelligencer* (Washington, D.C.), August 17, 1853.

18. Ibid., September 4, 1854; *Marcy and Neighbors Exploration of Big Wichita and Brazos Headwaters in 1854,* Western Americana Microfilm Series, Reel 5890.

19. *Report of Commissioner of Indian Affairs, 1853,* 373, 384.

20. *Fort Smith Herald,* April 30, 1853; *St. Louis* (Missouri) *Republican,* May 14, 1853.

21. Möllhausen, *Diary of a Journey,* 15; Lona Shawver, annot., "Stanley Explores Oklahoma," *Chronicles of Oklahoma* XXII, 3 (Autumn 1944):263–64; *Senate Executive Document No. 78,* 33d Cong., 1st Sess., "Report of Exploration and Surveys to Ascertain the Most Practicable and Economical Route for a Railroad from the Mississippi River to the Pacific Ocean" III, 19–22.

22. *Senate Executive Document No. 78*, 19.

23. Grant Foreman, ed., "The Journal of Lieutenant A. W. Whipple," *Chronicles of Oklahoma* XXVIII, 3 (Autumn 1950):262, 265.

24. *Senate Executive Document No. 78*, 19.

25. Foreman, "Journal of A. W. Whipple," 266–68.

26. Ibid., 269.

27. *Senate Executive Document No. 78*, 22.

28. Ibid.

29. Ibid.

30. Foreman, "Journal of A. W. Whipple," 272.

31. *Senate Executive Document No. 78*, 33.

32. *Southwest Independent* (Fayetteville), June 23 and August 3, 1854.

33. *Missouri Democrat* (St. Louis), July 28, 1855.

34. Robert S. Neighbors, who came to Texas just after the Battle of San Jacinto, served in the Texas Volunteer Army and the Texas Rangers. In 1843 he was one of forty-three prisoners taken at Bexar and imprisoned in Mexico. After his release, he entered the hotel business in Houston but did not like it. He accepted an appointment as agent for the Lipans and Tonkawas, quickly proving himself a just agent who was always considerate of his charges. In 1850 he was assigned the task of establishing the Santa Fe country as four Texas counties. He was elected to the Texas House of Representatives the following year, and in 1852 was Democratic presidential elector. See Williams and Barker, *Writings of Sam Houston* V, 165–67.

35. *Report of Commissioner of Indian Affairs, 1856*, 175.

Chapter 12. War on the Comanchería

1. James R. Mead, *Hunting and Trading on the Great Plains, 1859–1875*, 220. Strangely, no descriptive account of the trading post has yet surfaced, despite all of the Texas cattle traffic that passed by. Remnants of a well and broken pieces of china were found on the site when it was homesteaded in 1889 by J. A. Young. Through the efforts of the Oklahoma City Chapter of the D.A.R., a historic marker commemorating the site was placed just east and north of the Northwest Tenth Street bridge in Oklahoma City on April 22, 1941. In 1884 a sawmill operated there, and barracks were set up for Fort Reno troops detailed to cut wood at Council Grove. See James W. Moffitt, ed., "Historical Notes," *Chronicles of Oklahoma* XIX, 2 (June 1941):186, and "Chisholm Spring Trading Post," 200–201; Report of D.A.R. Historical Marker Committee, vertical files, LIB-OHS; Jim Cloud, "Jesse Chisholm's Old Ranch Located," *The War Chief of the Indian Territory Posse of Oklahoma Westerners* XIX, 3 (December 1985).

2. Thoburn and Wright, *Oklahoma*, appendix, 861. Some accounts say that Jesse hauled iron kettles to the location and manufactured salt in them. A National Register report by the Oklahoma State Historical Society states that two iron

vats were brought to the site in 1894 by Jeff Saunders, an old trail driver. The site of the salt springs is Section 23, T18N, R12W, southeast of Southard, Oklahoma. The salt could be picked up in chunks. Niel R. Johnson, in *The Chickasaw Rancher,* 26–27, tells how his father, who ranched near Council Grove in 1868, described the technique used to boil salt water in iron kettles, producing pure salt.

3. H. S. Tennant, "The Two Cattle Trails," *Chronicles of Oklahoma* XIV, 1 (March 1936):113–14. The Johnson ranch was originally due south of Council Grove and was called Johnsonville. Johnson later moved west along the river and established Silver City.

4. Neal W. Evans to F. G. Barde, June 26, 1912, Barde Collection, AMD-OHS; Captain George T. Robinson to George A. Reynolds, March 31, 1868, Correspondence of the Office of Indian Affairs (Central Office) and Related Records, Letters Received, Kiowa Agency (hereafter Letters Received, Kiowa Agency), 1864–1868, NA; James Wortham to N. G. Taylor, June 27, 1868, Correspondence of the Office of Indian Affairs (Central Office) and Related Records, Letters Received, Creek Agency, 1864–1868, NA.

5. *Leavenworth Daily Conservative,* September 28, 1867.

6. *Daily National Intelligencer* (Washington, D.C.), February 18 and July 11, 1857.

7. Ibid., July 11, 1857; Kenneth W. Porter, "Wild Cat's Death and Burial," *Chronicles of Oklahoma* XXI, 1 (March 1943):41–43.

8. Grant Foreman, ed., "A Journal Kept by Douglas Cooper," *Chronicles of Oklahoma* V, 4 (December 1927):385 n. 10.

9. *Daily National Intelligencer* (Washington, D.C.), April 5, 1858.

10. A. H. McKissick to R. P. Pulliam, April 15, 1858, Letters Received, Western Superintendency, 1847–1851, NA.

11. John S. Ford served in the Texas army from 1837 to 1840 before taking the profession of a frontier doctor. Finding this life too dull, he entered politics and served in the Texas Senate until the Mexican War, when he was with Scott's army on its march to Mexico City. In 1858 Governor Runnels placed him in command of the Texas frontier. Ford also served with the Texas Confederate Army and later reentered state politics. He was superintendent of the state Deaf and Dumb Asylum before dying at San Antonio in 1897. See Williams and Barker, *Writings of Sam Houston* VII, 391–94.
    Interestingly, among the Ranger guides were two Wacos named Sam Houston's Son and Sam Houston's Brother; List of Indians Who Served with Van Dorn and Ford in 1868, Letters Received, Kiowa Agency, NA.

12. John S. Ford to Gov. Runnels, May 22, 1858, "Protection of the Frontier of Texas," in *House Executive Document No. 27,* 35th Cong., 2d sess., 17–21; John S. Ford Memoirs IV, 676ff, BTHC-UT.

13. Foreman, "Journal by Cooper," 381–90; Cooper to Rector, July 24 and August 5, 1858, Letters Received, Southern Superintendency, 1858, NA.

14. *Daily National Intelligencer* (Washington, D.C.), August 23, 1858.

15. Joseph B. Thoburn, "Battle with Comanches," *Sturm's Oklahoma Magazine* X, 6 (August 1910):22–28.

16. Van Dorn to Withers, October 5, 1858, in *Senate Executive Document No. 1,* 35th Cong., 2d sess., II, 272–74.

17. Report of Agent Blair, December 1, 1858, Records of the Southern Superintendency, 1858, NA.

18. Grant Foreman, ed., "Survey of a Wagon Road from Fort Smith to the Colorado River," *Chronicles of Oklahoma* XII, 1 (March 1934):76.

19. *House Executive Document No. 42,* 36th Cong., 1st sess., October 28, 1858, 76–77.

20. Ibid., 14.

21. Ibid., 16.

22. Ibid., 17.

23. Ibid., 81.

24. J. R. Crump report in ibid., 57; *Report of the Commissioner of Indian Affairs, 1859,* 709–10. A group of Americans led by Colonel B.L.E. Bonneville and including Congressman John S. Phelps of Missouri and J. L. Collins, superintendent of Indian affairs for New Mexico, rode east from New Mexico just behind Crump. It has been misinterpreted that some of the party visited Chisholm's Ranch at Council Grove; but there is no evidence that either group did so, nor has any descriptive account of a visitation to Chisholm's post at Council Grove during this period surfaced. See Joseph B. Thoburn and Isaac M. Holcomb, *A History of Oklahoma,* 70–71; Ray Asplin, "History of Council Grove in Oklahoma," *Chronicles of Oklahoma* XLV, 4 (Winter 1967/68):437; and Moffitt, "Historical Notes," 186.

25. Letter from Fort Washita, March 2, 1859, published in the *Missouri Democrat* (St. Louis), March 6, 1859.

26. *Missouri Democrat* (St. Louis), March 2, 1859.

27. Joseph B. Thoburn, "Indian Fight in Ford County," *Collections of Kansas Historical Society* XII (1911–1912):312–29.

28. Richardson, *Frontier of Northwest Texas,* 195–96.

29. Ibid., 197.

30. Report of James Logan, Creek Agency, Letters Received, Western Superintendency, 1844–1845, NA.

31. Richardson, *Frontier of Northwest Texas,* 199–200.

32. Ibid., 202.

33. *Missouri Democrat* (St. Louis), July 25, 1859, citing *Fort Smith Times,* July 14, 1859.

34. Muriel H. Wright, "A History of Fort Cobb," *Chronicles of Oklahoma* XXXIV, 1 (Spring 1956):54–55; Chapman, "Establishment of Wichita Reservation," 1048.

35. Thoburn and Wright, *Oklahoma,* 292.

36. Wright, "History of Fort Cobb," 55.

37. Voucher, September 6, 1859, Correspondence of the Office of Indian Affairs (Central Office) and Related Records, Letters Received, Wichita Agency (hereafter Letters Received, Wichita Agency), 1857–1858, NA.

38. Thoburn and Wright, *Oklahoma,* 292.

39. Ibid., 293; Blain to A. B. Greenwood, July 3, 1860, Letters Received, Southern Superintendency, 1860–1861, NA; newspaper clipping re murder of Neighbors, Letters Received, Western Superintendency, 1847–1851, NA; William Burkett to Mrs. Neighbors, September 14, 1859, Robert S. Neighbors Papers, Letters File, BTHC-UT.

40. Rector to commissioner of Indian affairs, May 3, 1860, Letters Received, Wichita Agency, NA.

Chapter 13. Between Loyalties

1. Slave Schedules, Arkansas and Indian Lands, 1860 Census, Schedule 2, Creek Nation, 1, AMD-OHS.

2. Ibid., Cherokee Nation, 2.

3. Annie Heloise Abel, *The American Indian as a Slaveholder and Secessionist,* 86.

4. Slave Schedules, Creek Nation, 12, AMD-OHS.

5. Abel, *Slaveholder and Secessionist,* 193 n. 359.

6. Albert Pike, "Narrative of a Journey in the Prairie," *Arkansas Advocate* (Little Rock), April 17 and 24, May 1, 8, 15, 22, and 29, and June 5 and 19, 1835.

7. Report of Lt. Col. William H. Emory, May 19, 1861, in *The War of the Rebellion, A Compilation of the Official Records of the Union and Confederate Armies,* Series I, I, 648–49.

8. Report of Lt. W. M. Averell, April 17, 1861, in *Official Records,* Series I, LIII, 493–96.

9. *Lawrence Republican,* June 13, 1861.

10. It is probable that this route of the retreat went to the west of Council Grove but passed through the present site of Kingfisher, Oklahoma, and on northward to Kansas. It crossed the Arkansas just below the mouth of the Little Arkansas and headed on to the El Dorado site, where Lieutenant Averell left the command for Washington. See Report of Lt. W. M. Averell, in *Official Records,* Series I, LIII, 493–96.

11. *Emporia News,* June 8, 1861; *Lawrence Republican,* May 30, 1861.

12. The Creek chief Oketahhahshahhaw Choe referred to it as the Black Beaver Road; Annie Heloise Abel, *The American Indian as Participant in the Civil War,* 67.

13. Muriel Wright, "The Battle of Round Mountain," *Chronicles of Oklahoma* XXXIX, 4 (Winter 1961/62):383. Albert Pike reported to Jefferson Davis that a council of Creeks, Seminoles, Shawnees, Cherokees, and Delawares had been held with the Indians of the prairie on the upper North Canadian for the pretended purpose

of neutrality but in reality for siding with the North; Albert Pike, *Report on Mission to the Indian Nations,* 16.

14. *Report of the Commissioner of Indian Affairs, 1861,* 626.

15. E. H. Carruth to Tusaquach, September 11, 1861, in *Official Records,* Series I, VIII, 26.

16. *Galveston Weekly News,* September 3, 1861, in BTHC-UT.

17. Pike, *Report on Mission,* 8–19.

18. Ibid.

19. *Official Records,* Series IV, I, 542–54.

20. *Report of the Commissioner of Indian Affairs, 1865,* 519.

21. *Lawrence Republican,* February 6, 1862.

22. Abel, *Slaveholder and Secessionist,* 234–35.

23. Wright, "Battle of Round Mountain," 383.

24. Abel, *Slaveholder and Secessionist,* 254–59.

25. Geo. W. Collamore to Wm. P. Dole, April 21, 1862, in *Official Records,* Series II, IV, pt. 2, 11–13.

26. Angie Debo, *The Road to Disappearance,* 160.

27. Taylor, *Jesse Chisholm,* 177–78.

28. Elias Rector to Jesse Chisholm, December 1861, Letters Sent, Southern Superintendency, Confederate Records, NA.

29. Bill of goods purchased from J. Shirley by J. Chisholm, January 25, 1862, Letters Sent, Records of the Southern Superintendency, Confederate Records, NA.

30. Voucher by Jesse Chisholm, February 21, 1862, ibid.; Albert T. Page to Charles B. Johnson, Charles B. Johnson Papers, SCD-UA.

31. Albert Pike to Major E. Rector, January 28, 1862, cited in Abel, *Slaveholder and Secessionist,* 323–24.

32. Buffalo Hump and Jim Pockmark to John Jumper, December 15, 1861, cited in ibid., 337–38.

33. M. Leeper to Albert Pike, April 13, 1862, cited in ibid., 348–50.

34. Ibid.

35. Ledger, Shirley's Trading Post, Box 13, Item 4, C, Ross Hume Collection, WHC-UO.

36. M. Leeper to Elias Rector, September 15, 1861, cited in Abel, *Slaveholder and Secessionist,* 304–307; M. Leeper to Elias Rector, January 13, 1862, in ibid., 339–43.

37. *Lawrence Republican,* June 13, 1861.

38. Ibid., October 3 and 10, 1861.

39. Joseph B. Thoburn, "Horace P. Jones, Scout," *Chronicles of Oklahoma* II, 4 (December 1924):383–85.

40. S. S. Scott to Gen. Holmes, November 2, 1862, in *Official Records*, Series I, XIII, 919–21.

41. F. Johnson to William P. Dole, January 20, 1863, cited in Abel, *Slaveholder and Secessionist*, 329–30 n. 590.

42. Debo, *Road to Disappearance*, 151–52.

43. Charles B. Johnson Papers, SCD-UA (emphasis in original).

44. C. B. Johnson to Gen. William Steele, September 18, 1863, in *Official Records*, Series I, XXII, pt. 2, 1020–21.

45. James R. Mead, "The Little Arkansas," *Collections of the Kansas State Historical Society, 1907–08* X (1908):8–10.

46. H. W. Martin to W. G. Coffin, June 18, 1863, cited in Abel, *American Indian as Participant*, 275.

47. Mead, "Little Arkansas," 11; *Wichita Eagle*, March 7, 1890; *Daily Oklahoman* (Oklahoma City), November 17, 1907.

48. O. H. Bentley, ed., *History of Wichita and Sedgwick County, Kansas, Past and Present*, 126, citing James R. Mead manuscript; Henry Shanklin to James Wortham, September 1, 1867, in *Report of the Commissioner of Indian Affairs, 1867*, 322.

49. James Mead said in an 1890 address that the Wichitas suffered through the winter of 1863/64 at a place called Belmont, Kansas. This is supported by *Report of the Commissioner of Indian Affairs, 1863–1864*, 143. Mead also said the Wichitas arrived at the mouth of the Little Arkansas in the early spring of 1864, "destitute and mostly afoot."

    At other times Mead says the Wichitas came there in 1863 and Chisholm in the fall of 1864. However, on February 6, 1865, Chisholm made a claim to Wichita agent Gookins for taxes against the tribe for living on his land at Chisholm Ranch. This would imply that Chisholm, who was noted for his honesty, was claiming to have been there before the Wichitas. See C. Ross Hume Collection, Box 29, Item 12, WHC-UO.

50. Chapeyanechis, second chief Comanches, to chief and head men of Creek Nation, February 21, 1865, cited in E. E. Dale, "Additional Letters of General Stand Watie," *Chronicles of Oklahoma* I, 2 (October 1921):140–43.

51. Sam Peppard report, March 5, 1863, in *Official Records*, Series I, XLVIII, pt. 1, 1096–97.

52. Dale, "Additional Letters of Stand Watie," 141.

53. Sam Peppard report, in *Official Records*.

54. Petition of Chiefs, October 14, 1864, Letters Received, Wichita Agency, 1857–1866, NA.

Chapter 14. In the Cause of Peace

1. *Emporia News*, November 12, 1864.

2. *Leavenworth Times,* January 28 and February 8, 10, 12, 16, 17, and 28, 1864.

3. Mead account, in *Wichita Eagle,* March 7, 1890.

4. Ibid.

5. *Leavenworth Times,* September 8, 1865.

6. Joseph B. Thoburn, *A Standard History of Oklahoma,* 364–66.

7. When Donnell was interviewed by Neal W. Evans in 1912 he said that he had nursed Chisholm in 1865 after Jesse had been shot in the leg by a brother-in-law just after the close of the war. He did not say if the shooting was an accident. Evans to Barde, Barde Collection, AMD-OHS.

8. Bentley, *History of Wichita,* 118.

9. *Wichita Eagle,* March 7, 1890.

10. Mead account, in *Daily Oklahoman* (Oklahoma City), November 17, 1907.

11. Bentley, *History of Wichita,* 119.

12. Statement by Mix-with-water and Jesse Chisholm, in Winfrey and Day, *Indian Papers of Texas* IV, 94.

13. Chisholm to Leavenworth, February 15, 1865, Letters Received, Kiowa Agency, NA.

14. E. Kirby Smith to Albert Pike, April 9, 1865, in *Official Records,* Series I, XLVIII, pt. 2, 1266–69.

15. Ibid., 1266, 1305.

16. Anna Lewis, "Camp Napoleon," *Chronicles of Oklahoma* IX, 4 (December 1931):360–64.

17. J. H. Leavenworth to Gen. J. H. Ford, June 27, 1865, in *Official Records,* Series I, XLVIII, pt. 2, 1009.

18. Ibid., 687–89.

19. H. J. Tibbits to Gen. James H. Ford, June 28, 1865, in *Official Records,* Series I, LX, pt. 2, 1021.

20. J. H. Leavenworth to Gen. James H. Ford, June 27, 1865, in ibid., 1009.

21. Sam Peppard to Gen. James H. Ford, March 5, 1865, in ibid., 1096–97.

22. Jesse Chisholm to J. H. Leavenworth, July 14, 1865, Letters Received, Kiowa Agency, 1864–1868, NA.

23. *Washington Evening Star,* March 27, 1863; *Washington National Republican,* March 27, 1863; *Daily National Intelligencer* (Washington, D.C.), March 28, 1863.

24. Jesse Chisholm to J. H. Leavenworth, August 1, 1865, Letters Received, Kiowa Agency, 1864–1868, NA.

25. J. H. Leavenworth to Gen. J. B. Sanborn, August 10, 1865, in *Official Records,* Series I, L, 1176.

26. George E. Hyde, *Life of George Bent,* 246–47.

27. Inclosure B to letter of Gen. John B. Sanborn to Gen. G. M. Dodge, August 17, 1865, in *Official Records,* Series I, XLVIII, pt. 1, 362–63.

28. *St. Louis* (Missouri) *Democrat,* September 25, 27, and 29, and October 2, 1865.

29. Vouchers of Jesse Chisholm for services as guide, scout, and interpreter, Letters Received, Kiowa Agency, 1864–1868, NA.

30. J. H. Leavenworth to D. N. Colley, December 1, 1865, ibid.

31. Kappler, *Indian Treaties* I, 892–95; "Diary of Samuel A. Kingman," *Kansas Historical Quarterly* I, 5 (November 1932):44–50.

32. *Report of the Commissioner of Indian Affairs, 1866,* 709.

33. "Treaties with Arapahoes and Cheyennes, etc., No. 13," in *Report of the Commissioner of Indian Affairs, 1866,* 714.

34. Ibid., 718–19.

35. "Diary of Samuel A. Kingman," 447.

36. Ibid., 448.

Chapter 15. Trail to Immortality

1. Neal W. Evans to F. S. Barde, June 26, 1912, Barde Collection, AMD-OHS. Sheridan and his party chanced on the wild turkey roost on April 27, 1869; DeB. Randolph Keim, *Sheridan's Troopers on the Borders,* 303–304. The Barrett Survey of 1873 gives the location of Sheridan's Roost as the northeast corner, Section 36, T20N, R10W, and indicates there was a spring there. Later it was a watering place on the road between Camp Supply and Darlington Indian Agency. See Barrett Survey, Oklahoma State Archives.

2. Wayne Gard, *The Chisholm Trail,* 55, citing *Laws of Kansas, 1867,* 7th sess., 263–67.

3. Philip McCusker to Thomas Murphy, November 15, 1867, Letters Received, Wichita Agency, 1867–1875, NA. Jesse Leavenworth also used the title in a letter of April 23, 1868, instructing the shipment of Indian goods to the Wichita Agency "via mouth of Little Arkansas and the Chisholm Trail"; Letters Received, Kiowa Agency, 1864–1868, NA.

4. George W. Conover, *Sixty Years in Southwest Oklahoma,* 103–4; Bentley, *History of Wichita,* 119. According to Conover, Caboon (Vincente, or George Chisholm) claimed that a Delaware named Red Blanket had helped drive the first herd as far as the Canadian River from Texas.

5. Register of Traders Licenses, 1847–1873, NNR-852, NA.

6. *Leavenworth Daily Conservative,* July 2, 9, and 24, and November 7, 1867.

7. F. F. Jones, April 26, 1867, Letters Received, Kiowa Agency, 1864–1868, NA.

8. Winfrey and Day, *Indian Papers of Texas* IV, 94.

9. *Emporia News,* December 29, 1866.

10. Record Book of Chief Sam Checote, AMD-OHS.

11. Creek File, Foreign Relations file, AMD-OHS.

12. *Daily Missouri Democrat* (St. Louis), July 13, 1867.

13. Leavenworth to Mix, August 18, 1867, Letters Received, Kiowa Agency, 1864–1868, NA.

14. Ibid.; Hyde, *George Bent,* 280–81.

15. Leavenworth to Mathewson, August 5, 1867, Letters Received, Kiowa Agency, 1864–1868, NA.

16. William E. Chisholm, December 30, 1868, ibid.

17. Report of Wm. E. Doyle to A. G. Boone, March 1, 1869, ibid. Drover Andy M. Adams encountered Ransom and the herd while on his way back to Texas over the Chisholm Trail to purchase more cattle in March 1868. Adams statement, April 29, 1870, ibid.

18. James Mead, *Wichita Eagle,* March 7, 1890, says that it was a Colonel Daugherty who brought up the first herd from Texas; however, no absolute proof of this has been established.

19. Joseph G. McCoy, *Historic Sketches of the Cattle Trade of the West and Southwest,* 121–22. Captain Henry Sparks claimed that during May 1866 he accompanied a Texas trail herd that, guided by two Caddo Indians, passed by Chisholm's abandoned camp at Council Grove and followed the trader's wagon tracks north. See clipping from *Fort Worth Star Telegram,* Joseph B. Thoburn Papers, Jesse Chisholm File, AMD-OHS. It is doubtful that this took place during the spring of either 1866 or 1867. Gard, *Chisholm Trail,* 73, apparently misassumed that the Sac and Fox Indian Agency was in the Indian Territory in 1865 when he stated that Chisholm drove part of a herd of cattle over the route. The Sac and Fox Agency was then still in eastern Kansas.

20. *Leavenworth Daily Conservative,* September 9, 1867.

21. Henry Shanklin to James Wortham, September 1, 1867, in *Report of the Commissioner of Indian Affairs, 1867,* 321–23.

22. *Leavenworth Daily Conservative,* September 27, 1867.

23. McCusker to Murphy, November 15, 1867, Letters Received, Wichita Agency, 1867–1875, NA.

24. Kappler, *Indian Treaties* I, 982–84; Alfred A. Taylor, "The Medicine Lodge Peace Council," *Chronicles of Oklahoma* II, 2 (June 1924):98–118; *Daily Missouri Democrat* (St. Louis), October and November 1867 issues.

25. Kappler, *Indian Treaties* I, 987–89.

26. *Wichita Eagle,* May 9, 1890.

27. Ibid., May 23, 1890. This photograph has surfaced at various times and places. Former Wichita pioneer Milo Kellogg submitted a copy to the *Wichita Eagle* in May 1890, indicating that it was one of a lot of a dozen that were made — it is not clear whether he meant poses or copies of the same pose. A similar photograph was given to Velma Troxel Jayne by Jennie Chisholm Davis in 1911. This latter carried a notation that read: "E. E. Henry, Photographer, 42 Delaware St., Leavenworth." See Velma Troxel Jayne, *O County Faces and Places,* 6.

28. *Leavenworth Daily Conservative,* November 24 and December 15, 1867.

29. Aloise Hopkins to Joseph Thoburn, October 20, 1913, Edwards Trading Post File, Grant Foreman Collection, AMD-OHS. The writer states that her husband went to Council Grove with trader A. F. Greenway in 1869.

30. Johnson, *Chickasaw Rancher,* 29–31. According to E. B. Johnson, after Chisholm's death Montford purchased some logs that the frontiersman had cut preparatory to building a trading station on the west side of the Council Grove area. About 1873, Johnson used them to construct a ranch house in what is now west Oklahoma City in the vicinity of North MacArthur. See Asplin, "Council Grove," 443.

31. Johnson, *Chickasaw Rancher,* 27–29.

32. According to trader Henry Donnell, Chisholm maintained a temporary trading post at this location; Neal W. Evans, June 26, 1912, Barde Collection.

33. James Wortham to N. G. Taylor, June 27, 1868, Letters Received, Creek Agency, 1864–1868, NA; Geo. T. Robinson to George A. Reynolds, March 31, 1868, Letters Received, Kiowa Agency, 1864–1868, NA.

34. Captain George T. Robinson to George A. Reynolds, March 31, 1868, Letters Received, Kiowa Agency, 1864–1868, NA. Robinson reported that the surveyors arrived at the Seminole Agency near present-day Wewoka, Oklahoma, four days earlier, "a badly scared set of surveyors, I tell you — they had a narrow escape." It may well have been this survey that named present-day Chisholm Creek of central Oklahoma for the Scottish-Cherokee frontiersman.

35. *Wichita Eagle,* March 7, 1890.

36. Jesse Chisholm Papers, BTHC-UT.

37. According to an account in the *Leavenworth Daily Conservative,* May 8, 1868, Chisholm died "on the 4th inst.," which would have been May 4. It is doubtful, however, that the news reached Leavenworth in four days. Without question the date meant by the *Conservative* was April 4, the event being reported by William Greiffenstein, who arrived in Kansas with eight wagons of furs and buffalo robes in late April. He had sold his furs at Topeka and his buffalo robes at Lawrence before checking in at the Planters Hotel in Leavenworth on April 28.

   That Jesse was still alive in late March is evident by the March 31, 1868, letter of Captain George T. Robinson to George A. Reynolds (Letters Received, Kiowa Agency, 1864–1868, NA) stating that only four days earlier the survey party rescued by Chisholm had arrived at the Seminole Agency. It is reasonable to assume that the frightened surveyors, who came close to losing their scalps, lost no time in getting to the agency.

38. Mead, *Hunting and Trading,* 220–21. Donnell gave a similar account, saying that Jesse died from eating bear meat and honey; Neal W. Evans, June 26, 1912, Barde Collection.

39. Mead's account, *Wichita Eagle,* May 23, 1890.

Bibliography

Articles

Asplin, Ray. "History of Council Grove in Oklahoma." *Chronicles of Oklahoma* XLV, 4 (Winter 1967/68).

Barry, Louise. "Kansas Before 1854: A Revised Annals." *Kansas Historical Quarterly* XXIX, 1 (Spring 1963).

Benton, Lee David. "An Odyssey into Texas: William Quesenbury with the Cherokees." *Chronicles of Oklahoma* LX, 2 (Summer 1982).

Brown, John P. "Eastern Cherokee Chiefs." *Chronicles of Oklahoma* XVI, 1 (March 1938).

Buntin, Martha. "The Removal of the Wichitas from Butler County, Kansas, to the Present Agency." *Panhandle Plains Historical Review* IV (1931).

Bushnell, David I., Jr. "John Mix Stanley, Artist-Explorer." *Smithsonian Annual Report, 1924.*

Butler, Josiah. "Pioneer School Teaching at the Comanche-Kiowa Agency School." *Chronicles of Oklahoma* VI, 4 (December 1928).

Chapman, Berlin B. "Establishment of the Wichita Reservation." *Chronicles of Oklahoma* XI, 4 (December 1933).

"Chisholm Spring Trading Post." *Chronicles of Oklahoma* XLIV, 2 (Summer 1966).

"The Chisholm Trail." *Kansas Historical Quarterly* XXXIII, 2 (Summer 1967).

Clift, W. H. "Warren's Trading Post." *Chronicles of Oklahoma* II, 2 (June 1924).

Cloud, Jim. "Jesse Chisholm's Old Ranch Located." *The War Chief of the Indian Territory Posse of Oklahoma Westerners* XIX, 3 (December 1985).

Colket, Meredith B., Jr. "Chisholm Families in the American Colonies." *National Genealogical Society Quarterly* LXXII, 2 (June 1984).

"Corn Tassle Talk." *Calendar of Virginia State Papers* IV.

Dale, E. E. "Additional Letters of General Stand Watie." *Chronicles of Oklahoma* I, 2 (October 1921).

Debo, Angie. "The Location of the Battle of Round Mountain." *Chronicles of Oklahoma* XLI, 1 (Spring 1963).

"Diary of Samuel A. Kingman." *Kansas Historical Quarterly* I, 5 (November 1932).

Dott, Robert H. "Lieutenant Simpson's California Road Through Oklahoma." *Chronicles of Oklahoma* XXXVIII, 2 (Summer 1960).

Foreman, Carolyn Thomas. "Black Beaver." *Chronicles of Oklahoma* XXIV, 3 (Autumn 1946).

——, annot. "The Cherokee War Path." *Chronicles of Oklahoma* IX, 3 (September 1931).

——. "Colonel Jesse Henry Leavenworth." *Chronicles of Oklahoma* XIII, 1 (Spring 1935).

——. "Dutch, the Cherokee." *Chronicles of Oklahoma* XXVII, 3 (Autumn 1949).

——. "Early History of Webbers Falls." *Chronicles of Oklahoma* XXIX, 4 (Winter 1951/52).

——. "Israel Vore and the Levering Manual Labor School." *Chronicles of Oklahoma* XXV, 3 (Autumn 1947).

——. "John Jumper." *Chronicles of Oklahoma* XXIX, 2 (Summer 1951).

——. "North Fork Town." *Chronicles of Oklahoma* XXIX, 1 (Spring 1951).

——. "Pierce Mason Butler." *Chronicles of Oklahoma* XXX, 1 (Spring 1952).

——. "Report of Captain John Stuart." *Chronicles of Oklahoma* V, 3 (September 1927).

Foreman, Grant. "Early Trails Through Oklahoma." *Chronicles of Oklahoma* III, 2 (June 1925).

——, ed. "A Journal Kept by Douglas Cooper." *Chronicles of Oklahoma* V, 4 (December 1927).

——, ed. "The Journal of Lieutenant A. W. Whipple." *Chronicles of Oklahoma* XXVIII, 3 (Autumn 1950).

——. "The Journal of the Proceedings at Our First Treaty with the Wild Indians, 1835." *Chronicles of Oklahoma* XIV, 4 (December 1936).

——. "Our First Treaty with the Wild Indians." *Daily Oklahoman* (Oklahoma City), August 25, 1935.

——, ed. "Survey of a Wagon Road from Fort Smith to the Colorado River." *Chronicles of Oklahoma* XII, 1 (March 1934).

"A Fragment of History." *Chronicles of Oklahoma* XIII, 4 (December 1935).

Gipson, A. M. "Indian Territory United Nations, 1845." *Chronicles of Oklahoma* XXXIX, 4 (Winter 1961/62).

Goodpasture, Albert W. "The Paternity of Sequoyah, the Inventor of the Cherokee Alphabet." *Chronicles of Oklahoma* I, 1 (January 1921).

Hoig, Stan. "Diana, Tiana or Talihina, The Myth and Mystery of Sam Houston's Cherokee Wife." *Chronicles of Oklahoma* LXIV, 2 (Summer 1986).

———. "The Genealogy of Jesse Chisholm." *Chronicles of Oklahoma* LXVII, 2 (Summer 1989).

"John Mix Stanley." *Chronicles of Oklahoma* XXXI, 2 (Summer 1953).

Johnson, E. B. "The Two Cattle Trails." *Chronicles of Oklahoma* XIV, 1 (March 1936).

Jones, Harold W., ed. "The Diary of the Assistant Surgeon Leonard McPhail on His Journey to the Southwest in 1835." *Chronicles of Oklahoma* XVIII, 3 (September 1940).

"The Journal of Elijah Hicks." *Chronicles of Oklahoma* XIII, 1 (March 1935).

Lewis, Anna. "Camp Napoleon." *Chronicles of Oklahoma* IX, 4 (December 1931).

Mead, James R. "The Little Arkansas." *Collections of the Kansas State Historical Society, 1907–08* X (1908).

———. "The Wichita Indians in Kansas." *Collections of the Kansas State Historical Society* VIII (1903–1904).

Moffitt, James W., ed. "Historical Notes." *Chronicles of Oklahoma* XIX, 2 (June 1941).

Muckleroy, Anna. "The Indian Policy of the Republic of Texas." *The Southwestern Historical Quarterly* XXVI, 3 (January 1923).

"Notes and Documents." *Chronicles of Oklahoma* XXIV, 1 (Spring 1956).

Perrine, Fred S., ed. "The Journal of Hugh Evans Covering the First and Second Campaigns of the United States Dragoon Regiment in 1834 and 1835." *Chronicles of Oklahoma* III, 3 (September 1925).

Pike, Albert. "Narrative of a Journey in the Prairie." *Arkansas Advocate* (Little Rock), April 17–June 19, 1835.

Porter, Kenneth W. "Wild Cat's Death and Burial." *Chronicles of Oklahoma* XXI, 1 (March 1943).

Rucker, Alvin. "Jesse Chisholm's Grave." *Daily Oklahoman* (Oklahoma City), July 13, 1930.

Shawver, Lona, annot. "Stanley Explores Oklahoma." *Chronicles of Oklahoma* XXII, 3 (Autumn 1944).

Shirk, George. "Peace on the Plains." *Chronicles of Oklahoma* XXVIII, 1 (Spring 1950).

Taylor, Alfred A. "The Medicine Lodge Peace Council." *Chronicles of Oklahoma* II, 2 (June 1924).

Taylor, T. U. "Granite Marker to Jesse Chisholm." *Frontier Times* XVI, 10 (July 1939).

———. "In the Land of the Chisholms." *Frontier Times* XV, 11 (August 1938).

————. "Jesse Chisholm in Stone." *Frontier Times* XV, 11 (August 1938).

————. "A Reunion of the Chisholm Family." *Frontier Times* XVI, 2 (September 1939).

Tennant, H. S. "The Two Cattle Trails." *Chronicles of Oklahoma* XIV, 1 (March 1936).

Thoburn, Joseph B. "Battle with Comanches." *Sturm's Oklahoma Magazine* X, 6 (August 1910).

————. "A Campaign of the Texas Rangers Against Comanches." *Sturm's Oklahoma Magazine* X, 5 (July 1910).

————. "Horace P. Jones, Scout." *Chronicles of Oklahoma* II, 4 (December 1924).

————. "Indian Fight in Ford County." *Collections of the Kansas State Historical Society* XII, 1911–1912.

————. "Jesse Chisholm, a Stalwart Figure in History." *Frontier Times* XIII, 7 (April 1936).

Thompson, Isabel. "The Blount Conspiracy." *East Tennessee Historical Society Publications* II (1930).

"The Tribes of the Thirty-fifth Parallel." *Harper's New Monthly Magazine* XVII, C (September 1858).

Turner, Frederick Jackson. "Documents on the Blount Conspiracy, 1795–1797." *American Historical Review* X (1904–1905).

Van Zandt, Howard F. "The History of Camp Holmes and Chouteau's Trading Post." *Chronicles of Oklahoma* XIII, 3 (September 1935).

Webb, W. P. "The Last Treaty of the Republic of Texas." *The Southwestern Historical Quarterly* XXV, 3 (January 1922).

White, Kate. "John Chisholm, a Soldier of Fortune." *East Tennessee Historical Society Publications* I (1929); also *Chronicles of Oklahoma* VIII, 2 (June 1930).

Williams, Sam'l C., ed. "Tatham's Characters Among the North American Indians." *Tennessee Historical Magazine* VII, 3 (October 1921).

Winfrey, Dorman H. "Chief Bowles of the Texas Cherokees." *Chronicles of Oklahoma* XXXII, 1 (Spring 1954).

Wright, Muriel. "The Battle of Round Mountain." *Chronicles of Oklahoma* XXXIX, 4 (Winter 1961/62).

————. "A History of Fort Cobb." *Chronicles of Oklahoma* XXXIV, 1 (Spring 1956).

————, and George H. Shirk. "The Journal of Lt. A. W. Whipple." *Chronicles of Oklahoma* XXVIII, 3 (Autumn 1950).

Young, Otis E. "The United States Mounted Ranger Battalion, 1832–33." *Mississippi Valley Historical Review* XLI, 4 (December 1954).

Books

Abel, Annie Heloise. *The American Indian as a Participant in the Civil War.* Vol. 2 of *The Slaveholding Indians.* Cleveland, Ohio: Arthur H. Clark, 1925.

————. *The American Indian as Slaveholder and Secessionist.* Vol. 1 of *The Slaveholding Indians.* Cleveland, Ohio: Arthur H. Clark, 1915.

————. *The Indian Under Reconstruction.* Vol. 3 of *The Slaveholding Indians.* Cleveland, Ohio: Arthur H. Clark, 1919.

Acklin, Jennette Tillotson. *Tennessee Records, Tombstone Inscriptions and Manuscripts.* Baltimore, Md.: Genealogical Publications, 1975.

Agnew, Brad. *Fort Gibson, Terminal on the Trail of Tears.* Norman: University of Oklahoma Press, 1980.

Allen, Penelope Johnson. *Leaves from the Family Tree.* Easley, S.C.: Southern Historical Press, 1982.

Allsopp, Fred W. *Albert Pike, a Biography.* Little Rock, Ark.: Parke-Harper, 1928.

Anderson, William C., and James A. Lewis. *A Guide to Cherokee Documents in Foreign Archives.* Metuchen, N.J.: Scarecrow Press, 1983.

Baker, Jack, trans. *Cherokee Emigration Rolls, 1817–35.* Oklahoma City: Baker Publishing, 1977.

Barry, Louise. *The Beginning of the West: Annals of the Kansas Gateway to the American West.* Topeka: Kansas State Historical Society, 1972.

Bentley, O. H., ed. *History of Wichita and Sedgwick County, Kansas, Past and Present.* Chicago: C. F. Cooper, 1910.

Bible Records — Tombstone Inscriptions. Nashville, Tenn.: n.p., n.d.

Boddie, Mrs. John, ed. *Historical Southern Families.* Baltimore, Md.: Genealogical Publications, 1972.

Bolton, Herbert Eugene. *Texas in the Middle Eighteenth Century.* New York: Russell & Russell, 1962.

Brown, John Henry. *Indian Wars and Pioneers of Texas.* St. Louis, Mo.: L. E. Danielle, 1897.

Brown, John P. *Old Frontiers, the Story of the Cherokee Indians from Earliest Times to the Date of Their Removal to the West, 1838.* Kingsport, Tenn.: Southern Publishers, 1938.

Campbell's Abstract of Creek Indian Census Cards and Index. Muskogee, Okla.: Phoenix Job Printing, 1915.

Carter, Samuel, III. *Cherokee Sunset: A Nation Betrayed.* Garden City, N.Y.: Doubleday, 1976.

Catlin, George. *Letters and Notes on the Manners, Customs, and Conditions of the North American Indians*. 2 vols. New York: Dove Publications, 1973.

Claiborne, J.F.H. *Life and Times of Gen. Sam. Dale, the Mississippi Partisan*. New York: Harper & Brothers, 1860.

Clarke, Mary Whatley. *Chief Bowles and the Texas Cherokees*. Norman: University of Oklahoma Press, 1971.

Conover, George W. *Sixty Years in Southwest Oklahoma*. Anadarko: N. T. Plummer Book & Job Printers, 1927.

Cunningham, Frank. *General Stand Watie's Confederate Indians*. San Antonio, Tex.: Naylor, 1959.

Dale, Edward Everett. *Cherokee Cavalier, Forty Years of Cherokee History as Told in the Correspondence of the Ridge-Watie-Boudinot Family*. Norman: University of Oklahoma Press, 1939.

Debo, Angie. *The Road to Disappearance*. Norman: University of Oklahoma Press, 1941.

Eaton, Rachel Caroline. *John Ross and the Cherokee Indians*. Menasha, Wisc.: George Banta, 1914.

Fehrenbach, T. R. *Comanches, the Destruction of a People*. New York: Alfred A. Knopf, 1974.

Flint, Timothy. *Recollections of the Last Ten Years Passed in Occasional Residences and Journeyings in the Valley of the Mississippi*. Boston: Cummings, Hilliard, 1826.

Foreman, Grant. *Advancing the Frontier*. Norman: University of Oklahoma Press, 1933.

———. *Adventure on the Red River*. Norman: University of Oklahoma Press, 1937.

———. *The Five Civilized Tribes*. Norman: University of Oklahoma Press, 1934.

———. *Indian Removal*. Norman: University of Oklahoma Press, 1966.

———. *Indians and Pioneers, the Story of the American Southwest before 1830*. New Haven, Conn.: Yale University Press, 1930.

———. *Marcy and the Gold Seekers*. Norman: University of Oklahoma Press, 1939.

———, ed. and annot. *A Pathfinder in the Southwest, the Itinerary of Lieutenant A. W. Whipple*. Norman: University of Oklahoma Press, 1941.

———. *Pioneer Days in the Early Southwest*. Cleveland, Ohio: Arthur H. Clark, 1926.

———. *Sequoyah*. Norman: University of Oklahoma Press, 1938.

———, ed. *A Traveler in Indian Territory, the Journal of Ethan Allen Hitchcock, Late Major-General in the United States Army*. Cedar Rapids, Iowa: Torch Press, 1930.

Galvin, John, ed. *Lieutenant James W. Abert's March Through the Country of the Comanches in the Fall of the Year 1845.* San Francisco: John Howell Books, 1970.

Gard, Wayne. *The Chisholm Trail.* Norman: University of Oklahoma Press, 1954.

Gregg, Josiah. *Commerce of the Prairies: or the Journal of a Santa Fe Trader.* 2 vols. New York: Henry G. Langley, 1844. Reprint University Microfilms, Ann Arbor, Mich., 1966.

Gregory, Jack, and Rennard Strickland. *Sam Houston with the Cherokees, 1829–1833.* Austin: University of Texas Press, 1967.

Grinnell, George Bird. *The Fighting Cheyennes.* Norman: University of Oklahoma Press, 1956.

Harris, Rev. Nathaniel Sayre. *Journal of a Tour in the Indian Territory, 1844.* New York: D. Dana, Jr., 1844.

Hempstead, Fay. *Historical Review of Arkansas.* Chicago: Lewis Publishing, 1911.

Hildreth, James. *Dragoon Campaigns to the Rocky Mountains.* New York: Wiley & Long, 1836.

Hill, J. J. *Old Cherokee Families.* Norman: University of Oklahoma Press, 1968.

Hitchcock, Ethan Allen. *Fifty Years in Camp and Field.* Edited by W. A. Croffert. New York: G. P. Putnam's Sons, 1909.

Horan, James D. *The McKenney-Hall Portrait Gallery of American Indians.* New York: Crown Publishing, 1972.

Horr, David Agee, comp. and ed. *Cherokee and Creek Indians.* New York: Garland Publishing, 1974.

Hunt, Aurora. *Major General James Henry Carleton, 1814-1873, Western Frontier Dragoon.* Glendale, Calif.: Arthur H. Clark, 1958.

Hunt, David C. *John Mix Stanley.* Tulsa, Okla.: Thomas Gilcrease Institute of American Art & History, 1971.

Hyde, George E. *Life of George Bent.* Ed. Savoie Lottinville. Norman: University of Oklahoma Press, 1968.

Irving, Washington. *A Tour of the Prairies.* Ed. John Francis McDermott. Norman: University of Oklahoma Press, 1956.

James, Edwin. *Account of an Expedition from Pittsburgh to the Rocky Mountains.* 2 vols. Ann Arbor, Mich.: University Microfilms, 1966.

James, Thomas. *Three Years Among the Mexicans and the Indians.* Chicago: Rio Grande Press, 1962.

Jayne, Velma Troxel. *O County Faces and Places.* Enid, Okla.: H. Allen Printers, 1968.

Johnson, Niel R. *The Chickasaw Rancher.* Stillwater, Okla.: Redlands Press, 1961.

Kappler, Charles J., comp. and ed. *Indian Treaties, 1778–1883*. New York: Interland Publishing, 1972.

Keim, DeB. Randolph. *Sheridan's Troopers on the Borders: A Winter Campaign on the Plains*. Philadelphia: David McKay, 1885.

Kinietz, W. Vernon. *John Mix Stanley and His Indian Paintings*. Ann Arbor: University of Michigan Press, 1942.

Lewis, Thomas M. N., and Madeline Kneberg. *Hiwassee Island, An Archaeological Account of Four Tennessee Indian Peoples*. Knoxville: University of Tennessee Press, 1946.

Littlefield, Daniel F., Jr. *Africans and Creeks: From the Colonial Period to the Civil War*. Westport, Conn.: Greenwood Press, 1979.

Lottinville, Savoie, ed. *A Journey into the Arkansas Territory During the Year 1819*. Norman: University of Oklahoma Press, 1980.

Lucas, Silas Emmett, Jr., and Ella Lee Shefield, eds. *35,000 Tennessee Marriage Records and Bonds, 1783–1870*. Easley, S.C.: Southern Historical Press, 1981.

McCoy, Joseph G. *Historic Sketches of the Cattle Trade of the West and Southwest*. Ed. Ralph P. Bieber. Lincoln: University of Nebraska Press, 1985.

McLean, Malcom D., comp. and ed. *Papers Concerning Robertson's Colony in Texas, 1823 through September 1826*. 2 vols. Fort Worth, Tex.: Christian University Press, 1975.

McReynolds, Edwin C. *The Seminoles*. Norman: University of Oklahoma Press, 1957.

Malone, Henry Thompson. *Cherokees of the Old South — A People in Transition*. Athens: University of Georgia Press, 1956.

Masterson, William H. *William Blount*. Baton Rouge: Louisiana State University Press, 1954.

Mayhall, Mildred. *Indian Wars of Texas*. Waco: Texian Press, 1965.

Mead, James R. *Hunting and Trading on the Great Plains, 1859–1875*. Norman: University of Oklahoma Press, 1986.

Möllhausen, Baldwin. *Diary of a Journey from the Mississippi to the Coasts of the Pacific with a U.S. Government Expedition*. London: Longman, Brown, Green, Longman & Roberts, 1858.

Montaignes, François des (Isaac Cooper). *The Plains, Being No Less Than a Collection of Veracious Memoranda Taken During the Expedition of Exploration in the Year 1845*. Ed. and intro. Nancy Apert Mower and Don Russell. Norman: University of Oklahoma Press, 1972.

Mooney, James. *Historical Sketches of the Cherokees*. Chicago: Aldine Publishing, 1975.

Moore, Caroline T., comp. and ed. *Abstracts of Wills of Charleston District, South Carolina, and Other Will Records in the District, 1783–1800.* Columbia, S.C.: R. L. Bryan, 1974.

———. *Abstracts of Wills of the State of South Carolina, 1760–1784.* Columbia, S.C.: R. L. Bryan, 1969.

Morris, Lerona Rosamond. *Oklahoma, Land of Opportunity.* Guthrie, Okla.: Co-Operative Publishing, 1934.

New American State Papers, Indian Affairs. 13 vols. Wilmington, Del.: Scholarly Resources, 1972.

Newcomb, W. W., Jr. *The Indians of Texas from Prehistoric to Modern Times.* Austin: University of Texas Press, 1961.

Nuttall, Thomas. *Nuttall's Journal of Travels into the Arkansas Territory During the Year 1819* XVIII. *Early Western Travels, 1748–1846.* Ed. Reuben Gold Thwaites. Cleveland, Ohio: Arthur H. Clark, 1905.

Nye, Colonel W. S. *Carbine and Lance.* Norman: University of Oklahoma Press, 1940.

Owen, Narcissa. *Memoirs of Narcissa Owen, 1831–1907.* Washington, D.C.: n.p., 1907.

Pelzer, Louis. *Marches of the Dragoons in the Mississippi Valley.* Iowa City: State Historical Society of Iowa, 1917.

Pike, Albert. *Report on Mission to the Indian Nations.* Facsimile Reprint. Washington, D.C.: Library of the Supreme Council, 33 Degree, Ancient and Accepted Scottish Rite, 1968.

Portraits of North American Indians with Sketches of Scenery, etc., Painted by J. M. Stanley, Deposited with the Smithsonian Institution. Washington, D.C.: Smithsonian Institution, 1852.

Quaife, Milo Milton, ed. *The Diary of James K. Polk.* 4 vols. Chicago: A. C. McClurg, 1910.

Ramsey, J.G.M. *Annals of Tennessee, 1797–1884.* Knoxville: East Tennessee Historical Society, 1967.

Ray, Worth S. *Tennessee Cousins.* Baltimore, Md.: Genealogical Publications, 1971.

Richardson, Rupert Norval. *The Comanche Barrier to South Plains Settlement.* Glendale, Calif.: Arthur H. Clark, 1933.

———. *Frontier of Northwest Texas, 1846 to 1876.* Glendale, Calif.: Arthur H. Clark, 1963.

Ridings, Sam P. *The Chisholm Trail.* Guthrie, Okla.: Co-Operative Publishing, 1936.

Rister, Carl Coke. *Border Captives.* Norman: University of Oklahoma Press, 1940.

———. *Southern Plainsmen.* Norman: University of Oklahoma Press, 1938.

Rothrock, Mary U. *A History of Knox County, Tennessee.* Knoxville: East Tennessee Historical Society, 1946.

Royce, Charles C. *The Cherokee Nation of Indians.* Chicago: Aldine Publishing, 1975.

Smith, Dr. W.R.L. *The Story of the Cherokees.* Cleveland, Tenn.: The Church of God Publishing House, 1928.

Starr, Emmet. *Cherokees West, 1794–1839.* Claremore, Okla.: Emmet Starr, 1910.

————. *History of the Cherokee Indians and Their Legends and Folklore.* Oklahoma City, Okla.: Leander, 1921.

Steffen, Randy. *The Horse Soldier, 1776–1843.* Norman: University of Oklahoma Press, 1977.

Stuart, John. *A Sketch of the Cherokee and Choctaw Indians.* Little Rock, Ark.: Woodruff and Pew, 1837.

Taft, Robert. *Artists and Illustrators of the Old West, 1850–1900.* New York: Charles Scribner's Sons, 1953.

Taylor, T. U. *The Chisholm Cattle Trail and Other Routes.* San Antonio, Tex.: Naylor, 1936.

————. *Jesse Chisholm.* Bandera, Tex.: Frontier Times, 1939.

Thoburn, Joseph B. *A Standard History of Oklahoma.* Chicago: American Historical Society, 1916.

————, and Isaac M. Holcomb. *A History of Oklahoma.* San Francisco: Doub, 1908.

————, and Muriel Wright. *Oklahoma, a History of the State and Its People.* 2 vols. New York: Lewis Publishing, 1929.

Tyner, James W. *Those Who Cried.* Chi-ga-u, 1974.

————, and Alice Tyner Timmons. *Our People and Where They Rest.* 10 vols. Norman, Okla.: American Indian Institute, 1969–1978.

Wallace, Ernest, and E. Adamson Hoebel. *The Comanches, Lords of the South Plains.* Norman: University of Oklahoma Press, 1952.

Wallace, Grace Steele. *The Cherokees.* Norman: University of Oklahoma Press, 1972.

Wallis, Jonnie. *Sixty Years on the Brazos, the Life and Letters of John Washington Lockhart.* Los Angeles: Private Printing, 1930.

Washburn, Rev. Cephas. *Reminiscences of the Indians.* Richmond: 1869; reprint Van Buren, Ark.: Press-Argus, 1955.

Webb, Walter Prescott, ed. *The Handbook of Texas.* 2 vols. Austin: Texas State Historical Association, 1952.

————. *The Texas Rangers, a Century of Frontier Defense.* Austin: University of Texas Press, 1965.

Whitley, Edythe Rucker. *Tennessee Genealogical Records, Records of Early Settlers from State and County Archives.* Baltimore, Md.: Genealogical Publishing, 1980.

Wichita City Directory and Immigration Guide. Kansas City, Mo.: Tierman & Wainwright, 1878.

Williams, Alfred Mason. *Sam Houston and the War of Independence in Texas.* Boston: Mifflin, 1893.

Williams, Amelia W., and Eugene C. Barker. *The Writings of Sam Houston, 1793–1863.* 8 vols. Austin: University of Texas Press, 1838–1843.

Williams, Samuel Cole. *Dawn of Tennessee Valley and Tennessee History.* Johnson City, Tenn.: Watauga Press, 1937.

——. *History of the Lost State of Franklin.* New York: Press of the Pioneers, 1933.

——. *Tennessee During the Revolutionary War.* Nashville: Tennessee Historical Commission, 1944.

Wills and Administration of Arkansas County, Ark., 1814–19.

Winfrey, Dorman H., ed. *Texas Indian Papers, 1825–1843,* Austin, Tex.: Texas State Library, 1959.

Winfrey, James H., and James M. Day, eds. *Indian Papers of Texas, 1825–1916.* 4 vols. II: 1844–1845; III: 1846–1859; IV: 1860–1916; V: 1846–1859. Austin, Tex.: Pemberton Press, 1966.

Wisehart, M. K. *Sam Houston: American Giant.* Washington, D.C.: Robert B. Luce, 1962.

Worcester, Don. *The Chisholm Trail, High Road of the Cattle Kingdom.* Lincoln: University of Nebraska Press, 1980.

Collections

Barker Texas History Center, University of Texas at Austin
 Bexar Collections
 Robert S. Neighbors Papers
 Jesse Chisholm Papers
 Office of Indian Affairs Letter Books, 1838–1848, vols. 1–3
 T. U. Taylor Papers
 John S. Ford Memoirs

Kansas State Historical Society
 "Reminiscences of Frontier Life," James R. Mead

Knox County Archives, Knoxville, Tennessee
 Knox County Court Minutes

Oklahoma Historical Society
 Archives-Manuscript Division

B. W. Alberty Affidavit, Cherokee Files, Vol. 469
Barde Collection
Creek Old Settler Census Roll
Creek File, Foreign Relations
Fort Gibson Letter Book, 1834–1836
Grant Foreman Collection
Indian Archives File, Creeks
Joseph B. Thoburn Collection
Quapaw Agency Files, Vol. 81
Record Book of Chief Sam Checote
Shawnee War Claims File
Slave Schedules, Arkansas and Indian Lands
Starr Manuscript
Thompson McKenney Papers
Vincente Chisholm File
Whipple Collection
Library
Jesse Chisholm Vertical File
Oklahoma Territorial Census
Report of D.A.R. Historical Marker Committee

Oklahoma State Archives
Barrett Survey

Texas State Archives
A. J. Houston Papers
Indian Affairs Papers
Miscellaneous Indian Papers File
Record Book, 1844–1845, Texas Bureau of Indian Affairs
Secretary of State Papers, Indian Affairs
Texas Adjutant General Correspondence

Thomas Gilcrease Institute, Tulsa, Oklahoma
Fort Smith Traders' Books
Grant Foreman Papers
John Drew Papers

University of Arkansas, Special Collections Department
Albert Pike Papers
Charles B. Johnson Papers, 1859–1865
William Minor Quesenbury Diary, 1845–1861

University of Oklahoma, Western History Collections
C. Ross Hume Collection
Draper Collection
Lewis Cass Papers

Washington County Records, Jonesboro, Tennessee
McCown WPA Miscellaneous Records Book
Minutes Court Pleas Quarter Sessions County Court, I, 1778–1799

Dissertations/Theses

Lindsey, Virginia Lee. "History of the Western Cherokees," University of Oklahoma, 1935.

Markman, Robert Paul. "The Arkansas Cherokees, 1817–1828," University of Oklahoma, 1972.

Government Documents

Published

American State Papers, Congressional Series, Class II: *Indian Affairs.* 38 vols. Washington, D.C.: Gales and Seaton, 1832–1861; microfilm Ann Arbor, Mich.: University Microfilms.

Annals of Congress, Debates and Proceedings.

Bureau of Ethnology, Nineteenth Annual Report. 1900.

House Executive Document No. 27, 35th Cong., 2d sess. "Protection of the Frontier of Texas."

House Executive Document No. 42, 36th Cong., 1st sess. "Report of Lt. E. F. Beale on Wagon Road from Fort Smith to the Colorado River."

Marcy and Neighbors Exploration of Big Wichita and Brazos Headwaters in 1854. Western Americana Microfilm Series.

Report of Messrs. Butler and Lewis, Commissioners to Treat with the Camanches and Other Prairie Indians under Instructions from the War Department, September 13, 1845 (published 1846).

Reports of the Commissioner of Indian Affairs, 1826–1868.

Senate Executive Document No. 512, 23d Cong., 1st sess., IV. "Correspondence on the Subject of the Emigration of Indians between the 30th November 1831 and 17th December 1833."

Senate Executive Document No. 1, 23d Cong., 2d sess. "Colonel Henry Dodge's Journal from Fort Gibson to the Pawnee Pict Villages During the Summer of 1834."

Senate Executive Document No. 438, 29th Cong., 1st sess. "Report of Expedition Led by Lieutenant J. W. Abert, on Upper Arkansas, and Through Country of Comanche Indians."

Senate Executive Document No. 12, 31st Cong., 1st sess. "Report of the Route from Fort Smith to Santa Fe by Lieut. James H. Simpson."

Senate Executive Document No. 14, III, 32d Cong., 2d sess.

Senate Executive Document No. 78, 33d Cong., 2d sess. "Report of Exploration and Surveys to Ascertain the Most Practicable and Economical Route for a Railroad from the Mississippi River to the Pacific Ocean by Lieut. A. W. Whipple."

Senate Executive Document No. 1, II, 35th Cong., 2d sess. "Account of R. B. Marcy's March from Camp Scott to New Mexico and Return."

Smithsonian Report 1924, by David I. Bushnell, "John Mix Stanley."

Territorial Papers of the United States, comp. and ed. Edwin Carter. IV, XIV, XV. 1936, 1949.

The War of the Rebellion, A Compilation of the Official Records of the Union and Confederate Armies. 1880–1891.

Unpublished

National Archives
    Census Roll, 1835, of Cherokees East of the Mississippi, with Index
    Cherokee Old Settler Pay Roll Census, 1895
    Correspondence of the Office of Indian Affairs (Central Office) and Related Records, Letters Received, 1824–1881
        Arkansas Superintendency, 1824–1834
        Central Superintendency, 1860–1867
        Cherokee Agency, 1856–1864
        Cherokee Agency East, 1801–1835
        Cherokee Agency West, 1824–1831
        Cherokee Immigration, 1828–1864
        Creek Agency, 1834–1868
        Creek Agency West, 1826–1836
        Kiowa Agency, 1864–1868
        Sac and Fox Agency, 1865–1868
        Seminole Agency, 1824–1867
        Shawnee Agency, 1855–1857
        Southern Superintendency, 1863–1867
        Texas Agency, 1847–1859
        Western Superintendency, 1832–1851
        Wichita Agency, 1857–1866
    Documents relating to the Negotiations of Ratified and Unratified Indian Treaties with Various Indian Tribes, 1801–1869
    Drennan Roll, Records of the BIA — Cherokee's Old Settler Roll of 1851
    Eastern Cherokee Applications, 1906–1909
    Final Rolls of Citizens and Freedmen of the Five Civilized Tribes
    First Cherokee Commission (original document)
    Fort Gibson Letters Sent, 1824–1857, 1863–1890
    Fort Gibson Post Returns (original documents)
    Fourth Cherokee Commission (original document)
    Headquarters Records of Fort Dodge, Kansas, 1866–1882
    Index, Eastern Cherokee Applications of the U.S. Court of Claims, 1906–1909

Indexes to Letters Received, Adjutant General's Office (Main Series), 1846, 1861–1889

Letters Received by Adjutant General's Office (Main Series), 1822–1860

Letters Received by Secretary of War, Main Series, 1801–1870

Letters Sent by the Department of Texas, the District of Texas, and the 5th Military District, 1856–1858, 1865–1870

Letters Sent, Office of Indian Affairs, 1824–1829

Office of the Secretary of War, Letters Sent Relating to Indian Affairs, 1800–1824

Old Settler Cherokee Census Roll, 1895, and Index to Payment Roll, 1895

Ratified Indian Treaties, 1722–1869

Record of Proceedings of First Board of Commissioners Under Cherokee Treaty of 1835 — Reservation Claims

Records of the Central Superintendency of Indian Affairs, 1813–1859

Records of the Cherokee Indian Agency in Tennessee, 1801–1835

Records of the Southern Superintendency (Western Superintendency Letters Received, Southern Superintendency Letters Received and Letters Sent), 1832–1870

Records of the Superintendent of Indian Trade, Letters Sent, 1807–1823

Register of Traders Licenses, 1847–1873

Registers of Enlistments in U.S. Army, Indian Scouts, 1866–1877

Reports of Inspection of the Field Jurisdictions of the Office of Indian Affairs, Kiowa, Comanche, and Wichita Agencies

Special Files, Office of Indian Affairs, 1807–1904

Texas Census Records, Cherokee County, 1850

U.S. Court of Claims

Index

Bougie, Joseph, 18
Boundary Mounds, 118. *See also* Antelope
  Hills
Bowlegs, Jim (Seminole chief), 109
Bowles, John (Cherokee chief), 21–22, 49,
  52–53, 69; Texas colony of, 53
Brand, George W., 18
Brazos Reserve Indians, 73, 122, 126–28
Brazos Reserves, Texas, 112, 121–22, 127
Brazos River, 21–22, 29, 54, 57, 60, 62, 69–
  70, 72–73, 75–76, 79, 100, 108–10, 112,
  122, 128
Brooke, George M. (General), 109
Brown, H.M.C., 122
Brown, Patsy, 9; divorces John D. Chis-
  holm, 10
Brown, Richard (Cherokee chief), 9, 14
Bucksnort, Texas, 76, 81
"Buffalo Hump," as pseudonym, 81
Buffalo Hump (Comanche chief), 59–60, 64–
  65, 77, 83, 107, 138–39, 156
Bullet, George (Delaware chief), 38, 48
Burrow, James, 157
Bushman, John, 113
Butler, Pierce M. (Cherokee Agent), 54–56,
  60, 68, 74–75, 77–78, 87, 95; leads party
  to Cache Creek, 59
Byars, Indian Territory, 110

Caboon, 96. *See also* Chisholm, George
  (adopted son); de Demencio, Vincente;
  Juerus, Vincente; Vincente
Cache Creek, 59–60, 64, 72, 105, 152
Caddo Indians, 22, 55, 61–62, 71, 73, 77, 79,
  107, 112, 122–23, 136, 140, 142, 146,
  150, 152, 163–64, 166–67; language of,
  39; village of, 61
Calhoun, Tennessee, 14
California, 35, 74, 100, 107–8; emigrants to,
  105–6
California gold rush, 19, 100–106; trail of,
  124
Camp Arbuckle, Indian Territory, 95, 110,
  113, 134
Camp Canadian, Indian Territory, 33
Camp Holmes, Indian Territory, 43–44, 46,
  94, 104; Treaty of, 45, 100
Camp Mason, Indian Territory, 47
Camp Napoleon, Indian Territory, 152
Camp Radziminski, Indian Territory, 123,
  126
Camp Rendezvous, Indian Territory, 33
Camp Runnels, Texas, 122
Camp Supply, Indian Territory, 159
Canadian River, 26, 29, 31, 33–34, 39, 41,
  43, 45–46, 48, 50–51, 61–62, 77, 91, 94,
  100, 102–4, 106–7, 109–11, 113, 116,
  118–20, 122, 124–25, 130, 133, 139, 152,
  156, 163, 165–66, 169; as mail route,
  124; as wagon route, 100, 125
Cannibalism, 140; Tonkawas accused of, 106

Cantonment Gibson, Indian Territory, 17–
  19. *See also* Fort Gibson
Cantonment Towson, Indian Territory, 18.
  See also Fort Towson
Carey, William, 9
Carr, Eugene A. (Captain), 125
Carr, W. C. (Judge), 31
Carruth, Edwin H., 135
Carson, Kit, 145, 156
Cass, Lewis (Secretary of War), 31
Catlin, George, 32–33, 37, 39, 55; describes
  trek, 35; paintings of displayed at Capi-
  tol, 88
Cattle: drive of, 125; first herd over Chis-
  holm Trail, 165–66; of Indian Territory,
  146; Texas longhorns, 160; theft of, 146
Caunot, John, 48
Cedra Canales, 116
Center Market, Washington, D.C., 86
Charleston, South Carolina, 7
Chase County, Kansas, 163
Cherokee Advocate, 68–70
Cherokee Agency: at Calhoun, Tennessee,
  14; correspondence of, 11; at Tahlequah,
  54
Cherokee Indians, 20–21, 27–28, 30, 32–33,
  35, 38–40, 48–49, 51–52, 58, 61–62, 64,
  66, 68–70, 72–75, 79, 82, 89, 108, 112,
  116, 121–22, 135–36, 138; alphabet of,
  16, 66–67, 69; attack Tawakonis, 24–25;
  ball games of, 10; chiefs killed, 7; country, 58; as guides, 31; half bloods of, 132;
  hunting expedition of, 21; lands of, 6;
  language of, 67, 69–70, 115; in Mexico,
  69–70, 72; migrate west, 7; rebels
  among, 136; ritual of as told by Chisholm, 115; on St. Francis River, 11;
  slave party of, 51; Texas settlement of,
  52; at Treaty of Holston, 7. *See also* Arkansas Cherokees; Cherokee Old Nation; Texas Cherokees; Western
  Cherokees
Cherokee Nation, 11–14, 41, 57, 67–69, 110,
  131, 153; migration westward of, 5; National Council of, 50, 68
Cherokee Old Settlers, 110
Cheyenne Indians, 46, 122, 142, 145, 150,
  152, 155–56, 159–60, 163–64, 168–70;
  country of, 169; Dog Soldiers of, 160,
  164–65; reservation for, 168
Chickamauga Creek, 6
Chickasaw Bluffs, Tennessee, 85. *See also*
  Memphis
Chickasaw Indians, 48, 75, 82, 115, 122,
  127, 135, 138; language of, 115; nation
  of, 95, 111
Chikaskia River, 150, 166
Chishem, 153. *See also* Chisholm, Jesse
Chisholm, Albert Finney, 72
Chisholm, Deborah, 9
Chisholm, Eliza: death of, 91. *See also* Ed-
  wards, Eliza